100 YEARS OF
IRISH
FOOTBALL

The Moyola Park team which defeated Cliftonville in the final of the Irish Challenge Cup, in 1881. *Back row:* Thomas Houston, Willie John Houston, George Hewison, Robert Mackerill, (goalkeeper), Francis J. McLernon, Patrick Sloan. *Middle row:* Arthur Gaussen, (reserve), Daniel McKenna, W. J. Morrow (captain), Patrick McSwiggin, Robert Redmond. *In front:* Mitchell Redmond.

100 YEARS OF
IRISH
FOOTBALL

By
Malcolm Brodie

Published by the Authority of the Irish Football Association

Blackstaff Press

Published by Blackstaff Press, 3 Galway Park, Dundonald, Belfast BT16 0AN.

ISBN 08560 225 7

Printed in Northern Ireland by W & G Baird Limited.

Contents

ACKNOWLEDGEMENTS

The publishers gratefully acknowledge permission to reproduce extracts from the following books: *Attack* by Derek Dougan, published by Pelham Books Limited; *There's Only One United* by Geoffrey Green, © 1978 Manchester United Football Club Limited, published by Hodder and Stoughton Limited; *The Double and Before* by Danny Blanchflower, © 1961 Nicholas Kaye Limited, published by Nicholas Kaye Limited.

FIFA President's Greetings

At the time the Irish Football Association commemorates its centenary it is a great pleasure for me to congratulate it as president of Fédération Internationale de Football Association — FIFA.

The joys of our affiliated Associations are always shared by FIFA because, on the whole, National Associations through their strength and influence make us the highest authority in world football.

We are proud we have built up in more than eighty years a sports institution that, above racial, religious or political considerations, is an instrument to serve understanding and peace among people.

The ideal for which we have been working so hard gets more important every day in this disturbed world in which we live.

We will go on fighting for it with the support of all sportsmen who, through football competitions all over the world, increase their bravery and loyalty, thus improving their human, physical and moral qualities.

We know we can count on the Irish Football Association's valuable contribution to such a noble aim. It thus gives me great joy to present our congratulations and FIFA's at the festivities that commemorate the Irish FA's foundation.

Jaoa Havelange
FIFA President

Foreword

One definition of a holocaust must surely be a dinner table with Danny Blanchflower at one end and Derek Dougan at the other.

Idle rumours that footballers are to articulateness what George Best is to punctuality, would be submerged forever under an avalanche of anecdote, rhetoric, philosophy, wit and — on a good night — some splendid rip-roaring slander. You would reel from the table, deafened and exhausted, neck aching from the verbal overhead volleying of two maverick conversationalists who would almost certainly have spent all four courses speaking simultaneously. If talk were the criterion, Northern Ireland would win the World Cup more times than Brazil.

I can never understand why so many in my trade of sports writing are so reluctant to spend time in or around Belfast. There are Blanchflowers and Dougans everywhere. Stories grow on trees. The outrageous is common-place and the lies are often true. The welcome is invariably warm. I have never yet got home from Belfast on the scheduled plane, and on one occasion went AWOL for one whole week. Northern Ireland is that kind of place — and so is its sport.

I once asked Danny Blanchflower how a certain Irish soccer manager motivated his team. 'Well,' said Danny, 'By never so much as mentioning tactics. He simply sat us down in the dressing room and told us of the heroic deeds and legendary victories of Irish teams in the past. We'd look up the results later and discover that mostly Ireland had lost. But that was his way of firing us up and quite often it worked.'

A sport like that deserves a very special chronicler. Irish football, Northern Ireland, Belfast, and specifically the *Belfast Telegraph*, is blessed with such a man. Even the Queen acknowledged that in 1979 when she awarded him the MBE for his services to sport and journalism at a time and in a place which needed optimism, cool nerve and unerring judgment.

Malcolm Brodie, with his machine-gun speech, high humour, infectious laugh, ferocious capacity for work, and propensity for popping up at your elbow anywhere between Rio de Janeiro airport and what passes for the Kiev Hilton is as legendary in our game as many of the super stars he writes about are in theirs.

No journalist is so supremely equipped to write about Irish football. The first part of this book is a product of massively professional research, and second an incomparable account by a man whose eyes have seen the glories, the eccentricities and the sheer humanity of a large game in a small country which is never dull. Neither is Malcolm Brodie's apostolic record within these pages.

Ian Wooldridge, 'Daily Mail', London, January, 1980

Preface

To chronicle 100 years of Irish Football Association history has been an honour yet in a way a frightening task — frightening because it is impossible, short of going to encyclopaedic length, to record details of all those who have played such a vital part in the development of the game.

However, every effort has been made to capture the drama of the century, to profile those who have figured in the varied aspects of football, and to assess its complete evolution. From small beginnings has arisen an Association which now carries significance in the corridors of world football.

This has been a team effort — one in which every attempt was made to ensure complete accuracy, despite the fact that records are limited and in some cases non-existent.

I express my appreciation to the Irish FA secretary Billy Drennan and his staff at Windsor Avenue for their help and patience; to members of the Association Council, and Junior Committee, particularly President Harry Cavan and Vice President Sammy Walker; to the *Belfast Telegraph* management for their support, and especially the editor, Roy Lilley; my colleagues on the Northern Ireland Football Writers' Association, particularly Bill Ireland, Hamilton McDowell — 'Omar' of the *News Letter* and a companion in the 1958 World Cup series; the chief librarian of the *Belfast Telegraph*, Walter McAuley, and his staff; the Linen Hall Library; Roy Smyth (*Belfast Telegraph*) and his colleagues for their photographic guidance; R. Clements Lyttle, formerly official photographers to the Irish FA; to many players and ex-players for quotations from their autobiographies, my publishers Blackstaff Press and to those who inspired me to continue when the problems seemed so daunting.

There have been multiple sources of information as the research was carried out over two years. To them all I say thanks for aiding me in the compilation of this history — my humble contribution to the centenary of a game which has given us all so much pride and pleasure. It is a game which has personally been good to me.

Malcolm Brodie
Belfast, 1980

An impressive array of gifts presented to the IFA by associations and clubs throughout the world on display in the Trophy Room at the IFA headquarters.

The Beginning
1880-1900

When a group of progressive-thinking ambitious men, presided over by John Sinclair, met on Thursday, 18 November 1880, in the Queen's Hotel, Belfast, to form the Irish Football Association and frame its constitution they could not have envisaged the global ramifications which would arise, the crises to be overcome, and the glory to be achieved in 100 eventful years.

Viewed across a century, one might think that the actual business of founding was an enjoyable venture but there were the inevitable snags at that first meeting, including the fact that it had to be moved to a room away from the bar as the session had gone on beyond closing time! Still, the qualities of tenacity, panache and determination were evident among those men at that embryonic stage of the Association.

'If the spirit which prevaded those present be acted upon the result will be a strong Association for promoting the game which we have espoused,' wrote John M. McAlery, the hon. secretary, as an appendix to the minutes of that historic first meeting.

Major Spencer Chichester was appointed President. It was decided to adopt the Scottish FA rule books, and the clubs represented were Knock, Oldpark, Distillery, Alexander (Limavady), Moyola Park, Cliftonville and Avoniel. Although this meeting was the official drawing up of rules and regulations, football in Ireland had already been alive but, alas, in a haphazard, disorganised, almost chaotic fashion. An attempt had been made in 1887 to introduce soccer when Scottish FA secretary Willie Dick arranged an exhibition game but it fell through for some unknown reason: the idea was abandoned. Nevertheless, the seeds had actually been sown in 1878 when the resourceful McAlery, on his honeymoon in Edinburgh, arranged with the Scots to stage a game on 24 October 1878 at the Ulster Cricket Ground, Ballynafeigh, between selected players from Queen's Park and The Caledonians. It proved to be a game which captured the imagination of spectators, a superb exhibition of skills with the round ball as Queen's Park, a powerful force, triumphed 3-1. Then Lenzie, another Scottish club side, accepted an invitation to play the Ulster Football Club. Spectators laughed at and heckled the efforts of the local novices. It was obvious, however, that 'the Association' code, as it was called, had come to stay not only in Belfast but also in Dublin with the population responding to the Irishman's zest for finding something new. Cliftonville lost 9-1 in their first match against Caledonians. Balmoral Academy, Knock Lacrosse Club, and Albion, a rugby club, played some fixtures; so, too, did Windsor Rugby Club, while Major Spencer Chichester formed Moyola Park in Castledawson, Co Londonderry.

McAlery, manager of the Irish Tweed House, Royal Avenue, and later with premises in Rosemary Street, destroyed during the Second World War, was the Father of the Association. A dynamic visionary, he realised the potential of the game. Founder of Cliftonville, the first club, in 1879, he was the moving spirit in the formation of the Irish FA when, through the Reds, he issued an invitation to interested parties in Belfast and district for a meeting to be called.

John Sinclair (Knock) presided. McAlery and John Willis (Avoniel) proposed the resolution that the Irish FA be established. The conception completed, the birth had arrived with the way paved for the Irish Cup. The first round draw was made on 10 January 1881 involving the founder clubs — Distillery v Knock, Oldpark v Cliftonville, Moyola Park v Avoniel, bye Alexander (Limavady). Entry fee was a shilling, as was the annual subscription. It was a humble start to a development and progression of an Association which now has 900 member clubs, excluding those in the Army FA, Boys FA and Schools FA — all run by a forty-one-strong Council and thirteen members of the Junior Committee. Four Divisional Associations operate — North-West (five delegates), North-East (fourteen), Mid-Ulster (four), Fermanagh and Western (three); other representation is Junior Committee (one), Army FA (one), Schools FA (one) and twelve from the senior clubs of the Irish League.

McAlery retained the secretaryship until 1888 when he was succeeded by his assistant Jack Reid; although in retirement at Whitehead, Co. Antrim, he continued to take an active interest in the game which he had brought to his native land. This Irish Cup series, the McAlery brainchild, saw the first of many protests which were to become almost an integral part of Irish soccer history. Cliftonville preferred charges against Oldpark for 'ungentlemanly conduct' but this was allowed to drop and another protest from Avoniel that a Moyola Park player had 'worn boots with long studs' fell through but, in a generous gesture, the ten-shilling protest fee in each case was returned. And £1 was voted to Alexander for a player who had fractured his leg against Moyola Park whose players were warned for 'rough and brutal play'.

Moyola were the 'hard men', the power, defeating Cliftonville 1-0 in the first Cup Final played at Cliftonville on 9 April 1881. Gate receipts amounted to £8 and expenses to £2. 5s. 6d.

Events moved fast. Soccer had gathered momentum. There was no halting it now. A profit of £13. 1s. 5d. had been made by the IFA in the first year; here was a sporting baby vibrant with health, born into an amiable family in contrast to the contretemps which existed in England and Wales.

Internationals, the real crowd pullers, had been considered but the Irish FA's first match actually involved a Belfast and District side which lost 9-1 to Ayrshire at Cliftonville on 30 January 1882. This was but a trial for the opening international against England on Saturday, 18 February 1882, at the Knock Ground, Bloomfield, site of the former railway station. Only five members of that crushed and humiliated Belfast team remained.

What a disaster this international proved to be before a 'gate' of £9. 19s. 7d. England won 13-0 with Vaughton (5), A. Brown (4), J. Brown (2), Cursham and Bambridge scoring. For McAlery, captain of the Irish side, it was a sad day. As he sat dejectedly in the dressing room tears flowed down his cheeks. His task seemed hopeless; he had got soccer off the ground, the administration was right but the standard inept, bordering on the laughable. That lack of experience was cruelly exposed again a week later when Wales won 7-1 at Wrexham, Johnston (Distillery) getting his country's first goal in the international arena. For the Belfast game the minutes of the Association record that a quotation of 4s. 6d. per head for a meal was accepted and that the Irish players be charged 5s. per head!

Qualification for internationals was not nearly so strict or rigid as today. If they were born in Ireland, or had seven years residence, players could wear the St. Patrick blue jersey, the first colours — changed to green against England on 17 October 1931 to avoid a clash with Scotland's dark blue. Clubs were instructed to ensure players participating in the Irish Cup were eligible for Ireland; English-based players were not introduced until the 1898-9 season. It was the domestic game which flourished. Clubs came forward frequently seeking membership — Glentoran, Linfield, Mount Avon, Down Athletic, Churchtown Park, Clarence YMCA, Dublin University, Dublin Association, Sydenham Hertford, Victoria (Derry), St. Columb's (Derry), Magherafelt, Kilrea, Queen's Island, Malone, Belfast Academy, RBAI, St. Malachy's College, Belfast Mercantile Academy, Monaghan Diocesan School, Monaghan, Ormeau, Mossley, Albert, Rosemount.

The Irish Cup dominated the scene. By 1884-5 clubs from six districts — Belfast, North and South Derry, Monaghan, Banbridge and Dublin — were taking part. Still those protests kept pouring in. Just before the first tie between Sydenham and Hertford at Lisburn the referee was handed a protest stating that 'owing to the inclemency of the weather and that some players did not get their dinner' the match should be postponed. It was rejected as 'not only groundless but frivolous'. Once again the £1 fee was returned.

Gate receipts were high: for instance in 1887-8 takings at the Final were more than the combined receipts from internationals against England (£79. 9s. 6d.) and Scotland (£51. 14s. 6d.); in 1886 when Distillery won the Cup seven players who asked for money in lieu of gold medals were each paid £1.

Cup rules had been revised to permit 'foreigners'. This followed a request from the Belfast Scottish Association that Caledonians be allowed to play in the competition and they were altered so that a person of non-Irish birth would be eligible provided he had been in residence three months before the match. That year the Irish international side, for the first time, included players from Dublin University — F. W. Moorehead and A. L. Eames. At the Welsh game, played at Ballynafeigh, the goalkeeper A. W. Henderson left the field midway through the second half because of continued abuse from spectators; he was persuaded to return, only to be barracked again.

Professionalism became a debating point at the start of the 1885-6 season with Scotland inviting Irish FA delegates to a conference at Liverpool, but as England decided not to attend, there was no Irish representative there either. Professionalism, eventually, became legalised in England and Scotland that year. The Irish FA remained adamant that 'only amateurs should play in International Matches'.

An attempt to introduce professionalism failed in 1882; indeed it was not until the Association's annual meeting in 1894 that a proposal was pushed through on a 64-30 vote with the majority of clubs supporting the measure having no intention of adopting the system. Ironically, the proposal was moved by the delegate of Cliftonville, which was ardently all-amateur. As a gradual lowering of standards had emerged, professionalism was seen as the saviour.

Linfield's John Peden had the honour of becoming the first professional to be transferred to Newtown Heath, now Manchester United, that phenomenon of British football. And it was Peden who gave Ireland her first away victory in the Home championships by scoring the solitary goal against Wales, a team which included Billy Meredith (Manchester City) at Llandudno. Peden by then had returned to Distillery.

A Toronto side visited Belfast, defeating the County Antrim FA 5-2, Distillery 3-2 and Clarence 3-2. It was, however, the performances of Linfield which gripped the imagination: they defeated Bolton Wanderers 4-0, went to Nottingham and drew with Forest 2-2 and then triumphed 4-1 in Belfast.

Military sides, too, came into prominence — the Black Watch, Gordon Highlanders, 2nd East Lancs (Lilywhites), Lancashire Fusiliers, Sherwood Foresters. Preston played Linfield in Belfast in May 1889; managed by William

Suddell the English side were called 'The Invincibles', turning in a tremendous display to win 6-2. Linfield were now a dominant force. They moved their headquarters from The Meadow at Linfield Mill to a new stadium at Ulsterville, between Ulsterville Avenue and Dunluce Avenue.

The ground was opened in September 1889 and then in 1896 came the move to Myrtlefield Park, Balmoral. The Gordons beat Cliftonville 3-1 after a 2-2 draw in the 1890 Final, centre-half Bob Milne, later to join Linfield and play twenty-seven times for Ireland, winning his first Irish Cup Medal.

The year 1890 saw the introduction of the Irish League with eight clubs in membership, Cliftonville, Clarence, Glentoran, Distillery, Linfield, Milford, Oldpark and Ulster with W. McNeice (Cliftonville), the first president; Milford, who failed to win a match, dropped out after the first season along with Clarence. Of the original members only Cliftonville, Distillery, Glentoran and Linfield remain. Linfield, coached by Preston North End's Nick Ross, had three successful seasons, losing only two games, drawing four and in forty-one league matches hit an incredible 232 goals, conceding only thirty-nine. Junior clubs also got into the act. Inspired by Frank Osborne, a sports journalist, they formed a league with twelve clubs.

The IFA Council, January 1980. *Back row:* Maurice Masters, Knox Morrison, Charlie Ferguson, Raymond Kennedy, Bob Haslett, Hugh Heaney, Jim McDowell, Greer Walker, Gordon Ormsby, Stanley Forsythe, Wilfie Geddis. *Second row:* Herbie Johnstone, Claud Wilton, Joe McGorman, Billy Press, William Simms, Davy Campbell, Tommy Vaughan, Andrew Crozier, John Brown, Derek McKeague. *Third Row:* Ken Pritchard, Harry McNeely, Leslie McCullough, Sam Jefferson, Richard Holmes, Fred Duke, Derek Wade, George Pateman, Paul Metcalfe, William McElroy. *Front row:* W. J. Drennan (Sec.), Ivan Marshall, Jimmy Apperson, Brendan Keogh, Sammy Walker (Vice Pres.), Harry Cavan, OBE (Pres.), Eddie Barry (Hon. Treas.), Billy Carlisle, Jimmy Rock, Michael McColgan, John H. Lunn.

It seems incredible, but it is a fact that in 1891 two matches were played under electric lights at Cliftonville, Distillery defeating the Reds 4-2 with the Black Watch holding Cliftonville to a 2-2 draw. Kick-off in each case was at 8 p.m. with lights suspended across the pitch. These were dismantled later with the announcement that spectators found it difficult to follow the action and that 'players seemed to have all the fun in the middle!' It had been a bold experiment, but not a highly successful one, with the public sceptical, almost contemptuous of this enterprising project.

Goal nets were introduced in 1891 by John Arthur Brodie of Liverpool. This was the year which also saw the evolution of the penalty kick on the initiative of the Irish FA through William McCreery (Milford), first secretary of the mid-Ulster Association. He realised the value of punishing offences in the penalty area and his idea, looked upon with suspicion at first, became a reality and law.

Ireland received another 13-0 drubbing from England — this time at Roker Park, Sunderland, before 13,000. It was the first ever international staged on that famous pitch and on returning to Belfast the Irish team found their bags had been chalk marked with a huge '13' by disgruntled fans on the cross-channel ferry.

A Leinster delegate, Tom Kirkwood Hackett, described the Sunderland debacle like this: 'All this has come upon us because of the hidebound prejudice of five men who select the teams preventing anyone outside the close circle of Belfast being chosen to represent his country. Northern prejudice is the bane of Irish football.' So the Anglos, those who had decided to turn professional, got their chance against Wales in March 1899. Earlier, in 1893 Wales triumphed 4-3, a side captained by Frank Lea (Wrexham), a one-armed player.

Even in those distant days spectator trouble arose with disturbances at the Belfast Celtic-Cliftonville game. Posters had to be displayed at all grounds warning spectators of their conduct as well as threatening prosecution.

Rumblings of the Boer war could be heard, with only five teams competing in the Irish League after the departure of the North Staffords. In October 1899 the hostilities were declared and Irish football entered the twentieth century under dark, menacing clouds.

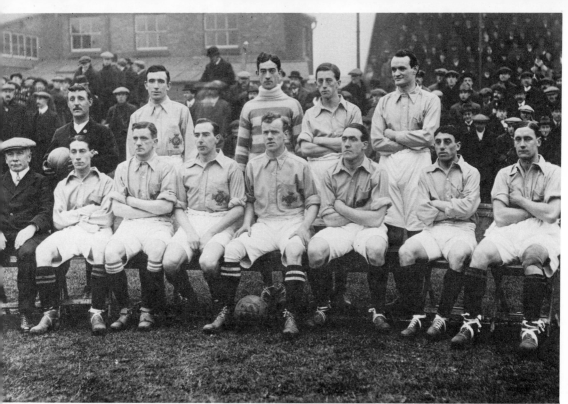

January, 1914. Ireland 2, Wales 1 — the battle for the British championship had begun. *Back row:* I. Baiter (referee), V. Harris, F. McKee, D. Rollo, P. O'Connell. *Front row:* D. McCann (IFA), E. H. Seymour, S. Young, W. Gillespie, A. Craig, W. Lacey, L. Bookman, W. G. McConnell.

1900-1920

With the Association's coming of age football flourished. The Munster Association had been formed, the Leinster clubs numbered 259 compared with 110 the previous year while the County Antrim Association rose dramatically from 32 to 161. The progress was tinged with sadness at the death of the first President, Lord Spencer Chichester, the Marquess of Londonderry being elected as his successor. Throughout this period and indeed until just after the First World War the President was, unlike today, merely a figurehead with the Council presided over by a Chairman. Alex Thompson occupied the chair for the first twenty years.

Belfast Celtic, admitted to the Irish League in 1896, moved from their first ground near Brighton Street, Broadway, to Celtic Park, forming a limited company to provide a 'first-class fully-equipped football and athletic ground having all the suitable and necessary accessories'. It was to cater for all sports with two tracks built — one of cinder for training purposes, the other for cycling. Whippet racing featured regularly in this opening era. Cult personalities arrived on the scene. John Kirwan (Tottenham Hotspur) who played fourteen times for Ireland, won an FA Cup medal in a 3-0 win over Sheffield United after a replay; Billy McCracken, the penalty king and the man responsible for the offside rule being initiated, revealed his class and assertiveness with Distillery. The name Scott, so traditionally associated with Irish football, became a household word.

Billy Scott (Linfield, Everton and Leeds City) kept goals for Ireland twenty-five times; his brother Elisha (Liverpool and Belfast Celtic), a renowned character with abrasive qualities and vituperative tongue which lashed those attempting to hide in a game, made thirty-one appearances, while Tom (Cliftonville) collected thirteen caps. These were achievements of considerable merit, bearing in mind that internationals were confined primarily to those in the Home championship: not for the Scotts, the McCrackens, the Kirwans, the delights of foreign travel. International football remained insular, played in the confines of the British Isles and, as a result, England, Scotland, Wales and Ireland had an inflated opinion of their skills compared with the European nations. How dearly were they to pay for this parochialism in later decades.

Ireland had a 3-0 success against Wales in February 1902 at Cardiff Arms Park with Alfie Gara (Preston North End) scoring three goals, but this was not the first hat-trick scored by an Irishman in an international. That honour went to William Dalton (YMCA) who hit three in the 7-2 win over Wales in Belfast, 1891, and who died in Toronto, Canada. And it was in 1902, during an England-Scotland game at Ibrox Park, Glasgow, that one of the stands collapsed, killing 25 and injuring 500. It was a horrific scene, to be repeated seventy years later at the end of a Rangers-Celtic New Year's clash, when a railing on a stairway collapsed. Ireland met the Scots in August, 1902 in aid of the Disaster Fund — the same day as King Edward VII and Queen Alexandra were crowned at Westminster Abbey.

Ireland won two internationals in 1903 against Wales and Scotland; the controversial McCracken got his first 'cap' at Wolverhampton. Later he refused to play unless he got £10, five times the normal fee, and quit the Irish party on the eve of a game with England, his place going to Tully Craig (Glasgow Rangers). For twenty years he remained out in the cold, a rebel ignored.

One of the biggest talking points then was the 1905 elimination of Linfield from the Irish Cup by Derry Celtic who had played eight League matches without a win. That year Windsor Park was opened — the actual ceremony being delayed for a fortnight because of a deluge of rain — and to celebrate it the Blues defeated Cliftonville 1-0. It was a magnificent arena, the ultimate and the obvious venue for international football, a tribute to the vision of the Linfield management committee members.

Yet another administrative change occurred as those who played a vital role in the formation of the Association resigned or passed from the scene. Jack Reid relinquished the post of secretary; Johnny Ferguson took over until February 1918, when he was to be followed by Charlie Watson. Ferguson's arrival coincided with the introduction of the electric tram service in Belfast, and, as a newspaper reported, it 'proved a a great boon to football enthusiasts as the cars moved considerably faster than the old horse-drawn vehicles and there were no stops for changing of horses!' Progress at last was being made.

FA Cup medals for Irish players were commonplace in this era — Billy Scott (Everton), Billy McCracken (Newcastle United), and Frank Thompson (Bradford City): all were honoured. Amateur internationals commenced in 1906 and operated until they were abolished in the 1973-4 season when they had outlived their usefulness in the new concept of modern day football.

The grip which the game had got on the public was amazing. Here, truly, was the sport of the people. More than 20,000 watched the international with England; membership of the Association rose to 334, the North East had 127 clubs, Leinster 90, Mid-Ulster 52, North West 13, Fermanagh and Western 16 and Munster 29.

Cliftonville and Celtic were suspended by the Irish FA for misconduct in a Charity cup tie but they refused to pay the fine, accept the decision and questioned the legal validity of the proceedings. For months the dispute dragged on until W. K. Gibson, a solicitor who had previously played for Cliftonville and Ireland, sorted out the complex tangle. Later he was to become a distinguished life member of the Association.

This was not the only row in the Irish soccer family. Players attending a Protest and Appeals Committee meeting became annoyed at having to wait outside while the committee debated field offences. Fist fights broke out, the anteroom was cleared and officials and members threatened. More trouble brewed. A separate Association was formed by clubs who had refused to compete in the Irish Cup; four members of the Linfield Management Committee were suspended for not granting Windsor Park to the Irish FA at ten per cent instead of twenty per cent requested by clubs. So on 22 February 1912, Distillery, Glentoran, Celtic, Derry Celtic, Cliftonville, Shelbourne and Glenavon formed the new Association, although the Irish FA remained adamant they were the governing body, the only people with power.

A new Irish Cup, now the Gold Cup, was instituted, Belfast Celtic defeating Glentoran 2-0 in the Final. The players wore crepe armlets in memory of those who had lost their life in the *Titanic* disaster. Neither the Irish Cup proper nor the County Antrim Shield was played: but in a series later that year Linfield got the main trophy.

A deep crisis existed. The game was tearing itself apart, and, after the 1912 annual meeting, there were suggestions that the English and Scottish FAs should act as a Commission of Inquiry; that the International Board fulfil the role of mediators. But, as happens so often in Irish disputes, the settlement was reached quickly, the heat taken from the crisis by John Sinclair, a Belfast Harbour Commissioner and the man selected as mediator.

These were the agreed terms: each senior club would have a delegate on the Council of the Irish FA and a sub-committee composed of seven delegates would manage the Irish Cup. Finalists would divide fifty per cent of the net receipts; all players guilty of misconduct in Irish League matches would be dealt with by the Senior Committee; ground rent for internationals would remain at ten per cent (it is now fifteen per cent at Windsor Park with Linfield awarded a twenty-year contract which expires on 31 December 1999) and all suspensions on those forming the new Association lifted. From the playing viewpoint life was much more pleasant. Ireland had the first victory — 2-1 — over England at Windsor Park with Charlie Buchan, later a respected sports journalist, scoring first for England, and Val Harris and Billy Gillespie. Ireland played for most of the game without inside forward Jimmy McAuley.

Ireland's playing fortunes had been mixed since those humiliating early defeats. There was the odd victory but, generally, they remained very much the underdogs. That is, until the 1913-14 season when for the first, and only, time Ireland won the international championship, just missing the Triple Crown as a result of a draw with Scotland. Ireland has shared the championship on five occasions — 1902-3 with England and Scotland, 1955-6 with England, Wales and Scotland, 1957-8 with England, 1958-9 with England, 1963-4 with England and Scotland.

The team which defeated England 3-0 at Middlesbrough in February 1914. *Back row:* J. MacBride (IFA), H. Hegan (President, IFA), A. A. Jackson (referee), H. Hampton, P. O'Connell, F. McKee, M. Hamill, W. McConnell, A. Craig, J. Clarke (linesman, IFA), R. J. Kirkpatrick (IFA). *Front row:* D. W. Foy (treasurer, IFA), D. Rollo, S. Young, W. Gillespie, W. Lacey, F. Thompson, R. Torrans (trainer). *On ground:* R. Norwood.

The Ireland team which drew 1-1 with Scotland at Windsor Park in March, 1914, to win the British championship. *Back row:* McConnell (Bohemians), referee, McKee (Belfast Celtic), Craig (Greenock Morton), O'Connell (Hull City), Lacey (Liverpool), Harris (Everton), H. McAteer (Cliftonville), trainer. *Front row:* Houston (Everton), Nixon (Linfield), Young (Linfield), Hamill (Manchester United), Thompson (Clyde), A. McAughey (linesman). This point actually gave Ireland the championship for the first and only time.

This 1913-14 season was one in which most people felt success could be attained. A blend had been found in the side; there were the experienced players such as Mickey Hamill (Manchester United) making almost as decisive an impact as did his illustrious if unorthodox countryman, George Best, four decades later.

The chapter of glory began with a 2-1 victory over Wales at Wrexham on 19 January 1914 even though Harris had been sidelined for the entire second half. A month later — on 14 February — came the clash with England at Ayresome Park, Middlesbrough, the thirty-third fixture of the series.

Ayresome burst at the seams. Ireland, despite that Wrexham triumph, were given little chance especially as some regulars had not been available and Davy Rollo (Linfield), hitherto considered a utility man, operated in the un-accustomed outside right position. What a performance he gave, as did the other members of the team to win 3-0, Billy Lacey hitting two of the goals. This was the side that defeated England that day: F. W. McKee (Belfast Celtic), W. H. McConnell (Bohemians), Craig (Morton), Hampton (Bradford City), O'Connell (Hull City), Hamill (Manchester United), Rollo (Linfield), Young (Airdrieonians), Gillespie (Sheffield United), Lacey (Liverpool), Thompson (Clyde).

Cliftonville, allocated the Scottish match, decided it should be switched to Windsor Park in view of the anticipated crowd. Saturday, 14 March, was a wet, miserable day, cutting the attendance to 27,000. Ireland, handicapped by McKee being injured before half-time forcing Billy Lacey to move into goal, did well to draw 1-1. It was a heroic feat to win the series, particularly as in all three games the original team chosen had been drastically altered by injuries and unavailability.

The final table read:

	P	W	L	D	F	A	Pts.
Ireland	3	2	0	1	6	2	5
Scotland	3	1	0	2	2	4	4
England	3	1	2	0	3	6	2
Wales	3	0	2	1	1	4	1

War again enmeshed the nation. Players, officials, spectators had joined the Ulster Volunteer Force. Captain James M. Wilton, later to be knighted and elected Association President, served with the 36th Ulster Division and was severely wounded at the Battle of the Somme. Internationals were suspended with a loss of revenue, but there was no general abandonment of competitive football. In fact, the Irish League lost 2-1 to England at West Bromwich Albion, while the Scots won by the same margin in Belfast. Nevertheless recruiting brought a decline in club membership from 221 to 140. So serious was the situation that an extraordinary meeting gave the Council power to suspend activities for the duration of the War if necessary, and agreements between clubs and players were put into cold storage during this period as well. A Belfast and District League was formed comprising Belfast United, Cliftonville, Distillery, Glenavon, Glentoran and Linfield who won the City Cup in 1915.

Clubs had to make do and mend, some living a hand to mouth existence: for example, a combined Linfield-Celtic team played The Rest in a match to liquidate an outstanding Irish League debt, and Irish and English women teams opposed each other at Grosvenor Park in aid of the Troops Fund. The Football League too made it clear players under their jurisdiction could only 'guest' for Irish clubs if they were signed under the proper arrangements. In other words there would be no 'open door'.

War creates comradeship, brings out the virtues in people faced with adversity and often there is a charitable approach. This happened when Billy McCracken apologised for his attitude in asking for that £10 international match fee so many years ago, and pleaded, for the first time by letter, for his suspension to be lifted; eventually it was on a 10-4 vote. Soon the redoubtable Billy, who lived until he was ninety-three, was back in action again — refereeing that women's international, and for a fee as well!

With the end of hostilities a civil problem arose. The 1919-20 season saw shots fired into a crowd during an Irish Cup semi-final replay between Belfast Celtic and Glentoran which had dramatic and far-reaching repercussions throughout the country. This could, in effect, be considered the first stage of

'The Split' with two Associations operating in Ireland although many contend the basic cause of this was the political formation of the Irish Free State.

Glentoran and Celtic had drawn 1-1 in an Irish cup semi-final at Windsor Park; in Dublin Shelbourne beat Glenavon 3-1 with the replay of the first game scheduled for 17 March, St. Patrick's Day, at Cliftonville. In the second half Celtic full back Fred Barrett was ordered off after bringing down a Glentoran player; spectators immediately invaded the pitch and the teams were instructed to seek the sanctuary of the dressing rooms. Hundreds spilled on to the turf. The 'Sinn Fein' flag was waved. There were choruses from the terracing of 'The Soldier's Song' and 'A Nation Once Again'.

Three days later Celtic were suspended, only to retaliate immediately, a protest being lodged claiming that Hugh McIlveen's name was not on the list submitted by Glentoran. The protest was upheld on this technicality, the Glens being dismissed from the tournament; Shelbourne's ground was also closed because of scenes during their game with Glenavon.

Celtic issued a writ against the Irish FA on their removal from the Irish Cup only to withdraw it after shareholders persuaded directors not to quit football. The signs were ominous. Unanimity no longer existed in Irish football. Hard line attitudes had developed between Belfast and Dublin. The split, admittedly minimal now, was soon to widen to a chasm.

One of the first Ireland teams after the First World War which drew 1-1 with England in October 1919. *Back row:* T. Dougray (referee), J. Harris, J. Gibson, V. Morgan, T. Chambers. *Centre row*: D. Fitzsimmons, J. Gowdy, D. Lyner, W. O'Hagan, M. Hamill, W. McCracken, C. Watson (IFA Sec.). *Front row*: W. McCandless, P. Gallagher, J. Ferris, W. Lacey (Capt.), W. Emerson, A. Snape.

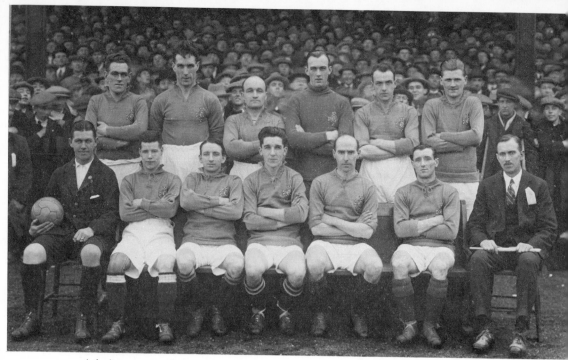

A losing team — defeated 3-0 by Scotland at Windsor Park in 1925. *Back row*: S. Irvine (Dundee), M. O'Brien (Leicester City), W. McCandless (Glasgow Rangers), T. Farquharson (Cardiff City), B. Manderson (Glasgow Rangers), H. Chatton (Partick Thistle). *Front row*: Noel Watson (referee), C. Martin (Boness), P. Gallagher (Glasgow Celtic), E. Carroll (Glenavon), W. Gillespie (Sheffield United), J. Toner (Arsenal), A. Jardine (IFA linesman).

The Split
1921-1930

'The Troubles' of this era disrupted football as groups of armed men engaged in ambushes and attacks on police, military personnel and barracks. The same shadow which later plagued the Seventies had fallen over the game with the Football League deciding not to send a team to Belfast due to what a spokesman described as the 'unsettled, volatile state of the country'. It was a difficult situation with various nations refusing to make the trip across the Irish Sea and the Province becoming an area of soccer isolation.

Dublin clubs declined to compete in the Irish League although Bohemians, Shelbourne, and St. James' Gate entered for the Irish Cup: Shelbourne, drawing 0-0 with Glenavon at Windsor Park in a semi-final, were ordered, much against public opinion, to replay the game there on St. Patrick's Day, 17 March 1921. Shelbourne would not obey; their delegates, protesting at a special Council meeting, got nowhere except to receive the expenses incurred when a military curfew forced an overnight stay in Belfast!

Ireland did send an amateur team to France in January 1921, winning 2-1 and, although political problems bubbled and boiled, clubs, in the tradition of

14

soccer, were able to devote time to their own brand of pressing issues — whether roulette tables or Crown and Anchor boards should be brought into grounds!

What caused the split? Was it the dispute over Shelbourne? That no doubt was a contributory factor but the prime reason appeared to be the formation of the Irish Free State and the desire of the Leinster FA to break away from the parent body. Eire newspaper advertisements described matches in Dublin as being under the 'Football League of Ireland' while games in Belfast were merely 'Belfast and District'.

The new Association in the South sought, without success, the support of England, Scotland and Wales. The Irish FA, determined to remain the governing body for the entire country, asked the Army FA to bar military players from assisting clubs under the jurisdiction of the new Association while the Football League agreed their member clubs would not sign a player from the new Association. Bitterness filled the air, acrimony the Council chamber, and complete deadlock existed in any attempt at conciliation.

To reconstruct the background to this complex issue is almost impossible. There are so many versions, so many theories, so many contradictions. In fact, research simply reveals that everyone possesses a different concept of what actually did happen.

A memorandum produced by the Irish FA and forwarded to the president and members of a FIFA Congress in Lisbon in 1954 when the Republic sought to be declared the only country entitled to use the name 'Ireland' pinpoints many of the complexities. I quote:

> To understand the relative position of the Irish Football Association and the Football Association of Eire, one has to go back a number of years and constantly keep in view the historical background connected with these Associations.
>
> The Irish Football Association was formed in 1880 with its headquarters in Belfast. Its membership was open to all clubs playing association football in Ireland. The Irish Football Association functioned harmoniously until a political movement caused re-adjustment of relations between Ireland and the British Government. Prior to this, International matches between Ireland and the other British Associations — which had been played continuously from 1882 — were arranged both in Dublin and in Belfast, under the control and jurisdiction of the Irish Football Association.
>
> The change came with the passing by the British Parliament of the Act constituting a part of Ireland as the Irish Free State. The Clubs whose headquarters were in the new Free State area and who were in full membership of the IFA seceded from the Association and formed a new Football Association for themselves. These clubs were at once suspended by the Irish Football Association, who desired to maintain the homogeneity of the Association, saw no reason why there should be two Football

15

Associations in an area which hitherto had been happy with one. The point which is vital here is that it was the clubs in the new Free State who left the Irish Football Association and thus made themselves non-members.

In 1922 the new body applied to the British Associations for recognition and membership of the International Board, which was refused. The Board came to the same decision in 1923 when they again sought membership. Following correspondence between FIFA and the Football Association (England) a conference was held in Liverpool on October 18, 1923 with the object of clarifying the position of football in Ireland. The four British Associations met representatives of the new Association, and decided that they should henceforth be known as the Football Association of the Irish Free State, which was the designation of that part of Ireland over which the new Association claimed jurisdiction and agreed that the two Associations would exercise full jurisdiction within their own areas, and would recognise each other's suspensions.

That conference further decided, and this is most important, that the Football Association of the Irish Free State would be recognised as an Association with Dominion Status. On that basis the Irish Football Association agreed to remove the suspensions to enable the new body and their clubs to have friendly relations with other Associations and clubs. But the Irish Football Association remained as the National Association and the only Association entitled to be "Ireland" and this was confirmed at a British Association's Conference held in Liverpool on 14th March, 1925.

From time to time various suggestions were made and conferences held

Another Irish success against Wales — this side won 3-0 at Windsor Park in February 1926. *Back row*: J. Torrans (trainer), M. O'Brien (Hull City), W. Brown (Glenavon), E. Scott (Liverpool), W. McConnell (Reading), T. Sloan (Cardiff City), S. Irving (Dundee), S. Moore (Belfast Celtic), Peter Craigmyle, (referee). *Front row*: T. Robbins (Sec. FAW), W. McCurley (IFA), A. Bothwell (Ards), A. Steele (Charlton Athletic), W. Gillespie (Sheffield United) (Capt.), S. Curran (Belfast Celtic), D. McMullan (Liverpool), C. Watson (Sec. IFA).

to formulate a working agreement between the two Associations. These conferences proved abortive, as they were bound to do with political influences as they existed in the Irish Free State.

But the position altered by the action of the government of the Irish Free State leaving the British Commonwealth. In consequence of this, the FA of the Irish Free State forfeited all claim to any connection with the Irish Football Association and the other British Associations.

The title taken by the once Football Association of the Irish Free State should be altered to the real name of the country over which they claim jurisdiction — that is Eire. It is important to point out at this stage that association football is not recognised as their national game — which is called "Gaelic" and is an amalgamation of association and rugby football. Although their territory may be greater in extent than that of the Irish Football Association, there are vast tracts of that territory in which no association football is played at all.

The position today is that the Irish Football Association remains the National Association, and indeed the only Association entitled to use the title "Ireland". Its territory may be reduced in size but in every other respect it remains unaltered. It carries the confidence of the other British Associations and it takes its place in the British International Championship as "Ireland" and is the only body competent to do so.

The Irish Football Association has suffered many attempts at interference with great tolerance but, in every instance, they have acted within

Ireland 0, Scotland 2 — Windsor Park, February 1927. *Back row*: F. Cochrane (IFA), J. Gowdy (Falkirk), A. McCluggage (Burnley), W. McConnell (Reading), T. Sloan (Cardiff City), D. McMullan (Liverpool), J. Devlin (Belfast Celtic) (trainer). *Front row*: G. Noel Watson (referee), J. McGrillen (Belfast Celtic), P. Gallagher (Falkirk), E. Scott (Liverpool), H. Davey (Reading) (Capt.), S. Irving (Cardiff City), J. Toner (St Johnstone), C. Watson (Sec. IFA).

the laws and within their rights with due regard to the rights of others.

The Irish Football Association has been accepted and recognised as one of the four British Associations since its formation seventy-four years ago, and is, in fact, the fourth oldest Association in the world. All it asks is to be left alone to conduct its own business in its own country as the National Association recognised by the other British Associations and FIFA.

Many efforts had been made to settle the dispute over a three year period, including a conference in the Shelbourne Hotel, Dublin. The Southern delegates issued their demands to the Irish FA led by Captain Wilton who had swiftly become an influential figure. He would not concede an inch. What baffled the Irish FA delegates, however, was the speed with which the Southerners had a statement available for the Press after the meeting. Could it have been prepared beforehand? Was it all a foregone conclusion? A mere cosmetic exercise to meet?

But the FA of the Irish Free State with Sir Henry McLaughlin, K.B.E., a Belfastman and former Cliftonville half-back, as its President would not budge either. One of their chief spokesmen — Larry Sheridan — summed it up like this: 'The cause of this dispute is that the Leinster FA is not prepared to play second fiddle to the Irish FA.' There were disputes on whether an Association like the County Antrim with 200 clubs should have the same representation on the Council as Munster with ten. Should the headquarters be in Belfast or Dublin?

The document issued after the hotel meeting spells out the Southern viewpoint. I quote:

1. All clubs and organisations having their headquarters in the Irish Free State to be under the control of the Football Association of Ireland.
2. Any club or organisation with its headquarters outside the Irish Free State to be eligible for membership of the FAI on the usual conditions.
3. The present Irish Football Association to become the North of Ireland FA (or some similarly named body).
4. The relations between the FAI and the Northern Ireland FA to be similar to the relations existing between the FA of England and the Army FA.
5. Except in competitions in which clubs from both associations participate, the North of Ireland FA to have full control over all clubs and other organisations directly affiliated to it.
6. In competitions open to and participated in by clubs from the two Associations and in all International matters the controlling bodies to consist of representatives of the two Associations and a scale to be arranged.
7. Suspensions of clubs, organisations and players, officials, etc., by the Association to which they are affiliated to be recognised and maintained by the other Association on a scale to be arranged.
8. The North of Ireland FA to have the right to nominate members on all International Selection Committees on a scale to be arranged.

Ireland 4, Wales 0: Windsor Park, December 1931. *Back row*: G. Greenwood (IFA linesman), R. Irvine (Derry City), M. Pyper (Linfield), E. Scott (Liverpool), J. McNinch (Ballymena United), W. McCleery (Linfield), W. Firth (Belfast Celtic) (reserve). *Front row*: P. Snape, (referee), J. Chambers (Nottingham Forest), W. Mitchell (Distillery), J. Bambrick (Linfield), R.P. Fulton (Belfast Celtic), (Capt.), W. Millar (Barrow), J. Kelly (Derry City), C. Watson (Sec. IFA), W Newburn (linesman).

'Impossible,' was the only comment by Captain Wilton who, with the other Irish FA delegates, left the conference immediately. He considered their demands 'out of the question'. They had advocated that instead of shifting the offices from Belfast to Dublin the IFA Executive Committee would meet alternately in Belfast and Dublin. That was rejected. So, too, was a promise that Divisional Associations in the South would have greater powers to deal with clubs under their control, and a guarantee that there would be a reasonable share of international matches in Dublin went unheeded as well. The gulf had widened.

The Irish Free State Association remained bitter. They requested meetings with England and Scotland to be recognised. All failed with the Irish FA the controlling influence in the corridors of powers. An indication of the feeling was revealed in the 1926-7 annual report which stated: 'It is regretted no improvement in the relations of the two Irish Associations can be recorded. The stupid policy of labelling the small Northern Province as Ireland continues to be favoured by England, Scotland and Wales so that the Northern Association has no incentive to come to an agreement. Significant comment on the quality of the game in the two areas is afforded by the fact that with the utmost ease the Football League of the Free State beat the Irish League 3-1.'

The dispute has never been settled. Relations now are much more cordial. There is co-operation on most issues while a dialogue at office-bearer level has started on the possibility of a united team for international matches, although political unrest makes any agreement unlikely in the foreseeable future.

Somehow the game itself survived. Distillery opened their new headquarters at York Park, Belfast, on 3 September 1922, but unquestionably the achievement of the year was Linfield's winning the seven trophies, a feat accomplished again in 1962 by Tommy Dickson's side. The trophies were the Irish Cup, Irish League, Belfast City Cup, Alhambra (Irish League) Cup, Irish Gold Cup, Belfast Charity Cup and the County Antrim Shield — and this was the Irish Cup winning side: Harland, Gaw, Frame, Wallace, Morgan, McIlveen, T. Cowan, McCracken, Savage, McIlreavey, Scott.

Celtic's new stand, accommodating 600, was opened in October 1926, and, at the same time, a severe gale ruined Distillery's unreserved stand at York Park; a 'back to Grosvenor' movement began. Queen's Island won the Irish Cup in 1924, Willowfield in 1928 — the year Ballymena United were formed and, within nine months they too had won the Irish Cup.

W. H. McClatchey, eventually a leading legislator who wrote under the *nom-de-plume* of 'Ralph the Rover' in the *Belfast Telegraph* was appointed secretary of the Northern Ireland Schools FA which he developed into a highly efficient organisation.

Willowfield — winners of the Irish Cup, Steel Cup, Irish Intermediate Cup, Intermediate League season 1927-28. *Back row*: H. McCullough, J. Higgins, N. Cromie, W. Neely, J. Millar, G. Best, T. Millar, J. Thompson. *Centre row*: W. Ritchie (trainer), H. Vance, J. Mallon, Dr. Gibson (Pres.), C. McFarlane, T. Conway, R. Young, R. Esdale. *Front row*: W. McCullough (Sec), J. Aicken, J. Hume, C. McClure, J. Kirkwood (captain), W. Kimlin, R. Shaw, W. Clarke (Chairman).

This, of course, was the spectacular era for international matches with Ireland defeating Wales 7-0 on Saturday 1 February 1930 at Celtic Park, Joe Bambrick hitting six, a record which still stands, and Andy McCluggage getting the other from a penalty. Joe, nicknamed 'Head Heel or Toe' scored ninety-four goals that season, a year later Fred Roberts (Glentoran) made it ninety-six, a record which stands to this day. Jackie Mahood (Belfast Celtic) scored fifty from the wing and, with his brother Stanley, formed an effective left wing partnership. A goal famine was something foreign to the Irish game then.

A historic day: Saturday, 2 February 1930, when Ireland defeated Wales 7-0 at Celtic Park, with Joe Bambrick scoring six of the goals. A historic team too. *Back row*: J.R. McFarlane (linesman), J. Jones (Linfield), A. Gardiner (Cliftonville), R.P. Fulton (Celtic), T. Sloan (Linfield), W. McCreery (Linfield), J. Devlin (trainer). *Front row*: T. Crewe (referee), J. Chambers (Bury), R. Rowley (Southampton), J. Bambrick (Linfield), A. McCluggage (Burnley) (Capt.), J. McCambridge (Ballymena), J. Mahood (Belfast Celtic), A. Bell (linesman).

Harry Cavan, IFA President since 1958.

The Era of Turmoil

The decades of the thirties, forties and fifties could be described as difficult. Thirty years of strife, unemployment, war, mediocre football and, of course, the post-war boom.

To study the minute books and the Irish FA annual reports is a fascinating exercise. For instance, there is reference in 1938 to 'tactics being employed which are not in keeping with the game'; that clubs were not receiving their due support due to 'the prevailing unemployment in the area'.

There was the 1939 Irish Cup 2-1 win by Ballymena United over Glenavon with gate receipts totalling £1,379 15s. 0d.; the operating of the Irish Cup on a two-round principle during the war years; Linfield defeating Glentoran 3-1 in the first final; the phenomenal success of the Regional League and the inter-city tournament. There was also the death of the President, Sir James Wilton, whose memory was commemorated by the endowment of two beds in the City and County Infirmary, Londonderry, and the unveiling of a portrait in the Irish FA headquarters. Austin Donnelly (1945-48) succeeded him followed by Fred J. Cochrane (1948-1957), Joseph MacBride (1957-58) and the present incumbent Harry Cavan (1958-   ). All made their contributions to the game in this island with their legislative know-how and ability to handle people and problems. They steered the Association into (no matter what the cynics may say) one of the most progressive-thinking in football.

Of them all, however, Harry Cavan has, without question, made the most decisive impact on world football. His diplomacy has earned him praise from many parts of the world where he has helped sort out disputes and age-old controversies such as sporting apartheid in South Africa or the Greek-Turkish conflict in Cyprus. He is an ideal leader, astute, shrewd, considerate.

That is not surprising for Harry Hatrick Cavan, a former coach builder and Divisional Officer for Northern Ireland of the Association of Scientific, Technical and Managerial Staffs, was always the man in charge. When at school he was invariably selected to collect the pennies to buy the ball; from those days his flair for organisation has always been recognised.

In one hundred years of Irish football there have been many great players and some have become superstars, but for influence and power in the Council chambers of football Harry Cavan, who began his career with his local club Ards (of which he still remains director and honorary secretary), has no peers. He has done everything at Castlereagh Park — from ball boy to painting the posts; indeed he still acts as the DJ and public address announcer there on match days.

He played in junior football until fracturing a bone in his right foot. He was then elected to the honorary secretaryship of Ards in 1942 when the club was competing in the Intermediate League; his thoughts, however, turned to legislation with all its problems and in December 1945, he entered the Irish FA.

He was overawed on the first night he took his seat in the Council Chamber, Wellington Place. Later these headquarters were situated at Ulster Chambers, Waring Street, Belfast, and then at 20 Windsor Avenue, Belfast.

Mr. Cavan, a realist, was a member of the International Committee responsible for the introduction of a team manager; he played a big part too in the development of coaching, and, with Victor Ferris, was for years selector in charge of the international team. After the 1958 World Cup series he returned home to be elected president of the Irish FA. It is a post he has filled with distinction; his award of the O.B.E. by the Queen in 1978 was just recognition of his services and his dedication to the game, not only in his native Province but wherever it is played. He has always held firm in the belief that international football and its administration can draw people together rather than drive them apart.

The first Irishman to be a Vice-President of FIFA, representing the four British Associations, after 20 years in that position, he is now the Senior Vice-President and Deputy Chairman of FIFA's Emergency Committee. A member of the World Cup Organising Committee since 1966, his other posts include Chairman of the Technical Committee of FIFA and of the Development Projects.

The task of presiding over the Organising Committee of the first and second

IFA Secretary Billy Drennan at work in his office in Windsor Avenue. He was the youngest soccer secretary in the world when appointed — now he is the longest serving, the elder statesman.

World Youth Tournaments in Tunisia in 1977 and Japan 1979 was entrusted to him. He is the Chairman of the Organising Committee of the third World Youth Championship to be held in Australia in 1981.

His career has run almost parallel with that of William J. (Billy) Drennan, a former local Government officer, who became the youngest secretary in football when appointed in 1950. Now he is the elder statesman, a member of the UEFA Clubs Cups Competition Committee and his contribution to the game has also been immense.

Billy Drennan captained the Belfast Battalion of the Boys Brigade team against the Glasgow Battalion at Hampden Park, Glasgow. It was this wonderful organisation in which millions of boys have served with benefit to themselves which formulated his principles of life, his honesty, his dedication, his sincerity. It gave him pride — pride to do a job thoroughly. Saturday, 28 September 1946, was the day when Billy Drennan really came to the attention of the Ulster public. A part-time sports broadcaster, he had been given the job of making the announcements over the public address system at the Ireland-England game. The schedule was normal until twelve minutes before kick-off; then, with the Windsor Park terraces packed to suffocation, many of the 57,000 crowd spilled over the parapets and on to the track as referee Willie Webb (Glasgow) pleaded hopelessly for them to return.

England players were instructed not to take the field until it was cleared. As the hands of the clock worked ominously to 3 p.m. Drennan grabbed the microphone. 'This match will not take place unless the crowd goes back,' he said. There were cheers from those on the terraces whose view had been obstructed. Still there was no movement. 'If those on the track are not back on the terraces within three minutes they will be removed by the police,' he repeated. One by one they obeyed as if hypnotised. By 3 p.m. it was all over. He was the man who had saved an international.

Since then Drennan has staged many internationals at Windsor Park as well as organising those played away from home during the height of the political unrest in the early and mid-Seventies. Tours abroad are meticulously planned so that each journey dovetails into the next; his ability has earned him the utmost respect from players, officials and the Press who always form part of the Irish FA international family and are not, as happens with other countries, kept in isolation.

Harry Cavan and Billy Drennan, backed by the Council, guided the Association during the Fifties to the 75th anniversary in August 1955, which saw the first team to play under the banner of the newly-formed European Football Union. Led by UEFA co-founder Joe Crahay (Belgium), and coached by French trainer Pierre Pibarot, it triumphed 4-1 before 58,000 at Windsor Park.

What was planned as Ireland's greatest ever soccer spectacular developed into a one-sided bore. Bernard Vukas (Yugoslavia) hit a hat-trick and Jean

IFA Council, 1955 (year of the 75th anniversary). *Front row*: J. Harrison, W.M. Wilton, W. Carlisle, W.A. Corry, J.B. Beggs. *Second row*: H. Dunlop, J.O. Bailie, J. Rock, A. Ferris, T.C. Mullan, J.N. Doherty. *Third row*: R. Peel, J.C. Williamson, J. Cull, F.J. Holland, H. Cavan, Major A. Dixon, W.J. Nicholl. *Fourth row*: W.J. Drennan (Sec.), T. Moorhead, W. McComb, T. Kerr, J.H. McMaster, M. McColgan, J. MacBride (Vice Pres.), F.J. Cochrane (Pres.), G. Jones (Treas.), W.A. McClatchey, G. Sidebottom.

Ireland's Saturday Night's story of the 75th anniversary game between the United Kingdom and Europe, Windsor Park, 13 August 1955.

Vincent (France), now manager of FC Nantes, hammered home the other goal; the Continentals remained supreme. The somewhat pathetic British side lacked spirit, strategy, skill: a collection of big names who never put it together. British footballers were seen to be very much the pupils — backward pupils.

The teams were:—

United Kingdom: Kelsey (Arsenal), Sillett (Chelsea), McDonald (Sunderland), D. Blanchflower (Tottenham Hotspur) *Captain*, Charles (Leeds United), Peacock (Glasgow Celtic), Matthews (Blackpool), Johnstone (Manchester City), Bentley (Chelsea), McIlroy (Burnley), Liddell (Liverpool).

Rest of Europe: Buffon (Italy), Gustavson (Sweden), Van Brandt (Belgium), Ocwirk (Austria) *Captain*, Jonquet (France), Boskov (Yugoslavia), Soerensen (Italy), Travassos (Portugal), Kopa (France), Vukas (Yugoslavia), Vincent (France).

Referee: M. J. Helges (Belgium).

The first football team to take the field under the banner of the newly-formed European Football Union played Great Britain at Windsor Park on 13 August 1955, in a match to mark the seventy-fifth anniversary of the Northern Ireland FA. The UEFA XI won 4-1.

UEFA XI. *Back row:* Pierre Pibarot (France) (coach), Alphonse Van Brandt (Belgium), Bengt Gustavsson (Sweden), Lorenzo Buffon (Italy), Jean Vincent (France), Pierre Jonquet (France). *Front row:* Bernard Vukas (Yugoslavia), Leslie Sœrensen (Italy/Denmark), Ernst Ocwirk (Austria) (Capt.), Vujadin Boskov (Yugoslavia), Raymond Kopa (France), José Travassos (Portugal).

Great Britain. *Back row:* Gerry Morgan (Northern Ireland) (coach), Tommy Docherty (Scotland), William Fraser (Scotland), Don Revie (England), Peter Sillett (England), Jack Kelsey (Wales), Roger Byrne (England), Walter Winterbottom (England) (team trainer). *Front row:* Stanley Matthews (England), Billy Liddell (Scotland), Joe McDonald (Scotland), Bobby Johnstone (Scotland), Danny Blanchflower (Northern Ireland) (Capt.), Bertie Peacock (Northern Ireland), Jimmy McIlroy (Northern Ireland), Roy Bentley (England), John Charles (Wales).

Two years earlier, the Irish FA embarked on a U.S.-Canadian tour — a coast-to-coast junket with travel by ship from Liverpool to Montreal. It was not an outstanding success from a playing viewpoint, with some disappointing results, especially in British Columbia. No manager accompanied the side, discipline was not what it should have been in certain cases, and many of the leading players were not available for the trip. It began with a 4-0 defeat by Liverpool at Ebbets Field, New York, former home of the Brooklyn Dodgers, ending a month later with a 4-1 thrashing by Berne Young Boys in Montreal where Sammy Hughes (Glentoran) broke his leg.

The Irish party in 1953 en route for Montreal and a two-month tour of the US and Canada. *Back row*: N. Uprichard, N. Lockhart, T. Casey, L. Graham, J. Scott, D. Blanchflower, E. McMorran, S. Hughes, A. McMichael, G. Morgan (trainer), J. McCabe. *Front row*: G. Bowler, F. McCourt, W.J. Drennan (IFA Sec.), A. Kennedy (IFA), F.J. Cochrane (IFA Pres.), S. Walker (IFA), R. Ferris, W. Neill, E. Crossan, J. D'Arcy.

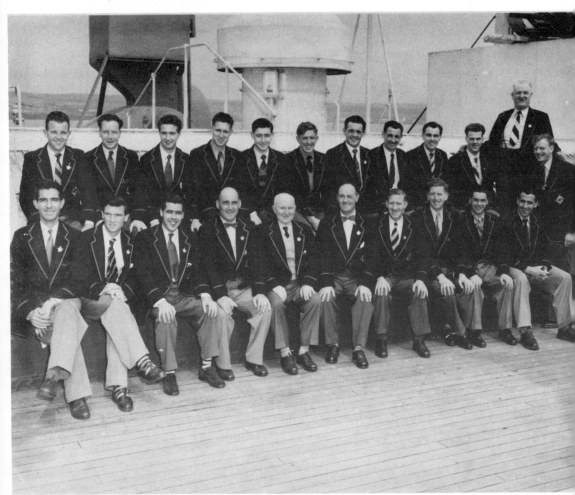

The results were:

May 14 (New York)	Ireland	0	Liverpool	4
May 18	Ireland	4	Hamilton and District	1
May 20	Ireland	2	Ontario	0
May 24	Ireland	2	Manitoba	0
May 26	Ireland	10	Saskatchewan	0
May 31	Ireland	3	Vancouver All Stars	1
June 7	Ireland	2	British Columbia	3
June 8	Ireland	9	Alberta	1
June 14 (Toronto)	Ireland	1	Liverpool	3
June 17	Ireland	1	Berne Young Boys	4

During this Cavan-Drennan reign Irish clubs decided to embark on the European club scene. Glenavon pioneered the way in the European Cup tie against Aarhus (Denmark) in 1957-8 and also in the Cup Winners against Leicester City (1961-2), while Glentoran were the first member club to compete in the old Fairs Cup (1962-3). No entry was made in any of the European competitions in 1972-3 because of 'The Troubles'; all matches were played before and since without incident, a tribute to how football can so often stand above the politics of a country.

There have been problems in this series, too. Glenavon withdrew in 1960-1 against Wismut (East Germany) because of visa difficulties; the following year Linfield travelled to Vorwaerts (East Berlin) and were defeated 3-0, but the East German Army side could not get travel documents for the West and the second leg had to be abandoned, Linfield eventually being compensated years later.

Linfield, who had ex-England centre-forward Jackie Milburn playing for them in the late Fifties and early Sixties, reached the quarter finals in 1966-7 only to be beaten by CSKA Sofia on the away goal principle. Glentoran drew 1-1 with Benfica in Belfast, and 0-0 in Lisbon in 1967-8 after their return from the triumphant US tour as the Detroit Cougars under the sponsorship of the Ford Motor Company who were then promoting the Cougar car. Distillery, with England winger Tommy Finney playing for them, drew 3-3 with Benfica at Windsor Park in 1963-4, but lost 5-0 in Lisbon.

Glentoran had also the distinction of being quarter finalists. That was in 1973-4, disposing of Chimia Rimnicu Vilcea on a 4-2 aggregate, Brann Bergen 1-1 and 3-1, but losing 2-0 and 5-0 to Borussia Moenchengladbach in the quarter finals. The Seventies were a difficult time for Irish football because of civil unrest. But competitions — the Irish League (Fiat), the Irish Cup (Bass) and the Gold Cup (Hennessy) — were all sponsored as commercial backing and flourishing social centres poured cash into the game. It survived the turmoil and that in itself was a feat. No doubt it will continue to do just that over the next ten years and the next century.

The Irish League side which defeated the English League 2-1 at Blackpool in September 1935. *Back row*: H. Bullock (Portadown) (reserve), E. Cassidy (Newry Town) (reserve), K. McCullough (Belfast Celtic), N. Millar (Glentoran); E. Scott (Belfast Celtic), C. A. Allen (Cliftonville), R. Browne (Derry City), H. Good (trainer), G. McAllister (Irish linesman). *Front row*: W. R. Hunt (English linesman), N. Kernaghan (Belfast Celtic), E. D. R. Shearer (Derry City), P. McNally (Distillery), J. Jones (Linfield), L. Conwell (Portadown), J. Kelly (Derry City), H. Nattrass (referee).

The Irish League

Next in legislative importance to the Irish FA is the Irish League, a body responsible for the League Championship, Ulster Cup and Gold Cup as well as competing — when the Province's political circumstances permit — in the inter-league series with England, Scotland and the Republic of Ireland. Delegates are sent from twelve senior clubs while the B Division is composed of representatives from twenty-eight, including the reserves of some senior sides. Its present chairman is Ken Pritchard (Larne).

It is a league with a colourful, if locally confined history, rarely venturing beyond its own boundaries. The inaugural meeting on 14 March 1890 was held in the Belfast Estate Office of the Marquess of Dufferin and Ava with eight clubs agreeing to participate — Cliftonville, Clarence, Distillery, Glentoran, Linfield, Milford, Oldpark and Ulster.

Twelve people actually attended that meeting — W. McNeice, a grandfather of present Glentoran director Tom McNeice, J. R. Spiller, W. Finlay, W. Couser, J. McClatchey, S. Monroe, J. McKnight, C. Birkby, J. Torrans, J. W. Gordon, J. Henderson and W. S. Dawson; first office-bearers were:— W.

McNeice (Chairman), W. Finlay (Treasurer), J. W. Gordon (Honorary Secretary).

Fourteen matches were played with Linfield as the first champions and Ulster as runners-up. This is how the League table for the 1890-1 season finished:

	P	W	D	L	F	A	Pts
Linfield	14	12	1	1	89	18	25
Ulster	14	9	3	2	72	39	21
Distillery	14	9	1	4	46	37	19
Cliftonville	14	7	3	4	37	46	17
Glentoran	14	6	1	7	40	38	13
Oldpark	14	4	2	8	22	48	10
Clarence	14	3	1	10	21	49	7
Milford	14	0	0	14	10	62	0

Linfield won the title the next season with virtually an unchanged team and in the season after that clubs were increased to ten: Clarence and Milford resigned. The Lancashire Fusiliers, Ligoniel, Milltown and Y.M.C.A. were admitted, but this number proved unworkable and it was later reduced to six.

Inter-league matches with Scotland were inaugurated in 1893, with Irish League winning 5-2; next season came a 4-2 defeat by England. Results in this series have, however, been lop-sided but there were a number of occasions against England which proved to be memorable. The first was in 1935-6 when Ireland won 2-1 at Blackpool; in 1936-7 there was a 3-2 triumph at home. And, of course, in 1955-6 the greatest victory of all was achieved — 5-2 against an English side — the basis of the national one to meet Brazil as well as tour West Germany and Spain.

The team at Blackpool was E. Scott (Belfast Celtic), Millar (Glentoran), Allen (Cliftonville), McCullough (Belfast Celtic), Jones (Linfield) *Captain*, Brown (Derry City), Kernaghan (Belfast Celtic), E. D. R. Shearer (Derry City), McNally (Distillery), Conwell (Portadown), Kelly (Derry City). McNally and Kelly got the goals.

George Eastham Jnr., later to be an England inside forward, inspired the Irish League, managed by Billy McCreery (Linfield), to that dazzling 1955-6 display before 25,000 at Windsor Park. One newspaper headline put it like this; 'Not luck, no fluke, but sheer soccer brilliance'. So stunned was an English columnist that he began his story with the words 'Shampoo me with a shillelagh'. The team was:— Russell (Linfield), Keith (Linfield), Davis (Crusaders), Corr (Glenavon), Hamill (Linfield), Cush (Glenavon), Hill (Linfield), Eastham (Ards), Jones (Glenavon), Dickson (Linfield) *Captain*, Weatherup (Linfield); *Reserve*: Newberry (Ards). Irish League scorers were Hill, Weatherup, Dickson (2) and Eastham.

Another match always figuring in discussions was the Irish League 1-0 success over the Combined Services XI at Cliftonville on 17 September 1945. Two days earlier the Combined Services played as England in a victory international, winning 1-0 at Windsor Park before 46,000 (gate receipts

One of the memorable Irish League victories: 1-0, against the Combined Services at Cliftonville on 17 September 1945. *Back row*: D. Maxwell (referee), S. McMillen (linesman), J. Wilson (Cliftonville), G. Bowler (Distillery), G. Matier (Glentoran), T. Aherne (Celtic), R. Langton (Glentoran), J. Deakin (Glentoran), F. T. Mowat (linesman). *Front row*: P. Bonnar (Celtic), S. McCrory (Linfield), W. McMillen (Celtic) (Capt.), J. Feeney (Linfield), J. McCarthy (Celtic).

£4,450). Stanley Mortensen (Blackpool) hit the winning goal with Peter Craigmyle (Scotland) acting as the referee.

Cliftonville was bursting at the seams with 15,000 crammed into the stadium in an atmosphere of anticipation as the crowd, starved of seeing the real stars, released those pent-up emotions of the War. Sammy McCrory achieved immortality with the winning goal, just as he did against England at Wembley more than a decade later.

For the record the teams that night were:—

Irish League: Matier (Glentoran), McMillan (Belfast Celtic) *Captain*, Feeney (Linfield), Wilson (Cliftonville), Bowler (Distillery), Aherne (Belfast Celtic), Bonnar (Belfast Celtic), McCrory (Linfield), McCarthy (Belfast Celtic), Deakin (Glentoran), Langton (Glentoran).

Combined Services: Swift (Manchester City), Scott (Arsenal), Kinsella (West Bromwich Albion), Soo (Stoke City), Franklin (Stoke City), Mercer (Everton) *Captain*, Matthews (Stoke City), Mortensen (Blackpool), Lawton (Everton), Wright (Wolverhampton Wanderers), Watson (Huddersfield Town).

Southern clubs eventually became members of the League in those formative years but, ironically, none of them ever won the Gibson Cup awarded to the Champions. It was a comparatively tranquil set-up then, with the same delegates returned year after year; in fact, Linfield's Sam Close missed only one meeting in thirteen seasons.

Still, problems were just around the corner. There was the 1912 dispute, mentioned in an earlier chapter, where senior clubs demanded the entire receipts from the Irish Cup final, and the proposal to play the Paris League on Sunday, a day prohibited then for football under Irish FA rules. Initially, the League approved the match but it was later overwhelmingly defeated on a proposal by Fred McKee and Bertie Andrews. As no new date could be found the match had to be cancelled.

Not until 1962 did the Irish League venture beyond the British Isles when they met the Italian semi-professional league at Arezzo, Florence, in a return fixture for the Italians' appearance in Belfast twelve months earlier. Over the years clubs have flourished, flickered and then faded out. Others continue to fold from season to season and of the original eight only Linfield, Distillery, Cliftonville and Glentoran are in existence today.

Lack of finance was the main cause of demise in the first forty years and then, as a result of the Second World War, a regional league was formed, through sheer necessity in 1940 after Linfield, Belfast Celtic, Distillery and Glentoran announced that they did not propose to take part in Irish League competitions but in a series more suited to the wartime conditions. Approval was given by the Irish FA to the new competition in which Belfast Celtic, Distillery, Linfield, Glentoran, Cliftonville, Glenavon, Portadown and Coleraine at varying times participated. This ran in conjunction with the lucrative, crowd-pulling North-South tournament until 1947 when the Irish League Championship was resumed once again.

The twelve clubs now in membership are Ards (formed 1902), Ballymena United (1934), Bangor (1927), Coleraine (1927), Cliftonville (1879), Crusaders (1909), Distillery (1880), Glenavon (1889), Glentoran (1882), Linfield (1886), Larne (1889), and Portadown (1924).. Glentoran claim they were the original Irish winners of a European competition — the Vienna Cup, a tournament staged in the Austrian capital during the 1913-4 season. In their boardroom is a photograph of the late Davy Lyner with the trophy.

Belfast Celtic withdrew in 1949, and, at the height of the civil unrest in 1972, Distillery were forced to evacuate Grosvenor Park, Belfast — now the site of a housing complex. They were accommodated by Crusaders at Seaview, by Brantwood at Skegoniel Avenue, then back to Seaview again and they hope this year to gain occupancy of a new stadium at Ballyskeag, Lambeg, a former pony trotting track, with considerable development potential.

Derry City (1928) withdrew in October 1972 after clubs had refused for security reasons to play at Brandywell where, earlier, the Ballymena United bus had been hi-jacked and burned; Derry directors, however, plan a return to senior football soon at a new stadium on the Buncrana Road.

Belfast Celtic (1891) were admitted to the Irish League in 1896, but, as a junior club, had defeated Linfield 1-0; it was the start of great rivalry, the true fabric of Irish football. They withdrew from 1915 until 1917-8; then again in 1920 until 1924, and finally once more in 1949 after the turmoil of the 1948 Boxing Day game at Celtic Park in which Jimmy Jones (Celtic) had his leg broken when attacked by the crowd.

Belfast Celtic photographed before their departure from Belfast for the United States in May 1949; on the extreme left is Mr. Austin Donnelly, Patsy McAlinden, and second from right, Elisha Scott.

They were the first Irish club to tour Europe, winning four out of five matches in an Austrian series during 1912. But it was not until 1949 when, touring the United States, they obtained a victory considered a high-water mark of local football — a 2-0 triumph over Scotland before 15,000 at the Triborough Stadium, New York. Johnny Campbell scored the goals in the 27th and 54th minutes.

29 May 1949 is a day of glory for all Celtic fans. The teams were:—

Belfast Celtic: McAlinden, McMillan, Aherne, Walker, Currie, Lawler, Moore, Dorman, Campbell, O'Flanagan, Bonnar.

Scotland: Brown, Govan, Young, Evans, Telfer, Cox, Waddell, Redpath, Thornton, Steel, McKensie.

The Tour record was: P10 W6 L2 D2 F30 A17.

May 8	(Toronto)	Ireland	2	American All Stars	2
May 12	(Toronto)	Ireland	5	Ulster United	0
May 14	(New Jersey)	Ireland	3	Kearney Scots	0
May 18	(Fall River)	Ireland	1	New England All Stars	2
May 25	(Philadelphia)	Ireland	6	Philadelphia All Stars	4
May 29	(New York)	Ireland	2	Scotland	0
May 30	(New York)	Ireland	3	Philadelphia Nationals	3
June 1	(Montreal)	Ireland	4	Montreal All Stars	1
June 5	(Detroit)	Ireland	4	Dave Kennedy Club	2
June 12	(New York)	Ireland	0	Kamratrna (Sweden)	3

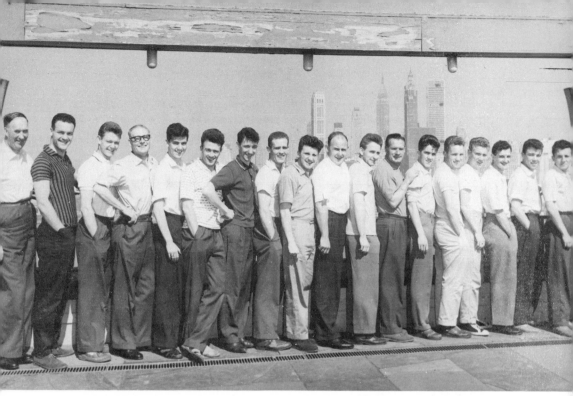

Glenavon competed in the 1960 New York Tournament. Here they are photographed on the roof of the George Hotel, Brooklyn. *From left*: Billy Walker (Secretary), Jim McKinstry, Jack McClelland, Jack Jones (Trainer), Derek Meldrum, Roy Rea, Hugh Forde, Sammy Wilson, Syd Weatherup, Jimmy Jones, Tommy Lucas, Jimmy McAlinden (Manager), Sammy Magee, Bobby Armstrong, Gerry Kearney, Stewart Campbell, Freddie Clarke, Ken Wilson.

Glentoran, the Detroit Cougars, before a match with Sunderland at the Varcity Stadium, Detroit. *Left to right*: Tommy Jackson, Billy Sinclair, Walter Bruce, Jim Weatherup, Roy Borne, Billy McKeag, Arthur Stewart, Eric Ross, Sammy Kydd, Tommy Morrow, Danny Trainor, Billy McCullough, Alan McNeill, Harry Creighton, John Colrain and John Kennedy.

Glenavon followed on the American circuit in 1960, competing in a tournament organised by millionaire entrepeneur Bill Cox, based on the Polo Grounds, New York, and the Roosevelt Stadium, Jersey City. This was their record — v New York 5-1, v Kilmarnock 0-2, v Bayern Munich 0-3, v Burnley 2-6 v Nice 2-3.

But perhaps the most outstanding tour of all — certainly the opposition was much more powerful — came in 1967 when Glentoran competed under the name of the Detroit Cougars in a tournament, operated on a coast-to-coast basis, and the forerunner to the present, widespread development of soccer in the States. Managed by John Colrain, ex Glasgow Celtic and Ipswich forward, they had a highly successful series; on their return home they were given a welcome by crowds lining the routes from the City Hall to the Oval. It was a phenomenal night reminiscent of that in 1962 when Linfield toured Sandy Row after winning the seven trophies.

Glentoran's results were: v Shamrock Rovers (Boston) 1-1; v Sunderland (Detroit) 1-1; v Shamrock Rovers (Detroit) 1-0; v Aberdeen (Detroit) 2-2; v Bangu Brazil (Detroit) 0-2 (abandoned with seventeen minutes left because of riots); v Wolves (Los Angeles) 1-4; v A.D.O. Hague (San Francisco) 1-6; v Dundee Utd. (Detroit) 1-0; v Cagliari Sardinia (Chicago) 1-1; v Cerro

Linfield's 1962 Seven Trophy Winning Team. *Back row (left to right)*: Leslie McClean, Jimmy McCune, Jim Reid, John Parke, Ken Gilliland, Bobby Irvine, Sammy Hatton, Jackie Graham, Billy Wilson, Ray Gough, Billy McComb, Tommy Armstrong. *Front row*: Isaac Andrews, Tommy Stewart, Billy Ferguson, Tommy Dickson, Hubert Barr, Bobby Braithwaite, Isaac McDowell.

Montevideo (New York) 1-0; v Stoke City (Detroit) 0-0; v Hibernian (Toronto) 1-1.

Unlike the Irish FA there have been many presidents in the League. Andrew Smith (Cliftonville) (1959-65) gained distinction in two sports as an Irish Cup medallist with Ards and a world-renowned international boxing referee. The list of presidents makes interesting reading:—

1890-3 W. McNeice (Cliftonville); 1893-7 J. McKnight (Glentoran); 1897-8 J. Johnston (Linfield); 1898-9 S. Monroe (Distillery); 1899-1900 C. McShane (Belfast Celtic); 1900-1 W. B. Burrowes; 1901-2 J. McKnight (Glentoran); 1902-3 W. Whitten (Linfield); 1903-4 S. Monroe (Distillery); 1904-5 A. Lockhart (Belfast Celtic); 1905-6 J. McAnerney (Derry City); 1906-7 S. C. Irvine (Cliftonville); 1907-8 T. D. Reid (Glentoran); 1908-9 D. McCloskey, J.P. (Bohemians); 1909-10 J. Gibson (Linfield); 1910-11 A. McAughey (Distillery); 1911-12 J. Price (Shelbourne); 1912-13 H. McAlinden (Belfast Celtic); 1913-14 J. Clarke (Cliftonville); 1914-15 T. H. Adams (Glentoran); 1915-16 W. Fitzsimmons (Bohemians); 1916-17 T. H. Chambers (Linfield); 1917-18 T. Topping (Glenavon); 1918-19 W. H. Stewart (Distillery); 1919-20 J. Walsh (Shelbourne); 1920-21 R. Barr (Belfast Celtic); 1921-22 J. Blair (Cliftonville); 1922-23 T. Moore (Glentoran); 1923-24 F. W. McKee (Linfield); 1924-26 N. Booth (Glenavon); 1926-31 G. I. Long (Distillery); 1931-37 J. Ferguson; 1937-40 G. Tate, J.P. (Linfield); 1940-41 Dr. N. E. Williams (Newry T.); 1941-42 J. T. Mercer (Glentoran); 1942-43 Dr. T. E. Hill (Distillery); 1943-44 A. F. Heggarty (Belfast Celtic); 1944-45 R. B. Andrews (Cliftonville); 1945-46 T. M. Harvey (Linfield); 1946-47 R. Patterson (Distillery); 1947-48 A. F. Heggarty (Belfast Celtic); 1948-50 R. B. Andrews (Cliftonville); 1950-56 Dr. G. Scarlett (Linfield); 1956-59 S. Walker (Coleraine); 1959-65 A. F. Smyth (Cliftonville); 1965-76 W. Kennedy (Glenavon); 1976- J. Apperson (Bangor).

The Irish side which defeated Wales 1-0 in March 1938 at Windsor Park. *Back row*: A. Lumberg (Welsh linesman), J. Leathem (Belfast Celtic), T. Brolly (Millwall), W. McMillen (Chesterfield), J. Twoomey (Leeds United), R.P. Fulton (Belfast Celtic), W. R. Browne (Leeds United), H. Webb (IFA linesman). *Front row*: J. Brown (Coventry City), P. Farrell (Hibernian), W. Cook (Everton), J. Bambrick (Chelsea), A. Stevenson (Everton), J. Coulter (Grimsby), R.E. Mortimer (referee).

The Greats:
1888-1930

Superstar is a catchword of the Seventies. Yet when one looks back at the first forty years of football in this country there were many who could have been aptly given that appellation. Players such as Olphie Stanfield, who won thirty caps; Sam Irvine, a Scot from Dundee who was eligible to play for Ireland; the Pyper brothers, John and James; John Peden; Johnny Darling; Bob Milne; Sam Torrans; Paddy O'Connell; Sam Young; Val Harris; Sandy Craig; English McConnell; Bobby Irvine; Johnny Houston; Billy Houston; Barney Moorhead (who often walked from Lurgan to Belfast to play for Linfield); that magnificent Glentoran half-back line of Johnny Scraggs, Billy Emerson, and George Ferrit; Jimmy Ferris whose career was cut short by ill health; to name but a few.

A player, however, who made a decisive impact was inside left Billy Gillespie, a brilliant individualist, a general. It was Gillespie and his left wing partner Fred Tunstall who engineered Sheffield United's FA Cup triumph in 1925 with a 1-0 victory over Cardiff City and he was, of course, a member of that Irish team which won the championship in 1913-14. A medal and a gold watch presented to him on that occasion were souvenirs which he cherished all his life.

Gillespie, discovered in Londonderry junior football, signed for Derry City, played a trial for Linfield who, much too dilatory in finalising an agreement, allowed Leeds City manager Scott Walford to snap him up. He stayed only a season and a half with City before joining Sheffield United, remaining there until 1932 when he returned to Derry as manager for nine years. Derry under his control finished runners-up in the Irish League on three occasions, won the City Cup twice and reached the Irish Cup Final only to be beaten by Linfield in a replay.

'I had a wonderful time playing with Sheffield United. I loved every minute of it. I broke my leg playing against Sunderland in 1914, missed the English Cup that season but from then on I never looked back,' said Billy, who was capped twenty-five times and would have earned many more honours if United had released him.

Perhaps, however, the real superstar arrived on the scene nearly a decade later — the legendary Joe Bambrick, prolific scorer of goals and a hero to this day. 'Slip it to Joe.' Four words which are part of Irish football history — and the story of Linfield. Bambrick is an immortal Irishman, an immortal Blueman. That day in 1930 when he scored those six goals for Ireland against Wales still raise innumerable queries. The date was 1 February. Was it a Saturday? Who scored the other goal? These points are forever raised. Well, yes, it was a Saturday. And Andy McCluggage (Burnley), the captain got the other.

Bambrick's feat that day has never been equalled in international football; perhaps it never will be either. Joe, even for those who never saw him in his heyday, possessed an idolatry, a charisma which never diminished with the passing of the years. Although Joe had a golden era at Windsor it was, ironically, with those arch rivals Glentoran that he first gained prominence as a shy young man with black hair and a penchant for scoring some remarkable goals. They came from the head, heel or toe. 'Bambrick shoots hard and often,' wrote a critic in April, 1927. 'He can distribute play with class, is always in position to finish off the work of colleagues. With experience he should go far.' How prophetic that comment proved, for Joe quickly developed into a cult figure.

His prowess with Bridgemount in the Belfast Combination soon flashed across the local grapevine; it was underlined also with Ulster Rangers and, briefly, with Broadway United and for that season at the Oval where he won an amateur international cap against England. Goal after goal was scored by him in amazing fashion: it was as if the centre-forward hero in those schoolboy books had arrived — Roy of the Rovers, the type who could do no wrong.

So, at the end of the 1927 season Joe Bambrick signed for Linfield to start a never-to-be-forgotten era; in his first match he hit a hat-trick against a visiting Everton side. That goal avalanche had started. In the 1929-30 season he established a record with 94 goals which were made up like this — Irish League

50, City Cup 10, Charity Cup 9, Irish Cup 7, Internationals 6, Inter-League 5, County Antrim Shield 5, Gold Cup 1, Condor Cup 1.

How did that catchphrase 'Slip it to Joe' originate? There are many versions, many claimants but research reveals it was the work of inside left Eddie Matthews. He had been rushed to hospital for a cartilage operation after his knee locked in a game. As Eddie came out of the anaesthetic he shouted, 'Slip it to Joe.' In the same ward was a comedian appearing on the bill at the Empire Theatre, who added the words 'Head, heel or toe'. So 'Slip it to Joe' became the catchphrase just as 'You'll never walk alone' and 'Que sera, sera' emanates from the terraces these days.

Joe's career was almost prematurely cut short when, on 8 December 1930, he cut his hand at the end of a training session when he accidentally put it through a pane of glass. A nerve in the wrist was partially severed but an operation saved the use of that hand; bulletins were issued daily from the hospital — an indication of the impact he made on the community.

Joe was unruffled by success, loved by the fans — and how could he be anything else for the joy he gave them? They came from everywhere to see him score those goals. He was in many ways the first pop idol of Irish football.

Joe was heralded in song and story. They wisecracked about him in the music-halls, his name was on the lips of everyone in shops, offices, factories, the shipyard in those dark days of the Depression. He was twenty-seven when he transferred to Chelsea in 1934 for £2,250 after manager Leslie Knighton had watched him in seven matches. His pal, Billy Mitchell, met him at St. Pancras Station and, within five days, he played against Aston Villa: in twenty-one League matches for Chelsea that season Joe scored fifteen goals, four of them in a 7-1 victory over Leeds and in 1935-36 he was Chelsea's top scorer with fifteen goals. Then came his spell with Walsall, and back to Linfield. No actual record of his scoring feat was ever kept but it could easily have been around 1,000 — the same as the fabulous Pelé. He was only ordered off once against Derry City for remarks made to a referee, but otherwise there was not a blemish, not a stain on that illustrious career. When he retired from active play he acted as a coach and scout for Linfield.

For more than ten incomparable years his name was mentioned with awe. Seeing him play was as compulsive as watching Matthews, Finney, Doherty, Best, Morton, Gallacher, James, Pelé, Di Stefano, Cruyff, Eusebio. He may have been a Blueman but to everyone in this community he was a football superstar. A measure of how he could break the barrier which has plagued this Province of ours for years could be seen when he walked up the Falls Road at Charlie Tully's funeral and passers-by stopped him to shake his hand. This is the stature of the man.

A close colleague of Gillespie was Billy Lacey, a quiet unassuming Wexfordman who, like Gillespie, was capped twenty-five times. He began an illustrious career with Shelbourne in 1906 when only sixteen and, after the 1908 Irish Cup Final replay which Bohemians won 3-1, was transferred to Everton but soon moved across to Liverpool, becoming an Anfield hero.

During the First World War Lacey returned to Ireland where he played for Belfast United and Linfield; winning that Irish Cup medal which eluded him at Shelbourne, thanks to a 2-1 win over Glentoran in the 1919 Final. Then it was back to Liverpool where he collected two League Championship medals; he had a short spell with New Brighton, and finished his playing days with Cork Bohemians.

There was the magic of Mickey Hamill, former Ireland, Belfast Celtic, Manchester United, and Manchester City centre-half, probably the greatest Irish player to occupy this key position. For twenty-one years he adorned first-class football, all his colleagues regarding him with awe and respect. Born in Cape Street, Falls Road, Belfast, a member of a family of five, Mickey was transferred from Celtic to Manchester United on 31 December 1910; he was a star with United; revealed unlimited ability and a perfect physique although he only stood 5ft. 8ins. Yet behind that rugged exterior lay great emotions, a fluctuation of feelings.

He was another member of that British Championship winning squad; with Celtic he gained Irish Cup and League medals and when his benefit match was arranged even world flyweight champion Jimmy Wilde visited Belfast to provide it with a publicity boost. Mickey tried his luck in the United States with

Ireland 0, Scotland 2, at Windsor Park, October 1938. *Back row*: W.R. Hamilton (linesman), H. Hayes (Huddersfield), W. McMillen (Chesterfield), T. Breen (Manchester United), M. O'Mahony (Bristol City), W.R. Browne (Leeds United), J. Horsburgh (linesman). *Front row*: J. Brown (Birmingham), J. McAlinden (Belfast Celtic), D. Martin (Nottingham Forest), W. Cook (Everton) (Capt.), A. Stevenson (Everton), J. Coulter (Grimsby), R.A. Mortimer (referee).

Fall River and Boston, then managed by Tommy Muirhead, ex-Scotland and Glasgow Rangers star. Afterwards he became Manchester City's Irish representative, Distillery's manager and, for a period Derry City's representative on the Irish League. His life ended tragically in 1943 when he was found drowned in the River Lagan. Did ever a better player leave Ireland? Billy McCracken, a colleague in those distant days who died in January 1979, nine days short of his 96th birthday, was quite emphatic. 'Hamill had no superior. You can rest assured of that.'

A remarkable man, even in his latter years Billy had in full measure many of the attributes most of those half his age have lost — vitality, a bubbling, mischievous sense of humour and a keen, penetrating mind.

William McCracken was born in Belfast on 29 January 1883. He transferred from Distillery to Newcastle United on 30 April 1904 for £50 and the promise that Newcastle would play the Whites in a friendly. Capped sixteen times for Ireland, he won three League championship medals, appeared in three Cup Finals, played until he was forty and then managed Hull City, Millwall, and Aldershot after which he became a talent scout for Newcastle United and Watford.

He will always be remembered as the man who made such a masterly art of exploiting the offside law that legislators changed it in 1925. An attacker was offside if he received a forward pass or interfered with the play when there were fewer than three opponents between him and the goal he was attacking. Thus, full-backs played well up field, lying diagonally, ready to catch the forwards like flies in a spider's web. Nobody could equal McCracken in this strategy; the key to his success was his keen understanding of tactics, superb anticipation of attacking moves. These were tactics which raised the wrath of the fans who booed and barracked him frequently.

At Villa Park he was hit on the head by a pipe; at Stamford Bridge a spectator spat on him and at Roker Park, Sunderland supporters, driven to frenzy by the success of Newcastle's offside entanglements, peppered him with oranges, apples, lemons and bananas. Bill thrived on it all. He was a born rebel, quite fearless. Once, after a referee had sent him off for questioning his decision, Bill wrote a four page letter to the referee. Instead of seven days suspension, he got a month!

Another star who spanned World War One was Patsy Gallagher who had a wriggling stop-go style. He never weighed more than eight stone and was only 5ft. 6ins. Fragile looking, slightly hunchbacked, his stamina, courage and skill more than compensated for any apparent physical deficiencies. The initial mocking laughter at Parkhead when he played his first home game for Celtic soon diminished and changed to adulatory cheers. Gallagher, born in Milford, Co. Donegal (which meant he could play for Ireland), went to Scotland when only a child, played with Juvenile Renfrew St. James' and Clydebank Juniors before joining Celtic in 1911 aged seventeen. He was employed as an apprentice shipwright in John S. Brown, Clydebank, birthplace of the *Queen* liners.

Between 1911 and 1926 Gallagher won four Scottish Cup winners and six League Championship medals. It was during the 1925 Cup Final against Dundee that he scored his most famous gaol. Celtic trailed 1-0; Gallagher beat four men but was brought down a yard from the goal; he emerged from the ensuing scramble with the ball wedged between his legs. He somersaulted over the line, finishing upside-down in the back of the net and Jimmy McGrory went on to score the winner.

Gallagher, capped eleven times for Ireland, spent six seasons at Falkirk, and a measure of his talent as a creator is that every centre-forward with whom he played became an international. He took over licensed premises in Clydebank but he was a soft touch to his customers any time they were short of a bob or two. Indeed, when Patsy died in 1953 one drawer in the safe at the pub was packed with IOUs amounting to hundreds of pounds. He had tucked them away over the years without attempting to collect.

Davy Rollo, former Linfield, Blackburn Rovers and Ireland international was another member of the championship winning side. A lightly-built youngster, he learned his football with the 24th Belfast Company of the Boys Brigade with his schoolboy pals Bertie Manderson (Glasgow Rangers) and Jimmy McKnight (Nottingham Forest). It was with Brantwood that he came to the notice of the public, developing at Linfield from December 1911 into one of the finest full backs in Britian.

He travelled to Wrexham for the opening match of the championship year as a reserve; Mickey Hamill dropped out through injury and Rollo played on the left. Despite an excellent performance he was only reserve for the England game at Middlesbrough, but here again fate took a hand with cry-offs and he found himself at outside right. Davy made 225 appearances for Blackburn Rovers before joining Port Vale and retiring to run licensed premises in Blackpool where he died in 1963.

This era also produced the half-back line of Billy McCleery, Jack Jones and Tommy Sloan. A prophet hath no honour in his own country. How often have you heard that phrase which could be applied particularly to Irish League players, many of whom had to join cross-channel clubs before being capped by their country. Not so McCleery, who was later to become manager of Linfield.

McCleery, from Rutland Street on the Ormeau Road, Belfast, was a shipyard worker playing along with 'Tucker' Croft, Joe Gowdy and Sammy McKeown for Queen's Island, which was then managed by Jimmy Magowan. They transferred him to Blackburn Rovers but a knee injury cut short his cross-channel 'life', and within twelve months Davy Emerson had him signed for the Blues with whom he won his international caps. He also played cricket for Ireland.

Jack 'Soldier' Jones, capped twenty-three times with Linfield, Hibernian and Glenavon came from a famous footballing family; his father and four of his uncles all gained Irish honours; there could be few families who have contributed so much to the game in Ireland as the Joneses and the Burnisons. They created a record by providing Ireland's middle line in a match against England in 1933 at Windsor Park: they were Jack, brother Sam (Blackpool) and brother-in-law Billy Mitchell (Chelsea and Distillery). Jones' four footballing uncles were Joe Burnison (Distillery and Bolton Wanderers), twice capped, Sam Burnison (Distillery and Bradford Park Avenue), eight times capped, Harold Burnison (Distillery), inter-league player, Johnny Burnison (Glenavon), Irish junior international.

Tommy 'Stickey' Sloan was a hero of the Cardiff City team which won the FA Cup in 1927. A rivetter in Workman and Clark's North Yard — the 'wee yard' as it was known to shipyard workers — he joined the Army in World War One; English clubs queued for his services but he came back to keep a promise — and sign for Crusaders chairman George Wilson, one of the stalwarts of Irish junior football.

He liked Cardiff, liked the Welsh and 'Land of Our Fathers' stirred him like any native of the Valleys; at Ninian Park he met up with Jimmy Nelson and Tommy Watson, two former Crusaders players, and with Ireland's goalkeeper Tommy Farquharson. He discovered Davy Cochrane hitting a ball against a gable wall in Jervis Street, Portadown, and when he went to Shamrock Park that night he told the others, 'Come with me and I'll show you a wee lad who really has ball control.' How right he was. Tommy managed Linfield for eighteen months but Portadown was his first love. There he was friend and counsellor to hundreds of budding stars down the years. He wanted them to have a chance just as he did with the greats of his generation.

Against the backcloth of the Oval, scene of so many of his achievements, Glentoran's renowned centre-forward Fred Roberts ponders on the past — and those six seasons in which he scored 250 goals for the club, including a record ninety-six in one season.

Peter Doherty, one of the greatest inside forwards of all time — a player who played a vital part in the development of Irish international football, both on the field and as a manager, particularly in the 1958 World Cup.

The Greats:
1930-1945

The years of the Depression preceded the Second World War, during which internationals were abandoned altogether from 1939 and 1946. However, the Thirties were a period producing outstanding players whose combined transfer market value in these days of highly inflated fees would be astronomical.

The prince, of course, was Peter Doherty, flame-haired inside forward genius. This priceless gem, born on 6 June 1913 in Magherafelt, Co. Londonderry, and whose first faltering steps in the game were with local Station United and Coleraine. There he was employed on a building site and then as a bus conductor. He was transferred in 1933 from Glentoran to Blackpool for a mere £1,500. Blackpool hit troubled times and he moved on to Manchester City for £16,000; his career glittered as he turned on a brand of football which many contend has never been bettered at Maine Road; with City he won a League championship medal in 1936.

Came the war, the interruption of organised football, a call-up to the RAF, 'guesting' for no fewer than sixteen clubs with the incomparable Stanley Matthews as his partner. Derby County was his next abode where he linked up with the silver-haired maestro Raich Carter; Doherty and Carter went together like bacon and eggs, Scotch and water — an irresistible combination. Derby, who won the first post-war FA Cup Final in 1946, had an international attack in those days — Harrison, Carter, Stamps, Doherty, Duncan. 'It is not generally known that I scored for both sides in that Cup Final against Charlton,' said Peter. 'I deflected a free-kick and wrong-footed the 'keeper. I got the equaliser which meant extra time and we won 4-1.'

As a player-manager he helped Huddersfield Town escape relegation, managed Doncaster Rovers to promotion, had a brief reign with Bristol City, decided to enter business but returned to soccer as assistant manager to Alan Ball at Preston North End. He played sixteen times for Ireland with, perhaps, his most memorable match on Guy Fawkes Day, 5 November 1947, at Goodison Park when he scored a dramatic last second equaliser after darting ten yards before heading Tommy Eglington's cross past the astonished Frank Swift. There was not even time to re-centre the ball; Doherty didn't know he had scored and was assisted to the dressing room by Gerry Morgan and Swift.

Doherty's work-rate was incredible; covering the pitch for ninety minutes with such fiery conviction that he was a manager's dream, an opponents' nightmare. In a word he played the total football which West Germany and Holland brought to a peak in the 1974 World Cup Final at Munich. An example was in the 1947 match at Windsor Park, which the Combined Services won 8-4; he picked up the ball in his own area, dribbled past four opponents and hit a tremendous shot. All four goals were scored by Peter the Great as he was dubbed by the fans. He was the master of the pass inside the back to send a winger away; he did not sway around an opponent but rather darted to leave them helpless. His ball control was exemplary, his 'reading' of a game unsurpassed. Few could handle him but topping his list of players who provided the most trouble to him were Bill Shankly, Joe Mercer, Wilf Copping, Ken Willingham and Stan Cullis.

Bernard Joy, a member of the Combined Services team and for years highly-respected soccer correspondent of the London *Evening Standard* summed up Doherty like this: 'There were some great inside forwards — Carter, Wilf Mannion, Bryn Jones, Tommy Walker, Billy Steel, but I rate Doherty the best of them all.'

Pipe-smoking Peter was Ireland's first manager in October 1951 and in this post by dedication, honesty, eloquence and a corps of excellent, responsible players led by Danny Blanchflower, he revealed just how a national side should be run. Those eleven years proved to be the golden period, with England defeated at Wembley and the team of which he was so proud reaching the World Cup quarter finals in Sweden in 1958.

He had the gift of being able to talk moderate players into believing they possessed greater ability than they really had. He inspired, he guided, he got success. To what had been a cavalcade of passing faces he had by a magnetic, buoyant personality created a team with unity and an identity.

Blanchflower in his autobiography *The Double and Before*, pays this tribute to him: 'He brought an understanding, a vitality, a touch of leadership to the players that had been so lacking before. Almost overnight he transformed the spirit of the team. We had a tremendous respect for him and with his burning enthusiasm, he urged us on to the extreme of our ability. He gave us encouragement and confidence and charged us with adventure; hammered home the idea we had nothing to lose and everything to gain and that we should throw caution to the winds. It worked. We didn't start winning all our matches; our successes were limited but we reduced the gap.'

Doherty resigned as manager in February 1962 because of his wife's health and his business commitments; his contribution had been incalculable. In this era there was also Jimmy Dunne (Sheffield United, Arsenal, Southampton and Shamrock Rovers), a brilliant inside forward, a strong, resolute player who had a wonderful flair for goal-scoring — a flair which entitled him to more than eight caps from 1928-33.

And Glentoran's Johnny Geary, a 5ft. 7ins. idol of East Belfast, whose spell was prematurely ended by injury. After playing for Linfield and Dundela, Johnny joined Glentoran, moving into the first eleven when centre-half Tosher Burns and inside forward Hugh Meek were transferred to Wolverhampton Wanderers. In his first season, playing alongside Davy Lyner and Bambrick, he hit forty-eight goals.

Rejecting a coaching offer from Springfield, Mass., U.S.A. —Tucker Croft had gone there — Johnny remained in Ulster. He won two international caps, both against Scotland at Ibrox Park and Windsor Park. Against Derry City in a Gold Cup match in September, 1932 he injured his knee, played much against his will after a plea from newly-appointed manager Jimmy McStay but broke down and was told by a specialist that further damage could cause permanent lameness. So at twenty-five he quit but, during the war, helped run Aircraft United with Albert Mitchell, and with Victor Ferris, assisted in the formation of Blyth Street Boys Club, Pitt Street Mission and Co-op Recreation clubs which were the fertile breeding grounds for internationals of the future.

Harold McCaw (Linfield), although first capped in 1927, played a big part in the Irish Soccer story of this time, appearing on four occasions for his country; Brantwood, Glentoran and Stockport County were his clubs but he really made his name with the Blues as an outside left.

Football has always had its controversial characters and I suppose it always will. Tommy Priestley (Linfield, Chelsea, Coleraine and Shelbourne) ranks among the greatest of them all, in this respect battling continually against officialdom, hypocrisy and cant. He was, like Billy McCracken, a rebel with many causes. Born in Belfast of an Irish mother and Scottish father, he could never be mistaken on the field, for no matter where he played he wore a rugby-type skull cap to cover his baldness. He played for Coleraine in 1932, didn't re-sign at the end of that season but Ireland, short of players, included him against Scotland in September although he had not kicked a ball or joined a club!

Linfield snapped him up, his class was such Sheffield United made him an immediate offer and Glasgow Rangers' Bill Struth came in with a £20 per-week five-year bid but these were declined. Chelsea manager Leslie Knighton eventually signed him for £3,000 with the promise of a schoolteacher's job thrown in.

His first match against Newcastle United was a near disaster with Irish international full back Jimmy Nelson subduing him. Up came Hughie Gallacher, renowned Scotland centre-forward who knew what was happening. In his broad accent he said to Priestley, 'Gie him a dunt with your shooder and knock him aff the baw.' It was a tactic which proved effective!

Chelsea got him that schoolteaching job all right but it was 1½ hours from his 'digs' on the Old Kent Road which meant he had to train at night. He walked out of Stamford Bridge, returned home and Chelsea retained him for twenty-eight years. Priestley simply went through the 'open door' to the Republic of Ireland signing for Shelbourne and playing for the League of Ireland against his fellow Ulstermen. But for the dispute he would probably have made an even greater impact on soccer; still he was one of the most accomplished wingers Ireland had produced.

Belfast Celtic's Bertie Fulton was another world-class exponent, an immaculate player whose knowledge was unrivalled. He was the brain behind the great Belfast Celtic team — the general.

'I never knew anyone who knew so much about football as he did. What's more he had the ability to impart it,' said his colleague Norman Kernaghan, also an Irish internationalist. 'He was years before his time. He would overlap on the touchline, crossing balls to the far and near posts — something reputed to be a post Second World War innovation. He operated 3-4-4 systems when they were unheard of in England.'

Fulton, like Priestley, was a schoolteacher, headmaster of St. Comgall's, Larne, playing for his home town and London Caledonians during his academic training, but his career revolved around Celtic. He won twenty-two international caps and twenty-one amateur, a place on the Great Britain side in the 1936 Berlin Olympics, Irish Cup and League championship medals, including four in succession. He never sought publicity, preferring to be remembered by what he gave to the game — and it was a lot.

Davy (Boy) Martin, a former drummer boy in the Royal Ulster Rifles who played for Celtic, Wolverhampton Wanderers, Nottingham Forest, Notts County and Glentoran was one of the limited number of Irish centre forwards capable of prolific scoring. Martin bought himself out of the army and signed for Celtic first as an amateur then a professional. He established himself as the permanent leader and, after scoring five goals against Derry City, Wolverhampton manager Frank Buckley, a man whose gland treatment and unorthodox methods created such a stir in the 1939 Cup Final with Portsmouth, paid £7,750 for his transfer and that of outside right Jack Brown. The previous records were £2,200 for Davy Rollo (Blackburn Rovers) and £2,500 for Billy McCandless (Glasgow Rangers).

Martin was not happy at Molyneux where there was steel discipline in dramatic contrast to the carefree atmosphere of Celtic Park; he was fined for reporting late at training and generally the regimentation was foreign to his make-up even though he had been a serving soldier. It was on to Forest, across the Trent to Notts County and back to the RUR during the war when he played for Glentoran with Peter McKennan and the Arsenal full back Jack Young, one of outstanding 'guest' players in Ulster. Davy, injured at Caen, recovered to continue his career until retirement.

From time to time there emerges in Irish football a player who stands out above his contemporaries for his ability, consistency and loyalty to one club. Such was Harry Walker who, thanks to the persuasiveness of Mickey Hamill, joined Belfast Celtic in 1929 when he was only seventeen. Yet, like so many youngsters, he could not find a place in any of the teams, and moved to Glentoran where he won a junior international cap. He played, too, for Broadway United, Linfield Swifts, Crusaders and the Celtic manager Jimmy McColl got him to return on Christmas Day, 1932.

He was then an inside right or a winger, but it was as a half-back that he made his mark — described as the best local player never to be capped at senior level. Much of Celtic's success was due to his distinguished play.

After Belfast Celtic dropped out of football in 1949 Harry joined Ards, then Glenavon, Portadown and finally Glentoran. He was a gem in the garland of jewels that was Celtic.

Another Celtic great was Jimmy McAlinden, an artistic inside forward who graduated from schoolboy to senior international, winning four caps and two with the Republic in 1946 — against Portugal and Spain. Wearing his first pair of long trousers he reported at Celtic Park to mix with Martin, Brown, Keiller McCullough and Harry Walker. Little notice was taken of him as he lapped the track so he quit for Sammy Weir to sign him for Glentoran, but after five months he returned to Celtic where Elisha Scott took him under his guidance. Then, in December, 1938, he figured in a £7,500 transfer to Portsmouth, managed by Jack Tinn and captained by Jimmy Guthrie. His arrival at Fratton Park coincided with a revival in the club's fortunes with the climax a 1939 Cup Final place against Wolves at Wembley, although he was doubtful almost until kick-off with a pulled muscle. For the boy from the Falls Road it was quite an exhilarating experience. A new world had opened up. To ease the pre-match tension Portsmouth brought a comedian into their dressing rooms but what eliminated the strain was an autograph book handed in from Wolves; the signatures were so illegible he knew his opponents were equally nervous.

After the war Jimmy, now happily recovered from a heart attack, played for Shamrock Rovers, managed Glenavon in the successful late Fifties and early Sixties, occupied a similar post with Distillery and finally Drogheda United.

When it comes to wingers Davy Cochrane (Portadown, Leeds United, Linfield and Shamrock Rovers) had few peers. They called 5ft. 4in. Davy 'the wee man with the big heart'. One of the best bargains to leave Ireland, he was so small when he reached England they thought he was a jockey instead of a footballer.

Davy, who runs a confectioner's shop in Leeds within walking distance of Elland Road where he spent six seasons, was selected for Ireland's schoolboy team but, as he was two years over the age limit, had to withdraw. As a seventeen year old he was positively scintillating, taking Celtic apart as Portadown swept to a 3-1 win; that day he really came of age.

It was a great Portadown side which included his uncle George Cochrane, Paddy Monaghan, Charlie Coull, Norman Cochrane, Jack McNally. Leeds manager Bill Hampson paid out only £2,000 for him; he spent his first season in the reserves but, once given the break, never looked back. His international debut was at Maine Road, Manchester, where Ireland lost 7-0 with Matthews rampant and Willie Hall hitting four of the goals; spectators that day thought Hall, later to have his legs amputated, could at last smash that six-goal record of Bambrick but it was not to be. An automatic choice for Ireland, he would, no doubt, have won every honour in English football had it not been for the war which brought him back to Northern Ireland. Portadown, alas, quit for the duration and, after their final match against mid-Ulster rivals Glenavon, he signed for Shamrock Rovers. It was with Linfield from 1942-45 that he re-established himself on the local scene.

Davy hit a hat-trick for an Irish FA XI against the Combined Services, was honoured by the Republic of Ireland but, due to dislike of flying withdrew. When only thirty he quit soccer and, no matter what persuasion was applied, wouldn't change his mind. 'I decided from the start that I would retire at the top and not let my career drag on an on. I had seen too many players slide downhill. It is always a sad sight.' He bowed out in glory, not in ignominy and embarrassment like some contemporaries.

The finest wing partnership was that of Alex Stevenson (Glasgow Rangers and Everton) — 'wee Alex' — and the man with the big feet, Jackie Coulter (Belfast Celtic and Everton).

Stevenson, now living at Bootle, Lancashire, and employed by the Corporation, is a Dubliner. He started with Dolphin who transferred him to Glasgow Rangers and, although such an integral part of Everton, he still considers Rangers as the greatest club — the Rangers in the years of Dougie Gray, Bob MacPhail, Alec Venters, Whitey MacDonald, Davie Meiklejohn, Jimmy Simpson, Alan Morton. Everton signed him in 1934 linking up with Coulter; week after week they prised open defences, had a telepathic understanding of each other's play and, as a result, became one of the most feared wings in the country. Stevenson played more than 400 matches for Everton, including the 1938 Exhibition Cup Final which they lost 1-0 to Celtic whose centre-forward Johnny Crum scored the goal in the 95th minute. Winning seventeen caps he had one regret when playing for Ireland — lack of preparation. 'We rarely had team talks. Often we arrived the night before a game or even on the morning of it. In fact, sometimes we were not introduced to colleagues until shortly before kick-off.'

Although he was one of the greatest Irish international forwards of all time it was as a roller skater that the young Coulter showed so much prowess. Success

Ireland 2, Scotland 1. Windsor Park, October 1934. *Back row*: W. McMillen (Manchester City), J. Mackey (Portsmouth), E. Scott (Belfast Celtic), R.P. Fulton (Belfast Celtic), W. Mitchell (Chelsea), J. Burns (linesman). *Front row*: J. Mackey (linesman), H. Duggan (Leeds United), W. Gowdy (Linfield), J. Jones (Linfield), D. Martin (Belfast Celtic), A. Stevenson (Everton), J. Coulter (Everton), H. Mee (referee).

eluded him in junior football until Belfast Celtic signed him on amateur forms; he was originally a centre forward but, in a moment of inspiration, Celtic switched him to the wing to become an instant hit. Everton paid £2,750 for Coulter after a match at Ballymena where he had been ordered off by referee Billy McClean; he found new friends in Dixie Dean, Ted Sagar, Torry Gillick and Cliff Britton.

He collected eleven Irish FA caps, playing a leading role in the dramatic 2-1 victory over Scotland in October 1934, a match in which Ireland was reduced to ten men, Walter McMillen (Manchester United and Chesterfield) going into goal for Elisha Scott. Coulter fractured his leg playing for Ireland against Wales at Wrexham — an injury which ultimately ended his career, although he went to Grimsby Town and non-league side Chelmsford. Exceptionally fast, he was deadly accurate with his crosses and, like so many other wingers of his generation, the essence of complete orthodoxy. Jackie Mahood (Belfast Celtic), was another in this mould; he won nine caps, the last in 1934, the first in 1927 when Ireland defeated England 3-0.

Mahood was a member of the Celtic side which in 1928-29 scored 116 goals with only twenty-three scored against them, picking up forty-eight points out of a possible forty-two, going through the season undefeated. Finally, Mahood went to Ballymena, where he fractured his leg in a collision with Tommy Breen in a match with Celtic. He never played again.

51

Arguments rage in football, but when the question is raised who possessed the most powerful left foot there can be only one answer — Jimmy Kelly who played twenty years for Derry City, scoring 363 goals, including forty-nine in the 1938-39 season. He was capped eleven times for Northern Ireland, four for the Republic, represented the Irish League on sixteen occasions and on three the League of Ireland. Cold statistics alone, however, don't tell the Jimmy Kelly story. It was in 1935-36 that he achieved his greatest individual triumph when scoring all three goals — a first-half hat-trick in the Irish League's 3-2 win over the Football League at Windsor Park. The team that day was Lambe (Portadown), Millar (Glentoran), Fulton (Belfast Celtic), Edwards (Linfield), Carlyle (Derry City) *Captain*, Walker (Celtic), Kernaghan (Celtic), Baird (Linfield), Shearer (Derry City), Duffy (Derry City), Kelly (Derry City).

A year earlier he scored the winning goal in the Irish League's 2-1 win at Blackpool and he got both goals which brought defeat to the Scottish League in 1931; Jimmy was then only nineteen.

Youngest of a family of eight, Kelly was born in Ballybofey, Co. Donegal and, strangely, the only member interested in football. He played for Stranorlar School, Long Tower Boys School, Foyle Stars, St. Columb's Court, Newry Town, Fulton Rovers, Coleraine and Liverpool. When he travelled to Anfield in May 1928, it was his first journey out of Ireland, and the first time, too, that he had been on a ship. He was disillusioned at Liverpool for, in almost three years, he had only four first team games with his activities confined to the Lancashire Central League. This was not his scene so he asked for a transfer.

A nominal fee of £100 was put on him with the stipulation he had to join an Irish League side. Derry, managed by Billy Gillespie, took up the option and thus began a twenty-one year association with the Brandywell club, apart, of course, from brief spells with Shamrock Rovers, Dundalk, Coleraine, Ballymena United and Ballymoney United. Jimmy, who played eleven times for Ireland and four for the Republic, would have been a sensation in modern soccer. He had one of the strongest shots in the game and scoring goals from forty yards was commonplace with him. He was fast, skilful, courageous, exciting. Not for him petty tantrums or harsh criticism of others. It was the twinkling feet of Bobby Ervine (Everton and Portsmouth) that 'made' Jimmy. Playing at inside right Ervine exploited the crossfield pass to perfection and Kelly, pounding in from the left wing, invariably met the ball first time in the penalty box.

Frank Curran, editor of the *Derry Journal* described Jimmy, who died in November 1970, like this: 'Anyone who never saw him play in his prime missed one of the most fascinating sights in football. He was a great player — but even more important he was a great person.'

The Thirties saw the greatest on-the-field tragedy in Scottish football, involving Rangers' Irish international striker Sam English and Celtic goalkeeper John Thomson. Only five minutes of the second half of the 'Old Firm' clash had gone on the sultry, windless afternoon of 5 September 1931. English went for a cross which landed in the Celtic goalmouth at the Copland Road end of the ground; his knee crashed against the keeper's head and the shot was diverted — but at a terrible price. Thomson never regained consciousness and died later that night in Glasgow's Victoria Infirmary. It was a pure accident with no blame attached to English but the memory lived with him for ever. Thomson fractured his skull and the inquest verdict said he had died while engaged in his employment. . . in an attempt to save a goal.

Ireland goalkeeper Ted Hinton grasps the ball while challenged by Tommy Lawton. England's Stanley Mortensen waits for an error. Peter Doherty scored the dramatic equaliser in this 2-2 draw with England at Goodison Park, Liverpool, in November 1947.

Peter O'Connor, Belfast Celtic forward, and holder of the individual goal-scoring record for an Irish League player — eleven in the 13-0 defeat of Glenavon at Celtic Park, Belfast.

The Greats:
1945-1957

Organised football in 1939 had ended with the sharpness of a power cut. Contracts had been suspended in England and Scotland, which meant players could appear for any team. Quick to realise this was Billy McCracken, manager of Aldershot, whose headquarters were close to the huge Army base. Some of the players he 'signed' were Tommy Lawton (Everton), Denis Compton (Arsenal), Stanley Matthews (Stoke) — who was described in *Picture Post* of those days as 'a football equation without an answer' — Stan Cullis (Wolverhampton Wanderers), Cliff Britton and Joe Mercer (Everton), Jimmy Hagan (Sheffield United), Tommy Walker (Hearts).

So to the new dawn. A new world. A free world. The great stride from war to peace had been taken. It was the start of the biggest boom football was to experience. Ireland's opening match in September 1946 at Windsor Park which England won 7-2 saw Johnny Carey (Manchester United) make his debut. This was the period of 'Bud' Aherne (Belfast Celtic and Luton Town), the bald Bill Gorman (Brentford), Willie Walsh (Manchester City), Norman Lockhart (Linfield, Coventry City, Aston Villa).

Carey can be classified as a 'great' and he had many claims to this. He was a versatile footballer, the complete all-rounder and an inspiration as captain of Northern Ireland (seven caps), the Republic (twenty-eight) and the Rest of Europe side which, through no fault of his, lost 7-1 to Great Britain at Hampden Park, Glasgow, immediately after the war in a match to raise funds for FIFA. 'He was a credit to football. No more honest man ever pulled on a pair of football boots,' commented Peter Doherty.

Carey joined United from St. James' Gate as an inside forward in 1936 for £250 and, during war service with the Army, played for several Italian professional sides. Converted to a half-back, he had the distinction of playing for the two Irelands against England within two days of each other — on 28 September 1946 at Windsor Park and on 30 September at Dalymount Park, Dublin. Voted 'Footballer of the Year' in 1949 he retired at thirty-four to enter management with Blackburn Rovers and then Everton, whose millionaire chairman John Moores sacked him in a London taxi after attending a Football League meeting. Orient and Nottingham Forest appointed him as a manager but now he has no official association with the game; indeed, rarely does he attend matches, a practice commonplace with so many ex-professionals.

Jackie Vernon (Belfast Celtic, West Bromwich Albion and Crusaders), was centre-half in the Great Britain team and captain of the Rest of Britain side which met Wales in the Welsh FA's 75th anniversary game at Ninian Park, Cardiff. Although he played Gaelic football at school, Vernon, now a Belfast butcher, preferred soccer and Celtic for whom he signed via Dundela. He gained all the domestic honours, guided them to win the war-time Inter-City Cup and, after a brilliant display for Northern Ireland against Scotland, West Bromwich Albion paid £10,000 for him. Vernon has many memories but one of the most outstanding was in January, 1941, when Celtic centre-forward Peter O'Connor scored eleven goals for Celtic in a 13-0 defeat of Glenavon, at Celtic Park, a nightmare day for goalkeeper Hugh Kelly. This is the highest individual club scoring record in Irish League football.

Arguably many will say Waterford-born Davy Walsh (Linfield, West Bromwich Albion, Aston Villa and Walsall) was the best post-War striker; he won eight 'caps' and there would have been many more if it had not been for 'the split'. West Bromwich signed him for £3,000 and, in his four years at the Hawthorns, he scored over 160 goals; in one season he was the joint leading English scorer with Charlie Wayman (Newcastle United).

Sammy Smyth (Distillery, Linfield, Wolverhampton Wanderers and Stoke City), scorer of one of the finest individual goals seen at Wembley (for Wolves in the 1949 FA Cup Final against Leicester) had a dramatic international debut. He was selected to replace the injured Peter Doherty, and celebrated with two goals which beat Scotland at Windsor Park on 4 October 1947.

Many new names emerged in the Fifties. Seamus D'Arcy (Brentford), Len Graham (Doncaster Rovers), Tommy Dickson (Linfield), Billy Dickson (Chelsea and Arsenal), Jimmy McCabe (Leeds United), Frank McCourt (Manchester City), Ray Ferris (Birmingham), and Bobby Brennan (Luton,

Ireland 0, Wales 2, Wrexham 1948. *Back row*: W. Gorman, P. Doherty, S. Smyth, T. Hinton, C. Martin, W. Walsh. *Front row*: D. Cochrane, T. Eglington, J. Vernon, P. Farrell, D. Walsh.

Birmingham and Fulham).

Peter Farrell (Everton) had some magnificent games for Northern Ireland. In 1946 he was transferred from Shamrock Rovers to Everton whom he captained for nine successive seasons, later becoming Tranmere Rovers player-manager for two years in 1958.

A fellow Irishman and lifelong friend at Goodison Park was Tommy Eglington, another Dubliner and, like Farrell, a product of Shamrock Rovers whose chairman Mrs. Mary Cunningham negotiated his move. Farrell and Eglington, a master of accurate centres, had careers which ran parallel both for Northern Ireland and the Republic; Eglington won six Northern Ireland caps and twenty-four for the Republic while Farrell's figures were seven and twenty-eight respectively.

Apart from the two 1946 games against Spain and Portugal when they enlisted the assistance of Tommy Breen, Jackie Vernon, Billy McMillan, Jimmy McAlinden, Walter Sloan, Hugh Kelly and Jimmy Kelly, the Football Association of Ireland relied entirely on their own resources for international football. An Ulsterman, Dickie Lunn (Dundalk) was also capped against Switzerland and Poland in 1939.

The Irish FA, by contrast, continued to select players on an all-Ireland basis which was acceptable to many but the winds of discontent were beginning to blow again in the late 1940s and it erupted into open hostility in 1950-51 season when Sean Fallon (Glasgow Celtic), chosen for a match against the British Army, refused to play. Pressure was applied on others and on 8 March 1950 at Wrexham the last all-Ireland side drew 0-0 with Wales; the Southerners on it were Bud Aherne, Con Martin, Reg Ryan and Davy Walsh.

Two players who made an immense contribution to the game then were Danny Blanchflower (Glentoran, Barnsley, Aston Villa, Tottenham Hotspur) and Charlie Tully (Belfast Celtic and Glasgow Celtic).

Blanchflower is a talker, a thinker, a man filled with words. They called him the Prince of Blarney with a captivating conversationalist gift. The late Nancy Spain once alleged he had actually swallowed the Blarney Stone!

Manager of the Northern Ireland international squad until November 1979, Blanchflower was one of football's most accomplished half-backs, a term he still uses, spurning the modern jargon of 'central defenders', 'strikers', 'functional play', 'zonal qualities'. Blanchflower, non-smoker, non-drinker, is an original; in 1961 his club Tottenham Hotspur became the first in the twentieth century to achieve the English League and Cup double. They won the FA Cup again the following season, defeating Burnley 3-1, while in 1963 Spurs were the first British club to win a major European tournament, the Cup Winners Cup.

Much of this success was due, of course, to Blanchflower's basic qualities, his perceptive leadership as captain, his belief that you must have responsibility and authority if you are to be in charge of a side. His principles, his opinions, his theories, so often the same as those of his idolised mentor Peter Doherty, come crashing at you like waves in a gale. Even a fairly simple question can evoke an answer via philosophy, logic and experience.

The maestro drops in for a chat. Peter Doherty, legendary player and manager, has a few words of wisdom for Dave Clements (back to camera) before the World Cup tie with Bulgaria (0-0) at Hillsborough, Sheffield, 1973. *From left*: Pat Rice, Bryan Hamilton, Tommy Cassidy, Sammy Morgan, David Craig, Iam McFaul, Liam O'Kane, Roy Coyle, Tommy Jackson.

That doyen of soccer journalists, Geoffrey Green, formerly correspondent of the London *Times*, aptly summed him up when he said, 'Words tend to run away with Mr Blanchflower, an Irishman who would be at home at Speaker's Corner. He tends to leap from one point to another like a grasshopper, often before one thought has been fully rounded off. But when all the pieces have been put together like some jigsaw puzzle, they offer sanity and integrity.'

Blanchflower, capped fifty-six times, was transferred from Glentoran to Barnsley in 1949; then two years later to Aston Villa for £15,000 and in 1954 began that illustrious career with Spurs. Twice voted England's 'Footballer of the Year', in 1958 and 1961, he played a key role in those Northern Ireland World Cup successes.

And he made history in February 1961, with his refusal to appear on Eamonn Andrews' 'This is Your Life' programme after being lured to a studio on the pretext of recording a soccer interview. 'A man's life is private. It was a matter of principle for me,' says Blanchflower who was appointed Northern Ireland's international team manager in 1976, a post to which he brought imagination, flair and an attacking concept. Successes such as the 2-2 draw in Holland, the win in Bulgaria, were mixed with mediocrity, even humiliation — the 1-0 defeat by Iceland in Reykjavik, 4-0 by Denmark in Copenhagen and by England at Wembley (4-0) and Windsor Park (5-1).

'When I was asked to take over the managership I felt I had a debt to repay. The Irish FA needed someone and I thought perhaps I could assist,' says Blanchflower who named Tommy Cavanagh (Manchester United), as his assistant.

His brief managerial spell at struggling, financially-stricken Chelsea throughout 1979 did not disillusion him; he would not change his values, something which had to be admired, nor did he lose his love of football. He wants always to be a part of it. For him the simplicity of football has made it the greatest game in the world.

A Blanchflower contemporary, Charlie Tully (Belfast Celtic, Glasgow Celtic) could perhaps be described as Ireland's leading soccer extrovert. Known as the Clown Prince of Football, a virtuoso in a jersey, he was an irrepressible, jovial character whose wisecracks and stories will forever be told when people meet to reminisce. Many of those yarns are fictional, many are true about a man who was the complete epitome of humour and gaiety.

Charles Patrick Tully died in his sleep in July 1973, a few hours after leaving his ex-clubmate and lifelong friend Jackie Vernon. 'It was strange he should have gone out so peacefully. It was not his way of life,' wrote the late John Rafferty in the *Observer*. The irrelevancies about him are always remembered. They still laugh at how Tully alleged he claimed tax relief for ten dependants in the Celtic team. They still recall too, pilgrims asking in St. Peter's Square, Rome, 'Who is that man on the balcony beside Charlie Tully?'

Charlie played for Whiterock, Forth River, Ballyclare Comrades, Clifton-ville and Celtic where he was the bane of manager Elisha Scott's life. Even as a youngster he had an extensive repertoire of ball artistry, tricks as he called them which prompted Scott to comment, 'Tricks? You should see him when he calls to collect his wages — that's the biggest trick of all.'

It was during the five-a-side matches at the RUC Sports, Windsor Park, where legendary Celtic manager Jimmy McGrory became impressed by Tully's gesticulating hands, the selling of 'dummies', the back heel flicks. Yet, when he stepped off the *Royal Ulsterman* at Broomielaw there was no welcoming party. Glasgow, that fanatical partisan soccer city, pockmarked then by the scars of war and with sooty forbidding tenements, did not know what was about to strike it.

His initial match for Celtic against Morton was not successful, and it was not until his sixth game that he came through — leaving those hard-boiled, knowledgeable fans gasping in bewilderment. For Celtic's legions it couldn't have happened on a more appropriate occasion — against those arch rivals Rangers. He shuffled with the ball, moved it both ways in the air, on the ground, his length was perfect, he waved his arms like a traffic policeman. Rangers obeyed his bidding. They were in disorder. They just couldn't take the ball from a Tully in full flight. He was a compendium that day of all the subleties in the homeland of ball artists such as Gallacher, Morton, James, Walker.

'Celtic fans immediately canonised him. This was the prophet they had waited for through many long, barren years. He did lead them to the promised land, kept the country talking. He was good for the game,' wrote Rafferty in the *Observer*.

Ireland 2, France 2, Windsor Park, 12 May 1951. *Back row*: W. Dickson (Chelsea), W. Bingham (Sunderland), L. Graham (Doncaster Rovers), T. Hinton (Fulham), D. Blanchflower (Aston Villa), W. Simpson (Glasgow Rangers), A. McMichael (Newcastle United), G. Morgan (trainer). *Front row*: K. McGarry (Cliftonville), J. McKenna (Huddersfield Town), J. Cull (Glentoran), J. Vernon (West Bromwich Albion) (Capt.), J. Beckett (Glenavon), W. Cush (Leeds United), R. Ferris (Birmingham). *Photograph*: Michel, Bangor.

Irish FA XI 2, Army 3, Windsor Park, September 1952. *Back row*: H. Bullock (linesman), J.O. Best (referee), J. Blanchflower (Manchester United), W. Cunningham (St. Mirren), A. McNeil (Sunderland), F. Mulholland (Middlesbrough), A. Montgomery (Coleraine), J. Arbuthnot (linesman). *Front row*: J. Scott (Manchester United), P. Tilley (Arsenal), D. McCabe (Leeds United), J. Clugston (Liverpool), F. McKnight (Blackpool), R. Peacock (Glasgow Celtic).

Fact must be kept apart from fantasy. So let's record two incidents. Celtic were two goals down against Falkirk at Brockville Park in the Scottish Cup: Tully, at outside left, floated a corner kick into the goal only to see the referee order it to be re-taken as it had been placed outside the arc. Tully obeyed, formed his fists into binoculars to ensure he was on target, put his right foot to the ball and again astonishingly curled it into the goal. That time it counted.

The second incident was on one of the infrequent occasions that Tully made Windsor Park his stage, but few people who saw him tease and tantalise England in 1952 are ever likely to forget the experience. Nor will Sir Alf Ramsey, the full back opposing him on that historic afternoon. 'I gave Alf a tough day but he never attempted to rough it up. It was not his style; he always played his football fairly,' said Tully. Tully scored both goals for Ireland in that 2-2 draw, one of them direct from a corner kick with Gil Merrick (Birmingham) mesmerised by the inswing. That was a scintillating performance measuring up — some say surpassing — to that of Best fifteen years later. Even the irritable Elisha Scott, a hard taskmaster who demanded exacting standards, agreed. His displays against Rangers were always the talk of Glasgow — at least with the Celtic fans. But how many know he actually played for Rangers, whose management always held this buoyant Ulsterman in such high regard?

It happened like this: when Rangers had been asked to play Highland League club Inverness Caledonians to celebrate new floodlights being installed, manager Scot Symon invited Charlie, a favourite in the North of

Ireland 2, England 2, Windsor Park, October 1952. *Back row*: W. Neill (reserve), two match officials, W. Cunningham, N. Uprichard, F. McCourt, W. Dickson, J. D'Arcy, G. Morgan (trainer), Referee. *Front row*: D. Blanchflower, J. McIlroy, E. McMorran, A. McMichael, W. Bingham, C. Tully, Irish Mascot.

Scotland, to make a guest appearance. 'I was appointed captain of the Rangers. They played in a red, white and blue strip. What a ribbing I had to stand,' said Tully. Rangers penalty kick expert Johnny Hubbard said he had never seen Charlie better dressed than he was when wearing that jersey.

Tully, who later managed Bangor, won only ten caps, the last when overweight and out of condition, against Spain in 1958-59. En route to Madrid he was asked if his Ireland recall had been a surprise.

'Surprised,' he said. 'I was walking down Argyll Street in Glasgow and noticed the newspaper bills. One said "Holy Father Dies in Rome". The other "Tully gets another honour!"'

It was a story so typical of the man who had so much natural ability: a man who had illuminated the game.

Sammy McCrory did the rounds of the clubs — Linfield, Swansea, Ipswich, Plymouth Argyle, Southend United, Cambridge United and Crusaders. He made a solitary appearance for Ireland — at Wembley on 6 November 1957 at the age of thirty-three, scoring one of the goals (Jimmy McIlroy and Billy Simpson got the others) in a 3-2 win over England at Wembley; McCrory, also a member of the 1958 World Cup party, never played in any of the Swedish matches.

Con Martin (Glentoran, Leeds United and Aston Villa) followed Carey as the all-rounder, operating at full back, centre-half or forward. Poison-pen letters didn't help the situation and he was one of the first players to decline an Irish FA invitation to play in their internationals.

'It all came to a head prior to a match between Northern Ireland and Wales at Wrexham in the late Forties. On the morning of the game I received a call from a then prominent FAI official urging me not to turn out for Northern Ireland,' says Martin, now owner of the 'Home and Away' lounge bar at Skerries.

'I listened to his argument but turned out just the same. It would have been unfair to my team-mates to pull out at that late stage. We drew with the Welsh but when I returned to Villa Park I had made up my mind that was the end of playing for the North. Villa chairman Fred Normansell was annoyed at his club being defeated 7-0 by Manchester United who had refused to release Johnny Carey for the international. Villa asked me not to play for Northern Ireland again.'

Larne also produced Eddie McMorran (Belfast Celtic, Barnsley and Doncaster Rovers) — very much a scorer in the Walsh mould. From Ballyclare Paper Mill he moved to Larne, then on to Celtic where, within three months, he had established himself as the regular centre-forward. Now employed as a crane driver at a Barnsley steel works, McMorran, holder of eighteen caps, was transferred to Manchester City in 1947; his other clubs were Barnsley, Doncaster Rovers, Crewe Alexandra, Leeds United — John Charles was on the ground staff — and finally player-manager of Yorkshire League club Bodworth.

Northern Ireland 1, Scotland 1, October 1957. *Back row*: Linesman, W. Cunningham (Leicester City), A. McMichael (Newcastle United), N. Uprichard (Portsmouth), J. Blanchflower (Manchester United), R. Peacock (Glasgow Celtic); Linesman, Referee. *Front row*: W. McAdams (Manchester City), W. Simpson (Glasgow Rangers), J. McIlroy (Burnley), D. Blanchflower (Tottenham Hotspur), W. Bingham (Sunderland), P. McParland (Aston Villa).

There are few players who can boast of scoring a hat-trick in an international against West Germany but one who had this magic moment was Billy McAdams (Distillery, Manchester City, Bolton Wanderers, Leeds United, Queen's Park Rangers, Brentford and Barrow). He was with Bolton when he snapped up those Irish goals at Windsor Park in October 1960, yet he found himself on the losing side; the Germans won 4-3 with goals from Doerfel (2), Bruell and the legendary Uwe Seller. He was capped seventeen times, a back injury ending his career.

The Manchester United air crash at Munich 1958 ended the career of many great footballers — some died on that snow covered runway; others lived, never to play again and in this category is Jackie Blanchflower, younger brother of Danny. Discovered by United's Irish talent-spotter, the late Bob Harpur, playing for Pitt Street Mission in the Belfast Boys Club League, it was evident almost immediately on arrival at Old Trafford he was 'Busby Babe' material. An Irish schoolboy international when only eighteen, he made his debut for United against Liverpool; was capped on eighteen occasions, including that infamous World Cup 'battle' against Italy in Belfast in 1957. In the same year he took over in the FA Cup Final as United's goalkeeper when Ray Wood was injured in a collision with Aston Villa's Peter McParland, so often a colleague on the Irish side.

It all looked so promising for Jackie Blanchflower, who could play either in defence or as a centre-forward, until that fateful return journey from a European Cup tie in Belgrade. He had eight broken ribs, two fractures of the pelvis, and kidney damage; he fought hard to make a comeback. . . but it was not to be.

Jimmy Jones (Belfast Celtic, Glenavon) only played three times for Ireland but will always be remembered as a fantastic scoring machine in domestic football; in a career spanning nearly twenty years he hit approximately 750 goals and he gave glamour and excitement to every game. Something always seemed to happen when Jones was around. Goals were his business. Never a brilliant ball player, this square-shouldered muscular man from Lurgan defined his function simply: 'I'm there to put the ball into the net — nothing else.' In one season alone he hit seventy-four and for years there was local rivalry between him and Sammy Pavis (Linfield) who scored 225 goals for the Blues and had a total of more than 500 in senior soccer.

Yet Jones' career looked like being dramatically brief. On 27 December 1948, he was the victim at the end of a Linfield-Celtic match at Windsor Park of what was probably the most vicious assault on any player in the history of British football. Linfield centre-half Bob Bryson had been carried off after an accidental clash with Jones and during half-time it was announced over the public address system by the late J. O. Mackey, Linfield secretary, that Bryson's leg was broken. Fans became incensed, tempers aroused, passions inflamed. The game, which ended in a 2-2 draw, exploded. Two players, Paddy Bonnar (Celtic) and Albert Currie (Linfield), were ordered off and at the finish Jones was attacked by fifty spectators as he ran from the far corner flag to the dressing rooms. He was thrown over the wall and, when prostrate, kicked viciously on the right leg. 'I tried to get up but the leg just hung limply,' Jimmy recalls. It took four manipulative operations to set the bone; he spent seven weeks in hospital, eight months encased in plaster and eventually the leg was half an inch shorter than the other. Damages for malicious injuries totalled £4,361.

With Celtic withdrawing from the Irish League his return to the game created further complications. Fulham signed him for £3,000 but, because of a technicality, the Football League would not accept his registration so he could only figure in London Combination matches. Back he went to Glenavon with whom he won his 'caps' and whom he also managed for several seasons.

The Duke of Gloucester, Patron of the FA, shakes hands with Jimmy McIlroy before the November 1957 game with England at Wembley. *Left to right*: Jackie Blanchflower, Dick Keith, McIlroy, Bertie Peacock, Billy Simpson, Sammy McCrory, Peter McParland.

Build Up to an Era of Glory

Northern Ireland's first real excursion into the colourful and explosive combat of the World Cup came in 1958 with the final series staged in Sweden. It was a never-to-be forgotten era, the zenith of Irish FA history. The team that was the joker in the pack became the shock one. Unheralded and unsung when they landed on Sweden's shores, they left as heroes who had won the respect of the public. The Cinderella nation had captivated the ball.

The story of Sweden, however, had its origin on a cold, bleak day — 9 January 1957 — at Lisbon where Northern Ireland, drawn in the same Group as Portugal and Italy, met the Portuguese with a 10-30 p.m. kick-off. It was a match which began on one day and finished the next! A match more like a display of unarmed combat than a ball game, or as Peter McParland described it, 'the dirtiest in which I've played'.

A valuable draw was earned here with a goal from Billy Bingham (Sunderland). It was a commendable goal but few thought it would lead to an era of glory. A flash in the pan? A fluke? An off night for a team which included European-class stars such as Aguas, Da Costa, Vasques, Virgile and Perdiace?

Many were convinced it was just that, but what really had happened was the emergence of a new concept of Irish international football through the partnership of Peter Doherty and Danny Blanchflower. Moves of fascinating beauty, both in creation and execution, came from players who had benefited from being kept together. Flair, imagination, unorthodoxy became part of the set up, with one tactical experiment after another tried out. Everyone enjoyed the simplicity of the game in such a carefree yet disciplined atmosphere.

Difficulty was experienced arranging a match with Italy but eventually it was fixed for Thursday, 25 April 1957 — three days after Easter. As Manchester United and Aston Villa had qualified for the FA Cup Final centre-half, Jackie Blanchflower and outside left Peter McParland could not be released, so it was decided to play the diminutive Wilbur Cush at centre-half and Bertie Peacock, normally a wing half, at outside left. The Italians, suspicious at the best of times, were intrigued by this ploy when the team flew into Rome. An inside forward at centre-half? A left half on the wing? Was it all a deadly Irish plot?

Italian pressmen, among the most persistent and, at times, abrasive in the world, could get no answer from Doherty; Blanchflower was glib with his replies and trainer Gerry Morgan — 'Uncle' to the players — put forward his own reasons! Still the Italians could not understand it. They were even more baffled when Morgan, on a stifling hot day, filled a bucket with eau de cologne and cold water. During moments of respite he wiped the players' faces with it.

Mystery may have abounded, but the Italians triumphed 1-0 from a thirty-yard Sergio Cervato free-kick which pierced the wall and shot past Harry Gregg. The Italians, World Cup winners in 1934 and 1938, were happy with this result but eyebrows were raised when, on 1 May, at Windsor Park, Northern Ireland defeated Portugal 3-0 with goals from Billy Simpson (Glasgow Rangers), Jimmy McIlroy (Burnley) and Tommy Casey (Newcastle United).

Italian qualification was not a foregone conclusion now, not the formality which everyone assumed when the draw was originally announced. And it became even more worrying for them when Northern Ireland defeated England 3-2 at Wembley, the first ever victory there which is described elsewhere in this book.

For Northern Ireland there could have been no greater boost to morale than this; no greater incentive to tackle the Italians at Windsor Park on 4 December 1957. Northern Ireland needed a win, their opponents a draw; this was the crunch, the turning point for Italy, the road to success or ignominy, with failure meaning a revolution in the corridors of Italian soccer power. The Italian Federation selected a powerful side which included Juan Schiaffino (Milano), a talented Uruguayan forward, who had won a World Cup medal in 1950, and

Right: Moment of drama in Northern Ireland's 3-2 win over England at Wembley in 1957 featuring three Manchester United stars — Harry Gregg, covered by Jackie Blanchflower, punches a Tommy Taylor header clear.

Taylor died in the 1958 Munich air crash. Blanchflower was so seriously injured he never played again and Gregg was one of the heroes, pulling victims from the crashed Elizabethan aircraft on the snow-covered Munich runway.

66

Argentianian forward Ghiggia (Roma). The journalist who called it a match between two continents and the six counties was not far wide of the mark.

The team arrived in Belfast to a fanfare of trumpets and a joyous welcome from Italians resident in Britain. The pressure for the game was on but suddenly there unfolded one of the most amazing behind-the-scenes drama known in football. A Hungarian, Istvan Zolt, manager of the Budapest Opera House, nominated as the referee, was fogbound at London Airport. Immediately the alarm bells rang, with Irish FA secretary Billy Drennan who had Arthur Ellis (Halifax), then the world's Number One referee, standing by to catch a train for Stranraer and the ferry to Larne.

No agreement could be reached with the Italian Football Federation President Ottorino Barassi who was confident the fog would lift and Zolt arrive next day. Arrangements had been made for the Belfast plane to be first off the runway at London airport when it got clearance; it didn't and by then it was too late for Ellis to make the journey. A local referee was ruled out so Drennan had an international incident of magnitude on his hands. The only alternative was to abandon the match but by then thousands of supporters were en route to Windsor Park.

A closed-doors discussion took place at the Midland Hotel, and eventually it was .decided to play a friendly game with the World Cup tie arranged for January. A document was drawn up signed by Dr. Barassi, Joseph MacBride, Irish FA president, and by the Lord Mayor of Belfast, Sir Cecil McKee.

At about 1.30 p.m. Northern Ireland's team was informed in the dressing room that it was a so-called friendly to be refereed by Tommy Mitchell (Lurgan). Fans, unaware of the circumstances, became irate; they felt they had been conned by the relegation in status, thus robbing the fixture of its true significance.

When the teams took the field howls of protest went up. They stopped during the playing of the British National Anthem but resumed again when the Italian Anthem began, although many did not realise what it actually was. There was an atmosphere of distrust, of anger, of antagonism, a far from satisfactory platform on which to stage any match. Naturally players reacted. Right half Chiapella caught Danny Blanchflower with a lightning hook which would have been applauded at Madison Square Garden; Schiaffino, contrary to his normal cultured play, brutally hit Cush and was immediately cautioned by the referee.

Schiaffino's eyes looked so blank, so expressionless that Jimmy McIlroy (Burnley) asked Blanchflower 'Is he drugged?' 'I don't know. I didn't expect *him* to do that,' replied the Ireland skipper, who told Cush to forget it and get on with the game.

Cush nodded his head but shortly afterwards he tackled the Uruguayan with a ferocity which made even those who knew the toughness of the little iron man from Lurgan wince. The Italians went about their business in a professional way giving as much as they got. They did not shirk. And, in the thick of the foray was the giant centre-half Ferrario (Juventus). One moment he pleaded with Blanchflower to keep the peace, the next he was engaged in acts of fury,

Glasgow Rangers' Billy Simpson scores a dramatic goal for Northern Ireland in the 3-2 win over England at Wembley, November 1957.

and, during a corner, kicked all around him with the ball nowhere in the vicinity.

When Ireland was awarded a free kick outside the penalty box they formed their defensive wall a few yards in front of the ball. They refused to move. Bingham paced out but they brushed him aside; Peter McParland (Aston Villa) eventually beat three defenders with the 'keeper Bugatti (Napoli) diving at his feet. Bugatti lay prostrate, McParland finishing in the back of the net. Chiapelli went berserk, jumping with his feet into the small of Billy McAdams' back — described by Blanchflower 'as the most dangerous act I've seen in football'.

The crowd invaded the pitch at the end of a 2-2 draw (Cush getting the Northern Ireland goals) attacking three Italians, including Ferrario, with police drawing batons to restore order. Questions were raised in the Italian Parliament, and, generally, relations between the two countries nose-dived to an all-time low. So it was back to Belfast — this time on 15 January 1958, but that match was a tame affair by comparison, although Ghiggia was sent off for no apparent reason in the second half.

Northern Ireland, wearing black armbands as a mark of respect to Jimmy Gibb, Irish League secretary who had recently died, won 2-1 before 40,000 with goals from McIlroy and Cush, Jackie Blanchflower playing a vital role as he kept the team, crippled with fatigue, together.

For the first time in the history of the Irish FA Northern Ireland had reached the World Cup Finals series; Italy, the side with the reputation, were out. This was how the Group One table finished:

	P	W	L	D	F	A	Pts
Northern Ireland	4	2	1	1	6	3	5
Italy	4	2	2	0	5	5	4
Portugal	4	1	2	1	4	7	3

Success was tinged with controversy. That never-on-a-Sunday rule passed so long ago reared its ugly head. Sunday matches were a must in Sweden, but, under the Articles of Association, these were banned. Critics claimed that the Irish FA were aware of this and should not have entered the preliminaries. It was a bitter feud between many leading Irish personalities but, eventually, a compromise was reached with the team permitted to play on Sundays and the rule unaltered. Fortunately since then the change has been made. Sunday soccer is now permitted outside Northern Ireland and no problem arises.

FIFA had arranged the draw in Stockholm on a Saturday in February — two days after the Manchester United air crash at Munich which decimated the 'Busby Babes' and wrecked British international football for a period. It robbed Northern Ireland of Jackie Blanchflower but Gregg, uninjured, made the journey to Sweden by sea and returned home by air, his first ever flight since that ill-fated trip to Belgrade.

Billy Drennan left immediately after the Group draw in which West Germany (1954 winners) and Czechoslovakia, and Argentina and Northern Ireland were paired. He had done his homework on the various team headquarters available, selected a magnificent centre at the seaside resort of Tylosand, near Halmstead. He got the manager out of his bed, made an inspection and then signed the agreement just as the Czechs came to book in!

It was an admirable choice, for Tylosand and Halmstad took the Irish to their hearts. Northern Ireland was their team with many lasting friendships formed. One pressman Terry Elliott (*Daily Express*) even called his new home 'Tylosand'. It was a perfect setting for what was to be a memorable adventure.

This was the pathway to Sweden. Wilbur Cush scores the final goal to give Northern Ireland a 2-1 World Cup victory over Italy at Windsor Park in January 1958, as goalkeeper Bugatti sprawls helplessly and full-back Corradi can only gaze in vain.

Tylosand, near Halmstad — Northern Ireland's headquarters during the 1958 World Cup final series in Sweden.

Sweden
1958

The date was Monday, 2 June 1958. Northern Ireland's World Cup party set out from London Airport for Sweden — first to Copenhagen and then by ferry to Malmo and eventually Tylosand. Nobody paid much attention to them when they landed; they mixed with tourists on the ship and indeed they looked like tourists themselves visiting those friendly shores.

Those were the days of the free-and-easy World Cup: a tournament which was a sporting occasion and not a huge commercial venture with blanket security as it is today. In many ways they were happier days, too, with greater enjoyment, greater fun, greater camaraderie. Football then had character, a substance, a warmth, a carefree, even capricious quality about it.

Munich had meant the unavailability of Jackie Blanchflower with seventeen players forming the squad — Danny Blanchflower (Tottenham Hotspur), Harry Gregg (Manchester United), Norman Uprichard (Portsmouth), Dick Keith, Alfie McMichael and Tommy Casey (Newcastle United), Derek Dougan (Portsmouth), Willie Cunningham (Leicester City), Bertie Peacock (Glasgow Celtic), Billy Bingham (Sunderland), Jimmy McIlroy (Burnley),

Off on the great adventure — Northern Ireland's squad leave for the 1958 World Cup. *From top*: Derek Dougan, Billy Bingham, the late Gerry Morgan, Norman Uprichard, Willie Cunningham, Peter McParland, Fay Coyle, Sammy McCrory, Jimmy McIlroy, Wilbur Cush, Jackie Scott, Danny Blanchflower, Tommy Casey, Billy Simpson, Bertie Peacock, and Peter Doherty (manager). The Newcastle United full-backs, Alfie McMichael and the late Dick Keith joined the party in Sweden after a club tour.

Billy Simpson (Glasgow Rangers), Wilbur Cush (Leeds United), Peter McParland (Aston Villa), Jackie Scott (Grimsby Town), Roy Coyle (Nottingham Forest) and Sammy McCrory (Southend United).

Frank Pearson, a young Swede, was appointed as the liaison officer. Quickly he became a member of the family led, of course, by the inimitable Gerry Morgan whose meet-the-Press interviews were quite hilarious. 'We'll equalise before the other team scores!' he told astonished West German journalists. And he managed to keep his face straight, too.

It was a little boy, however, who won the hearts of that party. His name was Bengt Jonasson, the thirteen-year-old son of a wealthy local businessman who visited the camp on the arrival day and never left. Bengt became the team's mascot, spoke perfect English, carried out errands for players and officials, guided them on shopping tours and actually stayed in the headquarters. Tears were in his eyes when he had to say goodbye as the train drew out from Norkopping for Stockholm after the quarter final defeat by France, but players and officials brought him as their guest to Belfast for the international with England in October.

Peter Doherty and Danny Blanchflower made the four-hour journey to Copenhagen to watch the Czechs, a team packed with outstanding, skilful players, who had arranged a warm-up match against a Danish select. There they conceived most of the tactical plans which were to pay off so handsomely in the later stages.

This was only part of the methodical approach to the tournament, with all the training carried out on a pitch secluded by a forest of trees. Set pieces were rehearsed and re-rehearsed, although Doherty found himself in a quandary when Simpson pulled a muscle and could not participate in the series. Doherty and Blanchflower formed a most effective partnership, and, with Morgan keeping spirits up over a three-week period, there was never a squabble, breach of discipline or the necessity for a reprimand.

Mickey McColgan, now an Irish FA Council member, and his friend Jim Nicholl arrived in Tylosand by motor-scooter, pitching a tent in the lawn of the luxury hotel. It was not the done thing — like placing a fish and chip stall outside the Savoy. When the manager attempted to remove them he was invited in and given a cup of tea brewed on a primus stove! So he let them remain and, on match days, even sent them off with carnations in their button holes.

The opening match was played at Halmstad on 8 June against the Czechs — the first ever occasion on which an Irish FA national eleven played on a Sunday. Services were organised that morning in a small church at Tylosand which had an amazing history. Apparently parts of it had been dismantled and taken to the United States as souvenirs; locals later decided to bring them back and rebuild the church. Appropriately the text of the sermon was 'Faith moveth mountains' and one of the hymns 'Fight the Good Fight'.

The centre-forward position provided the main problem for Doherty and the international selectors; eventually Dougan was preferred to Coyle. So this was

73

the team which met Czechoslovakia: Gregg, Keith, McMichael, Blanchflower, Cunningham, Peacock, Bingham, Cush, Dougan, McIlroy, McParland.

It was a scrappy game, hard to watch, but to the surprise of everyone, Northern Ireland, that joker in the pack, triumphed 1-0 with a goal from Cush after McIlroy had cut it back from the left wing.

'I knew Jimmy's left foot was his weak one. I wondered could he get it across to the far post. I darted to the near one and eased it in with a head flick,' said Cush.

Scrappy or not, it was victory for the Irish who celebrated that night in the Norre Kat Night Club, Halmstad; they took over the place with the Lord Mayor Sir Cecil McKee leading the group in singing and dancing. The music that night was intoxicating, the atmosphere perfect and everyone was in the mood to dance all night. The citizens of Halmstad lived it up, too, for *their* team had won.

Three days later came the match against Argentina, with Coyle taking over from Dougan. There was still scepticism about that Czechoslovak victory, but even more astonishment when McParland opened the scoring against the Argentinians who, twenty years later, were to win the World Cup themselves in the spectacular, colourful setting of the River Plate Stadium, Buenos Aires.

The Argentinians, 3-1 winners, who had introduced the veterans Angel Labruna at inside left and Nestor Rossi at centre-half, were much too good for Northern Ireland whose players became tension-filled and frustrated. 'There was a lot of strain and swearing. At one time I had to call the players together and tell them to shut up as they were only causing confusion among themselves,' commented Blanchflower in his autobiography *The Double and Before.*

Then it was on the Malmo for another Sunday match against the West Germans. For sheer excitement, superb football, and honest endeavour this game is unsurpassed. It is still talked about to this day by many Germans who consider it a classic in the mould of the Eintracht-Real Madrid European Cup Final of 1960.

Gregg was absolutely fantastic; his saves incredible, his reflexes amazing, and it was this performance which earned him the title of 'Goalkeeper of the Tournament'. There have been few, if any, better displays from an Irish or any other goalkeeper.

McParland scored two goals and with seven minutes remaining Northern Ireland led 2-1; the real shock of the series was about to materialise but then Uwe Seeler, a comparative newcomer, hit the equaliser. 'Uwe, Uwe, Uwe,' chanted the relieved West Germans who graciously stood and applauded Gregg and the Irish off the pitch.

Czechoslovakia, surprisingly, defeated Argentina 6-1, finishing equal on points with Northern Ireland which necessitated a play off at Malmo the following Tuesday. Instead of staying there the Irish party made the hundred mile journey back to Tylosand, a move which in retrospect was not conducive to proper preparation.

There were moments when glory, like grief, needs no audience. That was why the door of No. 1 dressing room at the stadium was locked on the Tuesday night. Inside the Irish team stood alone, savouring the greatest moment in the IFA history. The Czechs had been defeated 2-1 and Northern Ireland, this little country with a population of one and a quarter million, was through to the last eight.

Doherty lifted an empty lemonade bottle, cracked it against the massage table and the babble of voices, the singing of 'When Irish Eyes are Smiling' stopped. His voice was emotion-filled. Tears were in his eyes. Words almost failed him. 'Well done lads — you were magnificent,' he said. His tribute summed up the way every Irishman and woman felt about that team.

Gregg, his ankle swollen three times its normal size after twisting it against the Germans, bathed it for hours in the cold, salt water of the nearby beach but he simply could not make it and hobbled to the match with the aid of a stick. Centre-forward had, however, been the problem position. As neither Dougan nor Cush had been a success there it was decided to play Jackie Scott (Grimsby Town) in the middle. It was a tactical ploy by Doherty who had ordered him to switch to the left wing after the kick-off with McParland in the centre.

The terraces of the stadium were half empty, but in one corner the Ulster contingent stood and waved the Union Jack. Players were tired and it was a hard struggle for supremacy; those titanic efforts against the West Germans forty-eight hours earlier had taken their toll and there was no reserve strength in depth to ease the pain. The game was only in the eighth minute when

Caught off his line, Norman Uprichard stands no chance against Zikan's header which gives Czechoslovakia the lead in the 1958 World Cup tie.

A toothy grin from Billy Bingham — Northern Ireland are through to the finals.

Uprichard, going for a ball twisted his ankle but Ireland played superbly, with Blanchflower an inspiration, turning in his best game of the series.

After seventeen minutes Czech centre-half Popluhar hooked the ball twenty yards for outside left Zihan to head into the net — a goal which gave the Eastern Europeans confidence but did not deflate the Irish. They desperately needed to get back into the game and they did so a minute before half-time. Bingham raced down the right wing, pushed the ball inside for Cush who had three chances blocked, and, deciding against a fourth, flicked it across for McParland to hit into the net. The second half nearly proved a disaster. Uprichard smashed his hand against the post attempting to stop a shot from Dvorak and although he continued, it was later discovered that the hand was actually broken. Every time he grasped the ball the pain was excruciating.

That was not the only tragedy. Uprichard and Zihan collided with Peacock who had one leg in the air and the knee of the 'Little Ant' locked: an injury which side-lined him for the next three months. Let Blanchflower take over the story. He wrote in *The Double and Before*: 'I remember the scene as we paused on the field before extra time. Peacock was hurt, Uprichard's hand limp and useless. Peter Doherty and I tried to revive the boys with words of encouragement. "They are more tired than we are so keep plodding away" was the line we took.

'Uprichard suggested to me that he would be better playing out of goal but I urged him to stay. We moved Cush back to left half, Bingham to inside forward and Peacock to the wing. It was now or never.

'Extra time was gruelling. We got the vital goal in the hundredth minute, McParland hooking in a free kick which was one of the most accurate I have ever placed. I was ragged and tired as I went to take it. I recall urging myself that I must concentrate all the more and try to get it to McParland, one of our tactics at the time. With great deliberation I took the kick and it went away ever so sweetly right to the spot I had intended.'

Now only twenty minutes remained. 'When Irish Eyes Are Smiling,' sang the fans. 'Go on lads — keep at them,' shouted Doherty. Their response was instant, they fought until amost overtaken by fatigue. They tackled with ferocity but fairness and the Czech half-back Bubernik, an ice hockey inter-national, complained he had been pushed in the back but the referee brushed him aside. Bubernik again complained, gesticulated and spat in his face. Off he went and for the remainder of the match the Czechs were reduced to ten men.

Irish FA officials came down from their seats to the touchline. So, too, did the local pressmen. Harry Cavan, then a selector, and I sat with our backs to the play. We simply couldn't stand the tension. A roar from the crowd. Had the Czechs equalised? No — it was the hobbling Peacock who had hit the ball into the net only for the referee to rule it off-side. Then it was all over — 2-1 and those players had achieved immortality. As they left the pitch McMichael noticed Novak and Masopust behind him. He stopped, shook them by the hand and said, 'Hard luck fellows.' The Czechs forced a smile in that moment of disappointment and rejection. These were the section results:

Group One:

West Germany	3	Argentina	1
Northern Ireland	1	Czechoslovakia	2
West Germany	2	Czechoslovakia	2
Argentina	3	Northern Ireland	1
West Germany	2	Northern Ireland	2
Czechoslovakia	6	Argentina	1

	P	W	D	L	F	A	Pts
West Germany	3	1	2	0	7	4	4
Czechoslovakia	3	1	1	1	8	4	3
Northern Ireland	3	1	1	1	4	5	3
Argentina	3	1	0	2	5	10	2

Play Off — Northern Ireland   2   Czechoslovakia   1

It is interesting to note that under present FIFA regulations on goal difference Northern Ireland would not have qualified.

Northern Ireland had reached the quarter-finals but the limitation of players and the mounting injury list proved insurmountable. That night they drove back to Tylosand and the next day made a ten-hour journey across Sweden to Norkopping where they lost 4-0 to France, a team not nearly so accomplished as those they had previously played. Gregg, not fully fit, was drafted into goal as there was simply nobody else to take his place; Casey had stitched in a leg gash and finished with blood seeping through his sock.

Sweden had been the pinnacle but it had almost ended in tragedy. The plane carrying the team (fortunately Gregg, the hero of Munich, had gone home a day earlier with Irish FA selector Sammy Walker) had just taken off from Bromma International Airport, Stockholm, when the undercarriage failed to retract and it circled for almost an hour jettisoning fuel. Emergency services were called into operation on the airport apron with fire engines and ambulance standing by as the plane made its final landing and the white-faced passengers came off. Another possible Munich disaster had been averted.

Soon the plane took off again with everyone fortified by refreshments. The group returned home in glory. It was a group which became a legend.

Northern Ireland players take a breather during a training session at Ninian Park, Cardiff, before 1966 match with Wales. *From left*: Martin Harvey (Sunderland), Jimmy Nicholson (Huddersfield Town), John Parke **(Su**nderland), Jimmy Magill (Brighton), Terry Neill (Arsenal) (Capt.), Alex Elder (Burnley**)**.

1958-1970

Danny Blanchflower was the central figure of the 1958 team in Sweden but around him he had many outstanding competitors — probably the most accomplished group of Irish players assembled at the one time — Bertie Peacock, Jimmy McIlroy, Billy Bingham, Billy Cush, Peter McParland, to name but a few.

Peacock (Glentoran, Glasgow Celtic and Coleraine) was given the name of 'The Little Ant' in Sweden because of his magnificent tackling. Not many were so dedicated to fitness and football as Peacock, a member of the Great Britain side which met the Rest of Europe in the Irish FA's 75th anniversary match. He won every honour in the Scottish game and, oddly enough, it was against Scotland he earned the first of those thirty-two caps.

He returned to Coleraine as manager in 1961, a promise he made to club chairman Jack Doherty at the end of the World Cup series. He moulded it into one of the best sides in the country and over thirteen years achieved an amazing record — Irish Cup (1965 and 1972), Irish League championship (1974), Ulster Cup four times, Blaxnit twice, City Cup and Top Four once each. His

79

appointment as Northern Ireland team manager in 1962, as successor to Peter Doherty, was universally approved but, due to business commitments, he relinquished this in 1967 to be followed by Bingham, who took over the job again in January, 1980.

Bingham was the impish type, always smiling, but behind that cocoon of humour was a man of iron will. The stories about him when he was manager of Linfield are legion. Inside forward Phil Scott telephoned the ground to request a release from training as he had a cold. 'I'm terribly sorry to hear about your cold. Now blow your nose and get up here,' retorted Bingham.

He had the distinction with Blanchflower of winning fifty-six caps and his contribution to Northern Ireland in the late Fifties and early Sixties was invaluable. He brought solid endeavour to the game as an orthodox winger, an erudition which he carried into management despite the theory that soccer managers are invariably as thick as lodging house sandwiches. He was intelligent, level-headed. Bingham has a passion for antique books with a collection dating back to the early years of printing; he studies the topography of Ireland, listens avidly and contentedly to classical music and, strange as it may seem, loves watching Rugby Union.

Bingham and Jimmy McIlroy (Glentoran, Burnley and Stoke City) were inseparable on the field, a partnership which proved highly effective. A cultured, stylish inside forward, McIlroy was one of the outstanding tacticians of the Sixties. He took over at Turf Moor when Harry Potts was transferred to Everton; he played 440 league games, scoring 115 goals.

Here again was the classic example of a player who sparkled for his club but rarely for his country, which he represented fifty-five times. To contemplate Burnley without McIlroy was incredible, with chairman Bob Lord emphasising categorically that money would not buy him. Yet, in February 1963, he was placed on the transfer list after a series of hush-hush director's meetings. On a Monday morning when he reported at the ground Potts, by then manager, told him he could go. He spent over two years as manager of Oldham Athletic and for eighteen days was in charge of Bolton Wanderers but now he works as a journalist on a Burnley newspaper.

The other ever regular member of that attack was Newry-born Peter McParland (thirty-five caps). He was the hero of Aston Villa, winning an FA Cup Final medal with them against Manchester United. He scored five goals in the 1958 World Cup, managed Glentoran and then the Cypriot side with the intriguing name of Digenis Akritas of Morthou. He was the explosive element in the World Cup party, the man who could score goals. 'Everything was right with us. There is nothing better than to be in a team which is on song,' he says. 'Of course, Blanchflower and McIlroy were on top in English football and, basically, we were a team with a lot of gifts. But there was something more than that — a sort of magic.'

Atlanta Chiefs, Worcester City, Wolverhampton Wanderers, were some of his other clubs but he will always be remembered for that clash with United goalkeeper Ray Wood in the 1957 FA Cup Final. It was a controversial

The goal famine is over. Centre-forward Derek Dougan scores in the European championship match against Cyprus in Nicosia. Dougan swept the ball in after a shot from midfielder Jimmy Nicholson had rebounded from the bar. A 3-0 success was the first Irish victory in nine internationals.

shoulder charge on a day which gave him two goals and Villa's seventh FA Cup Final win.

Six minutes had gone and United, the favourites, were being pressurised. 'I tried a header at goal,' recalls McParland. 'Wood gathered the ball and carried forward by sheer momentum I went on to charge him. Our two bodies crashed with the side of my face hitting his jaw bone. Wood was carried off suffering from a cheek injury and I had a lump on mine.

'Pictures taken immediately after the collision show me sitting up apparently laughing but I wasn't. The expression was one of pain. Perspiration dripped down my fact and I had just wiped my hand across thinking it was blood. The whole stadium appeared to be going round. I felt terrible about Ray's injury. It was a pure accident. Every time I touched the ball United fans booed.'

One of Lurgan's greatest soccer sons was, of course, Wilbur Cush, a late developer. His career began with Carrick, winners of the Irish Schools Cup in 1941-2, 2nd Lurgan Boys Brigade, Lurgan Boys Club, winners of the Irish Junior Cup, Shankill Y.M., and then on to Glenavon with the late Willie Walker. He won Irish international recognition when at Mourneview Park and led Glenavon to become the first provincial side to take the Irish League championship.

'Too small' was often the criticism levelled at Wilbur but dynamic international and inter-league displays revealed that, although small in stature, he stood head and shoulders above the others in class. Skill, fearlessness, and honesty were his qualities. They came no harder than Cush. The Greeks knew that; in a match at Windsor Park one spat in his face. Cush saw red, hit him on the chin and down he went. The referee didn't notice, Cush walked away and Jimmy Nicholson, rushing over to see what happened, was sent off.

The iron man was Tommy Casey (Newcastle United) from Comber whose father was caretaker of the distillery there. He made his debut for East Belfast at Clara Park and then signed for Bangor who had Don McMillan, John 'Bap' Dunlop, Sammy Doak and Gerry Taylor on their staff with Andy Wylie as the manager. Next he joined Leeds United, had a row with manager Frank Buckley, and returned home. Then followed a spell with Fulham and on to Newcastle United, recommended by Billy McCracken; with them he won an FA Cup medal.

Casey continued in the game as manager of Distillery, as coach to Harry Catterick at Everton, in Iceland and Norway, and for a period he was in charge of Northern Ireland's youth team.

If Tully had extrovert qualities then Derek Dougan (Portsmouth, Blackburn Rovers, Aston Villa, Peterborough, Leicester City and Wolverhampton Wanderers) could be similarly classified. In the opening paragraph of his autobiography *Attack* he writes, 'Throughout my career since joining Portsmouth from Distillery I have been called a rebel, a show off, a belligerent non-conformist, a trouble-maker and a few unrepeatable names usually prefaced with the tag "Irish" which is supposed to explain, if not absolve, everything.'

Dougan won forty-three caps, playing mainly as a striker with a goal tally of five. His club record as a marksman certainly overshadowed that for his country as he played a key part in restoring Wolverhampton Wanderers to the First Division. 'The Doog' never seemed to be out of the headlines. He was a personality who shaved his head, grew a beard, became engaged to a beauty queen and fought for players' rights as chairman of the Professional Footballers' Association.

He posted a letter to Blackburn Rovers asking for a transfer on the mornng of their 1960 FA Cup Final against Wolves but he is now a big enough man to admit the error of his ways on that occasion. 'Looking back with a more temperate mind I acknowledge I did Blackburn Rovers a double disservice. I should not have asked for a transfer then and I should not have played in the Cup Final,' he wrote in his autobiography.

'As soon as I stretched my legs on the Wembley turf I knew I was the odd man out, that an injured leg would drag me down through the match. What should have been a professional climax became a frustrating anticlimax followed by an acute pang of conscience. It is too late to apologise, but for the record I must say that through selfishness I contributed to Blackburn's 3-0 defeat.'

Terry Neill, Northern Ireland captain (*second left*), demonstrates an exercise for strengthening the abdominal muscles. With him are Alex Elder, Jimmy McIlroy and Derek Dougan.

Dougan, who has given a lot to the game, is a strong advocate of an all-Ireland side which he sees as the springboard to Ireland making an impression on the world scene. Some years ago he got together an all-Ireland side which met Brazil at Lansdowne Road, Dublin.

There was, in this era, that full back partnership of the Newcastle United pair Alfie McMichael (forty caps), who was captain until Blanchflower took over, and Dick Keith (twenty-three). Keith was tragically killed in an accident at Bournemouth when a garage spring door hit him. They were a classic pair both of whom had gone to St. James' Park from Linfield, although at different times.

Willie Cunningham (St. Mirren, Leicester City and Dunfermline Athletic) also occupied the full-back and centre-half positions. Born at Mallusk, Co. Antrim, he was brought up from childhood in Scotland; a hard tackler, the essence of reliability, he got thirty caps and later became manager of Dunfermline, Falkirk and St. Mirren. In September 1971 he rejected a four-year contract at £8,000 per annum to manage Scotland's international team.

The Sixties saw the advent also of Alex Elder (Glentoran, Burnley and Stoke City) who took over from Keith; twice he captained the team. Transferred from Glentoran to Burnley in January 1959, for £4,000, he established himself as the regular left back at Turf Moor but fractured his leg in a pre-season match in August 1963 which put him out of the game for three matches, cost him three international caps and a place in the Rest of the World team against England. It took him months to recover fitness and confidence. With Burnley he won a League championship medal in 1959/60 and was also a member of the FA Cup side defeated 3-1 by Tottenham Hotspur in 1962.

'I've no grumbles about football,' he says. 'Some things could have turned out better. There were misunderstandings with clubs which hurt but I don't talk about that. Football gave me a lot which I wouldn't have had otherwise.'

Arsenal's Billy McCullough and Jimmy Magill, both products of Portadown, were full back partners for a considerable period, with Magill eventually taking up management in Denmark. Both were in the true tradition of Arsenal.

'Once an Arsenal player always an Arsenal player. Once you joined the club you felt a raise in stature and character,' said Jimmy. This was the period also in which Willie Humphries (Ards, Leeds, Coventry, Swansea) and Willie Irvine (Burnley, Preston and Brighton) made their mark.

It was in Bologna during the 1961 three-match tour of Italy, Greece and West Germany that Terry Neill (Arsenal and Hull City) played the first of his fifty-nine internationals, a record surpassing that of Blanchflower, Bingham and McIlroy — only to be beaten again by Pat Jennings (Tottenham Hotspur and Arsenal).

Neill has been one of Northern Ireland's greatest soccer ambassadors, centre-half and captain of Arsenal when only twenty. He is an example of the clean-cut sportsman parents would like their sons to emulate. He is proud of Ulster, of his parents and of his home life. Neill never failed to impress when wearing the green shirt; he had worked at his game to be competent and his greatest moment came in May 1972 when he scored the goal to give Northern Ireland victory over England at Wembley. He had not attained his 21st birthday in March 1963 when he was appointed Ireland's captain against Wales at Windsor Park.

'That day in Bologna I thought would be my last as an international player,' he recalls. 'Martin Harvey made his debut in that one, too, and the only experienced half-back we had was Bertie Peacock. Imagine that against a team which included Nicolai and the fabulous South American Omar Sivori!

'I was, however, selected against West Germany and asked to mark Seeler. Our nerves were shattered when a tramcar collided with our bus in West Berlin on the way to the Olympic Stadium. Fortunately, nobody was hurt.'

Neill went to Hull City as player-manager, succeeded Bill Nicholson at Tottenham Hotspur in 1974; two years later became the man in charge at Arsenal and, from 1971-5, managed Northern Ireland with distinction and complete professionalism.

And, as the Seventies approached, there was the courageous feat of Jimmy

England captain Bobby Moore, the Jules Rimet Cup in his right hand, leads out his team for the October 1966 game with Northern Ireland at Windsor Park — their first after winning the World Cup. On the left Derek Dougan, Willie Irvine, and right Sammy Todd, Billy Ferguson, John Parke, George Best and Alex Elder. England won 2-0.

McLaughlin, now manager of League of Ireland double champions Dundalk, who scored two goals against England in 1964 despite dislocating two fingers of his left hand after a challenge from Maurice Norman (Tottenham Hotspur).

For consistency of performance it would be difficult to surpass Martin Harvey (Sunderland) who made 300 League and Cup appearances for his club. We had the impish class of Eddie McMordie (Middlesborough), labelled 'The Ferret' by his team-mates, and the iron will of Dave Clements (Coventry City, Wolves, Everton), 'The Farmer', who succeeded Terry Neill as captain and eventually as manager of the Irish international side before joining New York Cosmos and Colorado Caribous. There was, too, the brilliance of the 'Busby Babe' Jimmy Nicholson who began as a teenager with Manchester United and continued with Huddersfield Town.

This was an era which produced quite a battle for the right back position between David Craig (Newcastle United), who came into the side in the late Sixties, and Arsenal's Pat Rice.

85

A gentleman of soccer is, of course, a cliché but it epitomises David Craig about whom a London journalist once commented, 'If he had been a Cockney instead of from Comber he would have played for England.'

He won only twenty-four caps; the number could have been much higher if injury had not plagued him. One could get the impression from statistics of a player rarely off the treatment table, prone to the slightest knock and unable to cope with the rough-hewn life of professional football and all its subtleties of tackling. That would be wrong. Few players contributed more to the team than Craig, who possessed technical know-how, superb defensive qualities and a capacity to recover quickly.

Rice is an Ulsterman with a Cockney accent. His father, a Belfast engineer, died when he was only three years old; he left the city at the age of ten to live only a hundred yards from Highbury.

'I won no honours at school. I learned my football kicking about the street with my pals,' says Rice, who joined Arsenal as an apprentice professional after he had been discovered by Mickey Dulin, a former Tottenham Hotspur winger and talent spotter for the Islington school teams.

Rice started work in a greengrocer's shop, and on becoming an Arsenal player, his greatest ambition had been achieved, particularly, when he established himself in the 1970-71 double season. His international debut was against Israel in Tel Aviv in 1968; from then on the right back position was Pat's for keeps except when injury struck.

'His secret could be summed up in one word — dedication,' said ex-Arsenal goalkeeper Bob Wilson. 'He would spend hours trying to iron out all the faults in his play, give up his free afternoons and his days off. He decided his left foot was not strong enough so he would tackle and practice with this in a private session. He would go on as long as there was anyone around to pump balls at him.'

Dave Clements was also the epitome of professionalism, of principle and integrity. His breakthrough came against Mexico at Windsor Park in 1966 and eventually he won forty-eight caps, as well as succeeding Neill as captain of the side and manager. But in 1976 the authorities decided his managerial contract could not be renewed because 'a manager located in the USA was not in the best interests of the Irish FA'.

Jimmy Nicholson left Belfast as a fifteen-year-old for Manchester United and when he was seventeen years and eight months played left half in the first team; he won the first of forty-one international caps against Scotland at Hampden Park. By fulsome effort and a sharp, positive, attacking approach, he brought a high degree of authority to the mid field game. His departure from Old Trafford for £50,000 came after the arrival of Pat Crerand (Glasgow Celtic).

The Northern Ireland team beaten 2-1 by England at Goodison Park, on Saturday, 12 May 1973 — one of the matches switched from Belfast because of the civil unrest. *From left*: Terry Neill (Capt.), Pat Jennings, Dave Clements, Sammy Morgan, Bryan Hamilton, Trevor Anderson, Allan Hunter, David Craig, Tommy Jackson, Martin O'Neill, Pat Rice.

1970-1980

The Seventies saw the establishment of such players as Bryan Hamilton, (Linfield, Ipswich, Everton, Millwall, Swindon Town), Liam O'Kane (Derry City and Nottingham Forest), Tony O'Doherty (Derry City), Tommy Jackson (Glentoran, Everton and Manchester United), Tommy Cassidy (Glentoran and Newcastle United) and Warren Feeney (Glentoran and Linfield) who followed in the footsteps of his father, Jimmy, capped as a full back with Linfield and Swansea Town.

Boys Brigade football in the Co. Londonderry village of Sion Mills set 6ft. Allan Hunter (Coleraine, Oldham Athletic, Blackburn Rovers and Ipswich Town) on the road to fame as his country's central defender. At seventeen he joined Coleraine, where his brother Vic was the goalkeeper and also an Irish International. His sheer strength, his razor-sharp tackling, his commanding presence, made him an instant success, and with the club he won an Irish League medal and a runners-up medal in the League championship series.

Jimmy McIlroy, when manager of Oldham Athletic, realising his potential, signed him in 1967. During two and a half seasons with the Lancashire club he

Shopping in Moscow before the September 1971 match with the Soviet Union at the Lenin Stadium — George Best with Iam McFaul, Martin Harvey and Eric McMordie. Russia won 1-0.

played seventy-four matches, a period dogged for him by injury. Blackburn Rovers paid £25,000 for him, trebling their money when Ipswich Town moved in two seasons ago. He was transfer-listed in September 1973 at £200,000 but taken off by manager Bobby Robson after behind-the-scenes talks. His club and international performances prompted Sir Alf Ramsey to nominate him for the 'Three v The Six' match at Wembley to mark Britain's entry into the European Economic Community and 'The Big Man', as he is called by team mates, also topped the fifty cap mark.

Then came the concentrated supply from Manchester United — Sammy McIlroy, Jimmy Nicholl, David McCreery. McIlroy, a seventeen-year-old whose father played for Linfield, was pitched into the Manchester derby with City for his baptism in English football and it turned into a dream start when he scored United's first goal in a 3-3 draw; how appropriate too, that it was George Best who initiated the move.

McIlroy, ex-schoolboy international with Ashfield, joined Old Trafford in June 1963 and entered the senior side as a replacement for Denis Law; a serious car accident in January 1962 when he received multiple injuries and a punctured lung almost ended his career.

He first wore the green jersey against Spain at Hull — this was one of the matches switched from Belfast because of the political unrest. McIlroy was a mere 17 years and 198 days old, which made him the third youngest Irish international debutant; Norman Kernaghan (Belfast Celtic) was 118 days

Top Right: Windsor Park, May 1975 — and yet another Irish attack fails. England's Emlyn Hughes flykicks the ball away from Bryan Hamilton to bring the move to a halt.

Bottom Right: Scotland forward Denis Law whips round Northern Ireland goalkeeper Pat Jennings and prods the ball into the net, only to be given offside. Scotland, however, won 2-0. The year — May 1972.

Hands up... as Chris McGrath dashes to the centre after scoring against Iceland at Windsor Park in September 1977 (2-0). His gesticulating colleagues are, from the left, Sammy McIlroy, Trevor Anderson and Sammy Nelson.

younger when he became an international in 1936. W. K. Gibson (Cliftonville) 16 years and 240 days when he played against Wales in 1894 and Jimmy Nicholson 17 years 255 days against Scotland in 1960.

Jimmy Nicholl is another who made his pathway to fame through schoolboy and youth international football. He is a valuable asset of Old Trafford and a possible future captain of his country and it was in 1975 that David 'Wee Dee' McCreery played for Manchester United's First XI. Another Bob Bishop capture, he is precocious without being brash, his enthusiasm is infectious. Manager Tommy Docherty always had a special place for McCreery and it was not surprising that when 'The Doc' took over at Queen's Park Rangers, McCreery, a member of an East Belfast footballing family, eventually joined him.

His midfield partner has been Martin O'Neill (Distillery and Nottingham Forest) who quit law studies at the Queen's University, Belfast, to enter professional football. His dynamic play had galvanised Distillery into a team

Left: Holland's superstar Johann Cruyff failed to win this battle with Jimmy Nicholl in the 1977 World Cup tie with Holland at Windsor Park. The Dutch won 1-0 and finished defeated finalists to Argentina in Buenos Aires a year later.

It's not often a full back scores but here is the moment of triumph for Sammy Nelson, his arms raised, as he beats the Welsh goalkeeper in the 1977 match at Windsor Park. It ended 1-1.

The Irish squad relaxing at their St. Alban's headquarters before the May 1978 match with England at Wembley. *Left to right:* Peter Scott (York City), Chris McGrath (Tottenham Hotspur), Martin O'Neill (Nottingham Forest), Tom Connell (Manchester United), Trevor Anderson (Swindon Town).

No luck here for England's Butch Wilkins as Jim Nicholl gets in a timely tackle watched by Allan Hunter, his face revealing his determination, during the European championship game with England at Windsor Park in October 1979.

good enough to win the Irish Cup; he hit two of the goals in the defeat of Derry City and in the European Cup games with Barcelona revealed his potential in the Camp Nou stadium where he was given the title of the 'White Pelé'.

His progress was slow at Forest — so much so that he was on the verge of a transfer until the arrival of Brian Clough changed all that. Clough and Peter Taylor ignited the spark which turned him into one of Britain's best soccer properties.

These years saw the appearances of Danny Hegan (West Bromwich Albion and Wolverhampton Wanderers); Sammy Nelson, the Arsenal full-back who became a regular with Rice for club and country; Roy Coyle (Glentoran and Sheffield Wednesday), the Linfield manager since 1976; Chris McGrath (Tottenham Hotspur and Manchester United); Hugh Dowd (Glentoran and Sheffield Wednesday); Trevor Anderson (Manchester United and Swindon Town); Tom Finney (Cambridge United) and Ronnie Blair (Oldham Athletic).

Vic Moreland (Derby County) sends Peter Shilton the wrong way to score Northern Ireland's solitary goal in the 5-1 European championship defeat by England in October 1979.

Strikers have always been a major problem with Northern Ireland international teams. Many were tried in the Seventies — Derek Spence (Bury, Blackpool, Southend), Gerry Armstrong (Bangor and Tottenham Hotspur) who, like so many professionals in the Irish League, graduated from Amateur League side Cromac Albion, and Sammy Morgan (Port Vale) who switched to football after qualifying as a schoolteacher. Morgan always wore contact lenses when he was playing and was in the mould of most Northern Ireland international strikers, a bustler with an infinite capacity to rumble the opposition.

The Republic's Liam Brady and Northern Ireland's Derek Spence challenge during the September 1978 game at Lansdowne Road, Dublin. Each side failed to score.

Northern Ireland striker Gerry Armstrong (right) heads the ball into the net for the solitary goal in the defeat of the Republic of Ireland at Windsor Park in November 1979. Could there be any more joyous expression than that of clubmate Derek Spence?

Northern Ireland midfielder ploughs through against Wales as Peter Rodrigues slips on the Windsor Park pitch. The game ended in a scoreless draw.

Northern Ireland striker Sammy Morgan, rebuked by Scotland's Billy Bremner, is about to be booked by the referee for a challenge on Scotland goalkeeper David Harvey during the game at Hampden Park, Glasgow, in 1974. Wisely Tommy Cassidy walks away from the action — and later scored the goal to give Northern Ireland a 1-0 success.

Irish FA president Harry Cavan, a senior vice-president of FIFA, presents Arsenal goalkeeper Pat Jennings with a gift of Tyrone crystal to commemorate his record eightieth international appearance — before the European championship game with the Republic of Ireland at Windsor Park, November 1979.

The Great Goalkeepers

Ireland may have had a paucity of players for some key positions but certainly not the goalkeepers. Indeed, there has been a plethora of them — all with class. Arguments will rage as to who was the greatest. Elisha Scott? Or Harry Gregg? Or Pat Jennings who, with eighty-two caps by the start of 1980, had established an all-time record. There will always be a web of conflicting opinion — that is the basic essence of football — but nobody can provide a definitive answer when assessing the cavalcade of the past. They all had their part in the story of Ireland's international football.

Many are the legendary characters but few approach Elisha Scott (Liverpool and Belfast Celtic), famed not only for his brilliance, his professionalism, but also for the vituperative manner in which he assailed colleagues and opponents. Scott — or Lee as he was known to friends — was the man in black; he played in Liverpool's first team on 429 occasions, won thirty-one Irish international caps and for years was manager of Belfast Celtic. Story after story is told of his prowess as a player and how he obtained discipline and loyalty as a manager.

An historic picture as two great rivals, Dixie Dean (Everton), on the left and Elisha Scott (Liverpool), lead out the teams for a 'derby' game in October 1932. It was the 400th League appearance of Scott.

One can never think of Scott without coupling his name with that of Dixie Dean, renowned Everton and England forward. There could have been no greater rivals or friends; they made football vibrant on Merseyside. Anecdotes about the pair are endless. Like the one about a meeting in a Liverpool street when Dixie nodded and Scott, in an instant reaction, dived through a shop window. Not true, of course, but it showed the adulation in which Scott was held by the fans.

Dean often played tricks on Scott: one Friday night Scott received a parcel in a hotel before a derby game with Everton. It contained Aspirin and this note: 'Get a good night's sleep. You'll need it when I'm around tomorrow!'

Scott was a centre-forward with the 4th Belfast Company, Boys Brigade, and at the age of fourteen became so disgusted with the manner in which his side's goalkeeper was continually beaten, he went into the goal himself. That was the beginning of an illustrious career which saw spells with Irish Junior Cup-winners Broadway United and then, of course, Liverpool. His brother Billy, a goalkeeper with Everton, recommended him to Liverpool on a trial basis, and so in 1912 he went to Anfield, making his debut on New Year's Day, 1913, against Newcastle United.

Altogether he spent twenty-two years with Liverpool before returning to Northern Ireland — and Belfast Celtic — as a player and then from 1936 as manager, a post he held until his death at sixty-six in 1959, even though Celtic

99

Harry Gregg (Manchester United) clutches the ball as the late John White (Tottenham Hotspur) challenges during the 1959 international with Scotland at Windsor Park. The Scots won 4-0.

had left football ten years earlier. During his spell with Celtic they won the Irish League in 1936, 1937, 1938, 1939, 1940 and 1945 and on 29 May 1949 his team defeated Scotland 2-0 at Triborough Stadium New York. Internationals always brought out the best in Scott.

Scott at his peak was described as the world's outstanding goalkeeper — as is Pat Jennings (Newry Town, Watford, Tottenham Hotspur and Arsenal) today. There is no flamboyance about Pat, no extrovert qualities. He remains still the quiet, 6ft goalkeeper from Newry, with the largest and safest pair of hands in the game. His modesty is appealing and in striking contrast to the abrasive, often arrogant approach of some professionals.

'Soccer provided me with everything and for that I am grateful. I always remember that I was a labourer before football gave me the break,' says Pat.

Pat is a legend now at White Hart Lane, at Highbury and at Windsor Park. Ask most fans and they will say he rarely has a bad game. He is the essence of consistency — so much so that he is almost taken for granted. Strangely enough Pat's greatest moment was not performed at White Hart Lane but away from home... at Anfield on Grand National Day in March 1973.

His performance against Liverpool was phenomenal, reminiscent of the feats of that unbeatable goalkeeper hero in the schoolboy thrillers. He stopped

100

two penalties, brought off remarkable saves and was applauded by the 48,477 spectators, and by the opposing players as he left for the dressing room at the finish. Pat recalls that match in typical fashion. 'The penalties were not too difficult. I just happened to have a good day,' he says. Nobody privileged to be there, however, will ever forget it.

It was the same, too, when Northern Ireland defeated England at Wembley in 1972. Although suffering from the effects of a smallpox inoculation, he was, to put it mildly, astonishing. It prompted Derby County manager Brian Clough to make this comment: 'He stopped everything England could throw at him. He also made a one-handed save of which Gary Sobers would have been proud.'

At school Pat concentrated on Gaelic football, as soccer was not permitted in those days. Eventually he went to work for a timber gang, felling trees in the forests of Down which enabled him to have Saturdays off for playing football. But it was the 1963 European Youth Tournament final against England at Wembley which brought him into the spotlight. Coventry City's manager Jimmy Hill wanted him; so did many others but in stepped Watford with a £6,000 fee. Just thirteen months later Spurs signed him for £27,000. There is not a single flaw in the Jennings' make-up. He catches the ball superbly; cuts off centres with uncanny judgment, punches when prudent and every clearance is made with a purpose. He never forgets that humble, happy background which is part of the charm of Pat Jennings, goalkeeper supreme and a gentleman of football.

A jovial smile and the safe hands of Norman Uprichard, another of Northern Ireland's 1958 World Cup heroes and a legendary goalkeeper.

Hugh Kelly, ex-Belfast Celtic, Fulham and Southampton goalkeeper.

The name Harry Gregg (Coleraine, Doncaster Rovers, Manchester United and Stoke City) will inevitably be associated with a superb display against West Germany at Malmo during the 1958 World Cup in which he was voted the outstanding goalkeeper; the 1957 defeat of England at Wembley and his heroism after the Manchester United air crash at Munich when he went back to the shattered Elizabethan aircraft to save a child.

Gregg played at all levels for his country as well as winning inter-league honours, too. His career was one of outstanding merit with his £24,000 transfer from Doncaster Rovers to Manchester United in December 1957 a world record for a goalkeeper; the previous highest had been £20,000 paid by Coventry City for Reg Matthews a year earlier. Gregg played for Linfield Rangers and the Swifts but was persuaded to return to Coleraine who transferred him in October 1952 for £1,200; his first international appearance was in March 1954 when Ireland defeated Wales at Wrexham.

Ted Hinton (Fulham and Millwall) framed in his garden. His lasting memory is that 2-2 draw with England at Goodison Park, Liverpool, in November 1947.

He had succeeded Norman Uprichard (Distillery) who occupied the position from 1952. Uprichard was a genial character, but then that could be said of most of the goalkeepers — Hugh Kelly (Belfast Celtic, Glenavon and Fulham) whose verbal battles with Scott were renowned; Tommy Breen (Manchester United, Belfast Celtic, Newry Town, Linfield and Glentoran) who began as a forward with Drogheda United and switched to goalkeeper by accident after the regular 'keeper had been injured. His command of the goal-mouth area was complete and few opponents would ever challenge him. If they did there was no second time!

Fred McKee, who played for Cliftonville, Belfast Celtic and Linfield during the years 1906-1914, was 'Lizzie' to the fans. He wore long black stockings which went up below his pants; his red, white and blue hooped jersey was unique. A cigarette holder always projected from the side of his mouth and every day he wore a carnation in his Savile Row cut suits.

Ted Hinton (Glentoran, Distillery, Fulham, Bangor and Ballymena United) was the hero of the 2-2 draw against England at Goodison when he saved the day with a spectacular dive at a Wilf Mannion shot. The Second World War years fractured his career as it did with thousands of his generation and, but for this, he would probably have picked up more than seven international caps.

Goalkeepers are a breed apart. Ireland has been blessed with many of those eccentrics — and geniuses — as well.

103

Allan Hunter (Northern Ireland) and Mick Martin (Republic of Ireland) lead their sides on to the pitch before the European championship game at Windsor Park, November 1979. Behind Hunter are Gerry Armstrong, Jim Nicholl and Derek Spence and following Martin are Mick Kearns, Frank Stapleton, Steve Heighway and Gerry Daly.

Matches to Remember

Ask any football fan his match to remember, his match of the century, of the decade, of the year. The answers are varied, surprising, sometimes astonishing, but by general consent the outstanding game in the Irish FA annals was that 2-2 draw with England at Goodison Park, Liverpool, on 5 November 1947. Sweden (1958) produced brilliant, exciting, nerve-tingling spectacles which are dealt with elsewhere but it was this Goodison Park encounter which captured the imagination.

'A writer of schoolboy thrillers would have given ten years of his life to have thought up the plot of this, one of the greatest internationals ever staged in England,' wrote one English critic.

This game had everything — skill, high speed, movement, great football, equally great goalkeeping, the odd note of anger, a penalty miss, signs of the great English machine cracking. Then came England's recovery, a magnificent goal by Tommy Lawton eighteen minutes from the end, the equaliser from Peter Doherty with forty seconds to play — and the greatest of all moments after the whistle had blown.

This is what happened. Doherty, in a last despairing effort, threw himself at a ball floating across the English goal-mouth. In a flash it was in the back of the net off Doherty's head with the player lying unconscious on the pitch. Team mates hugged him, tried to bring him round, hammered each other, shouting inarticulately while the crowd roared. The referee ticked away the few remaining seconds as the England goalkeeper Frank Swift, the ball forgotten in the back of the net, tried to lift his former Manchester City team-mate. The whistle went, the crowd streamed over the barriers and in the surging mass Swift and Irish trainer Gerry Morgan both supported the sagging Doherty. As they reached the tunnel England captain George Hardwick, in torn shorts, came up. 'Well done,' he said grasping Doherty's hand.

Partisans will argue long over this game — that England should have won in the first twenty minutes; that Ireland, having taken the lead and playing like a winning team, should never have been caught; that Johnny Carey's plan of keeping out the England machine for the first twenty minutes succeeded beyond belief and that England could battle when the chips are down. All these remained lasting memories in the minds of the watching 67,980 — 179 short of the Goodison record.

England's selectors paid a tribute to eleven home players by choosing them en bloc for the match against Sweden later that month on 19 November; Irish selectors could do no more than to declare 'no change' for the next match against Wales. Outstanding were the two centre-halves Neil Franklin and Jack Vernon; the ever young Carey who slipped only near the end against the genius of Stanley Matthews; the flame-haired Doherty who inspired the Irish rallies; the twinkling feet of Billy Wright, Tom Finney and Tom Eglington, and the brilliance of Wilf Mannion.

Individual performances did not, however, count against the goal in a million from Lawton; the flying header of Doherty, the penalty save of Hinton from Mannion, the break in the ice calm of Vernon in his appeal against the referee's decision. For the record, the penalty, hotly disputed by the Irish players, was awarded against Vernon for a foul on Matthews twenty-one minutes from time.

Seven minutes after half-time Willie Walsh took a free kick; Doherty beat Taylor to the bouncing ball and Davie Walsh diverted his pass into the net from four yards. Eight minutes to go and Hardwick for the first time upset the Irish defence with a free kick. Wright pulled the ball down; a short pass inside from him and Mannion forced it over the line. Three minutes to go. Matthews beat Carey on the right, a studied cross and Lawton on the turn volleyed a smashing shot into a corner of the net. Then came the Doherty equaliser. History had been written.

Ireland's only British championship win was in the 1913-14 season with wins over Wales 2-1 at Wrexham, a 3-0 triumph against England at Middlesbrough with two goals from Billy Lacey, another from Billy Gillespie and a 1-1 draw against Scotland in Belfast which prevented them from winning the Triple Crwn. To this day Irish fans contend they should have been awarded a penalty which would have given them the Treble.

105

Not until 20 October 1923 did Ireland have another victory over England. 'Tucker' Croft (Queen's Island) scored the winner but knew nothing about it. It was a dramatic goal, for he took the ball three times around English right half Tommy Meehan (Chelsea), then goalkeeper Eddie Taylor (Huddersfield) rushed to the near post, leaving three quarters of the net unguarded. Cröft, however, did not hit the ball into that gap; instead he contemptuously chipped it over Taylor's right shoulder. It was a never-to-be-forgotten goal.

The next success against England was at Belfast in October 1927. Ted Hufton (West Ham United) had his arm fractured when going down to stop Jackie Mahood (Belfast Celtic) from scoring, but Mahood got the winner in a 2-0 victory. Ireland's centre-forward Hugh Davey still vividly recalls that match, for which players were given a £6 fee. 'I have the jersey I wore and a photograph of the team, nearly all of whom, alas, have passed on,' he says.

'That victory was the greatest and most satisfying I experienced in international football because in those days England were just as difficult to beat as they are now. It is impossible to put into words the emotion and delight you feel when winning against England in front of your own countrymen.

Ireland 2, Scotland 3; Windsor Park, Belfast, February 1946. *Back row:* W. McMillan (Belfast Celtic), J. Vernon (Belfast Celtic), T. Breen (Linfield), J. Feeney (Linfield), S. Todd (Blackpool), T. Aherne (Belfast Celtic). *Front row:* K. O'Flannagan (Arsenal), D. Walsh (Linfield), A. Stevenson (Manchester United) (Capt.), J. Carey (Manchester United), P. Bonnar (Belfast Celtic).

'Windsor Park was packed that afternoon. I would not go as far as to say that 'e played England off the park. We actually won by good all-round team-work nd our support of each other rather than in flashes of individualism.'

Alas, Ireland, later went down 2-1 to a mediocre Welsh side with Elisha Scott wice beaten from twenty yards by Willie Davies and Windsor Lewis.

The February 1925 game with Scotland produced one of the most fierce shots seen in international football. Scotland centre-half Davie Meiklejohn (Glasgow Rangers) hit a forty-yard drive from a quick throw in which flashed past Tom Farquharson (Cardiff City). 'It was a mere blur,' commented the astonished 'keeper.

And talking about powerful kicks that of Belfast Celtic full back Fred Barrett must be supreme. Playing for Ards in a Gold Cup Final against Linfield, he hit a free kick which bounced off Tommy Frame, rose a foot, smashed against the crossbar and rebounded to the centre circle!

But back to the international scene and to Firhill Park, Glasgow, in 1928 where a strong Scots side lost 1-0 to a goal by Jimmy Chambers (Bury and Nottingham Forest). That day Scott gave the display of his life — so much so that a Glasgow newspaper published a contents bill with this wording: 'Great Scott beats the Scots'.

This Irish team, mainly second and third choices, triumphed against the odds with Barney Moorhead (Linfield) eliminating all the menace from Jimmy McGrory (Glasgow Celtic) who never got his famous head or foot to the ball.

There was, of course, the day when Joe Bambrick hit the six goals against Wales at Celtic Park, on Saturday, 1 February 1930. And that match against Scotland at Windsor Park, on 20 October 1934. An overhead cable fault at Shaftesbury Square led to a breakdown in the tram service which meant thousands streaming late into Windsor Park. The first half was uneventful, mere run-of-the-mill with Scotland taking the lead. Only ten Irishmen came out for the second half and there were gasps of dismay when the crowd realised Scott was the missing player; Walter McMillen (Manchester United) deputised, for in those days substitution was not permitted.

The selection of Joe Gowdy (Linfield), a right-half at inside-right, had earned considerable criticism on the International Committee but it was a move which paid off for he produced a classical display of attacking and defensive football.

McMillen saved everything that came at him. Gradually the 40,000 crowd, earlier subdued and despondent, realised Ireland were in with a chance. Prompted by Gowdy, Ireland mounted attack upon attack; Martin missed an easy chance; Jackie Coulter smacked the crossbar and with five minutes remaining Martin hit the equaliser.

It was a perfect setting for a finale. Gowdy picked up the ball in mid-field, beat two Scots and floated across to the left of the goal, leaving Coulter to come in and finish it off with a header. Hats were thrown in the air by thousands of Irishmen who did not care if they ever got them back again.

Northern Ireland have twice won at Wembley — first in 1957 with a 3-2 success: a Jimmy McIlroy penalty went in off the upright; Alan A'Court (Liverpool) equalised thirteen minutes into the second half and it seemed the inevitable would happen but it was not to be with Sammy McCrory (Southend United) getting a second and Billy Simpson (Glasgow Rangers) a third; England's second goal came from Duncan Edwards (Manchester United). Fifteen years later — on 23 May 1972 — Northern Ireland triumphed again by 1-0 thanks to a thirty-third minute goal from player-manager Terry Neill, Danny Hegan (Wolverhamption Wanderers) created the opening, curling the ball to the near upright where Willie Irvine (Brighton) narrowly missed it, but the ball dropped perfectly for Neill to beat Peter Shilton (Leicester City) from close in.

Charlie Tully often graced the international scene, and his supreme moment came on 4 October 1952 when he gave England's Alf Ramsey an afternoon of horror. Tully hit both goals — one from a corner kick. His impertinence on the ball delighted the fans and irritated the English who, however, at the finish applauded the genius of the immortal Charles Patrick.

Rain cascaded relentlessly from the leaden skies. It was one of those gloomy, bleak days which mark the onset of winter — not the setting for the return of the conquering heroes. Yet it was just in such an unpromising situation on 4 October 1958 that Northern Ireland met England at Windsor Park — their first match since the epic days of Sweden. Rain-drenched fans saw the teams share six goals and provide them with imperishable memories. There was the indomitable courage of the Irish; the fantastic form of Bobby Charlton and a majestic display by Tom Finney, then nearing the finish of a wonderful career.

Northern Ireland led three times. England hit back three times. Such was the standard of play that the result was relegated to an irrelevancy. Charlton scored two of the England goals; Finney got the other. Wilbur Cush, Bertie Peacock, who suffered an Achilles tendon injury, and Tommy Casey, operating at centre-forward, were Ireland's marksmen. Casey's tenacity and bustling tactics worried Jackie Charlton and the entire England defence. Surely this must have been the most glorious mud battle in all the years of international conflict at Windsor Park. That year Northern Ireland shared the championship — an indication of the sterling quality of the Swedish squad.

'Here comes the hero,' quipped fellow Derryman Johnny Crossan when his international colleague Jimmy McLaughlin arrived at the Northern Ireland team headquarters to prepare for a World Cup tie with Switzerland at Windsor Park in October 1964. Jester 'Jobby' Crossan was referring to the acclaim won by McLaughlin two weeks earlier — his name being splashed over all the newspapers after he had scored two goals against England.

This was an extraordinary feat in any circumstances, the first time Gordon Banks had been beaten twice by the same player since becoming established in the England goal, but McLaughlin did it under an extreme handicap. The live-wire winger, then a twenty-three-year-old with Swansea Town, played for most of the match with two fingers of his left hand dislocated. He had fallen heavily when challenged by Maurice Norman.

Northern Ireland hero Jimmy McLaughlin is helped off by trainer Jimmy McCune (left) and his England counterpart Harold Shepherdson after breaking two fingers of his left hand. He returned to score two goals in a dramatic second half at Windsor Park where England won 4-3 in October 1964.

'It happened after only five minutes but I did not know the extent of the injury until the hand was X-rayed in hospital,' recalls Jimmy. The Derry youngster courageously played on and had a memorable part in what must rate as the most amazing comeback ever staged by Northern Ireland. The *Belfast Telegraph* that night called it a rags to riches story — and there could be no more appropriate comment.

Northern Ireland were 4-0 down at half-time when that arch-poacher Jimmy Greaves, who made a habit of producing his most devastating form against the Irish, hit a hat-trick. Although racked by pain with only a light bandage covering those swollen misshapen fingers, he miraculously kept going. 'I did go off at one stage but thought I would be more use out on the field. We were in a really desperate plight,' said McLaughlin.

The indomitable spirit of the slender Derryman provided Northern Ireland with the inspiration to overcome that calamitous first half. They set about England with renewed determination and vigour. An inviting right wing cross by Crossan was brilliantly headed in by centre-forward Sammy Wilson, a goal praised afterwards by England manager Sir Alf Ramsey. Northern Ireland had at last drawn blood, but it seemed incredible that they would score twice more and almost snatch a draw. Yet that is exactly what happened.

McLaughlin, who said his role was to roam free as a front runner, stole through the middle to score with a fierce shot. 'I still look back on that goal as the high point of my career. It gave me tremendous satisfaction,' remembers Jimmy, manager of League of Ireland side Dundalk.

That made it 4-2 but the fireworks were far from finished. McLaughlin, that left arm hanging limp and useless at his side, struck again in the dying minutes as excitement built to fever pitch. Wilson, who played a leading part in the Irish recovery, put the ball back from the left wing and McLaughlin was on the spot to stab it in. The score was at 4-3 with still time left. And what a dramatic finish. England back-pedalled furiously as Northern Ireland attacked, but that elusive equaliser would not come. The first England goal had been scored by Blackburn Rovers centre forward, Fred Pickering, a converted defender.

It was on 21 October 1967, that Ireland defeated Scotland 1-0 at Windsor — the George Best match. What a show it was from the Manchester United superstar. The whole fascination of his performance was like a dream; this was his thirteenth international appearance and for him not an unlucky one. He had everything — elegance, skill, ball control, superb passing, pace. Adjectives could be trotted out by the dozen in paying tribute to the player who was the real basis of Irish success. It was all so staggering. He entranced the crowd with those delicate touches as he dispossessed Scottish players to begin his build-ups, for he rarely got a service from his colleagues. He had to do it alone, do it his way.

The Scots attempted to stop him by every conceivable means. He was 'lifted', sent crashing with head-on tackles but it made no difference. He reigned supreme from the sixty-eighth minute when he pushed the ball into the middle for Dave Clements (Coventry City) to score. This was Ireland's third successive victory over the Scots on the day Windsor Park belonged to George Best. But there have been the disappointments and the depressions, such as a World Cup tie 1965 (1-1), in Tirana, Albania, a city where life seemed to have stood still for a century; losing 1-0 to Cyprus in Nicosia, 1973, on a pitch resembling Ballyholme beach with the tide out; in Reykjavik, Iceland, 1977 (1-0) where hopes of qualifying for the 1978 World Cup finals ended.

Perhaps Ireland's most amazing game, however, was staged during the 1953 US and Canadian tour at Moose Jaw, Saskatchewan. Local officials had spent weeks on the pitch; the rains came and overnight the turf became a quagmire of gumbo. So a new pitch had to be found with players almost becoming lost in the grass near the corners.

From the start a dog pranced along with the players. Where the ball went so did Bonzo as they labelled him; he was struck once or twice but it did not deter him and he maintained the pace to the end.

The Saskatchewan All Stars, some of them Ukrainian immigrants with bands around their long hair, lost 10-0. So disgusted were they with their first half performance that they substituted the entire team in the second. Of such bizarre happenings football is made.

Joker in the pack ... that's Johnny Crossan as he shows his hand to newly-wed clubmate Martin Harvey who is also congratulated by Bobby Braithwaite (Middlesbrough) with a smile from trainer Jimmy McCune.

The Johnny Crossan Saga

Friday, 30 January 1959, was a typical mid-winter day. Heavy night fog enshrouded Londonderry as Johnny Crossan made his way through the city's narrow streets from his home. He had arranged to take a telephone call at a newspaper office.

When it came Crossan, a twenty-year-old inside forward with Coleraine, quickly became ashen faced. His normal smile, his humour vanished. Six words told him his fate — banned for life from British football. A decision had been made by the Irish League — guilty of being paid as an amateur and asking for more than the £750 permitted from a transfer fee.

That night his world collapsed around him. Yet, in retrospect, it was only one of many incidents which were to pockmark the career of an Ulsterman who had more ups and downs than an elevator operator.

Just what was his misdemeanour? What crime had he committed to merit such a sentence? It was a complex issue which became more entangled with every statement issued. Put simply, he had asked for what many others had already obtained but unfortunately he got caught.

Crossan, a member of a family of five — his eldest brother Eddie played for Blackburn Rovers and Tranmere — joined Derry City as an amateur at the age of fourteen, a few months before going to work in a record-player factory. His ability with a ball was immediately recognised by the English and Scottish scouts who honeycomb Northern Ireland in their never ending search for embryonic George Bests.

The name Crossan filtered into many boardrooms. Sheffield United, Stoke City, Nottingham Forest, Birmingham and Sunderland all made offers with Sunderland even offering £60,000. But Crossan declined as he felt the Roker Park club were doomed to relegation.

His relationship with Derry City deteriorated, his form slumped, culminating in his being dropped for an Irish Cup semi-final against Ballymena United. Nottingham Forest invited him for an interview that weekend; instead of talking to Crossan, however, they spoke to relatives — and then dropped out of the bidding.

Against this background of bargaining in stepped Coleraine secretary Jack Doherty, now chairman of the club, to sign Crossan as an amateur. On 11 June 1958 Derry City, amazed and upset, addressed a letter to the four British Associations and to the English, Scottish, Irish and Republic of Ireland Leagues. This stated they had been prepared to offer Crossan £3,000 on the completion of his transfer to a cross-channel club, subject to the approval of the League, although the maximum permitted was only £750. Agreement had been reached with some English sides on this; Crossan, too had been offered £9 per week in the playing season and £5 per week in summer as a full-time professional.

Not until October did the Irish League appoint a five-man committee to investigate 'all aspects of the circumstances arising from Derry City's letter and the signing of Crossan by Coleraine'. What sparked them into action was this: Crossan had been transferred to Bristol City, then managed by Ireland's Peter Doherty, for £7,000 but the registration was not accepted by the Football League who, in a general circular, had stated that if Crossan signed for any club under their jurisdiction an investigation might follow. So the Irish authorities were forced at last to act.

For two months the Committee heard evidence. Twice Crossan appeared before them. 'Questions were fired at me by every member. . . my tongue was dry answering them. The questions covered every aspect of my career,' recalls Crossan, who says he never broke any rules which justified such a severe punishment.

The League's findings were released in a statement which gave the bare facts of the case. Crossan was suspended permanently 'from taking part, as a player or in any other way, in connection with Irish League football affairs or competitions'. Derry were fined £256 for making the offers and Coleraine £5 for inadvertently putting the wrong date on the transfer form — an offence described as 'technical'. Crossan still did not know why he had been banned.

Eventually it leaked out that the verdict had been taken on two grounds:

firstly, for accepting expenses as an amateur and secondly, because he had asked for a share from the fee.

Appeals to the Irish FA were rejected. So Crossan was driven to the Continent; the only way he could earn a living was by the magic in his boots and he required a platform. He signed for Rotterdam Sparta on 27 August 1959 to become a football cosmopolitan, a seeker of fortune. He worked during the day in the Rotterdam dry dock, trained at night and played once a week. He learned French, German and Dutch and, to his astonishment, found himself capped by Ireland against England in November — a selection frowned upon by the English and Irish Leagues who contended that no player banned by them should represent his country.

Again fate took a hand for Crossan, pilloried and now pardoned, was goaded by some England players into indiscretions and had his name taken for a tackle on wing-half Ron Flowers (Wolverhampton Wanderers). It was his last appearance in the green shirt until 1962 when he was chosen against Poland in Katowice — the second of twenty-three caps.

Crossan established himself as a player above the ordinary. Standard Liège paid £10,000 for him in 1961 but still the ban remained despite two appeals by Coleraine to the Irish League for it to be lifted. They felt, as did most people, that Crossan had suffered enough. Legislators, however, remained adamant.

Then the action moved to Lima, Peru, where England were playing a friendly fixture en route to the 1962 World Cup in Chile. Irish FA president Harry Cavan and Sunderland chairman Syd Collings, an England selector, sat over coffee at a pavement café. Crossan was the subject.

Collings said they would like to sign him and what were the chances of the ban being lifted? Cavan explained that a letter to the Irish League could, perhaps, end the ban provided Crossan had a definite offer and the Belgians were willing to transfer the player. Six months later the suspension was lifted; automatically Crossan could return from exile. He did just that with Sunderland handing out a £30,000 fee. Immediately he became an over-night idol at Roker Park with his goals helping the club gain First Division promotion.

Then came a slump in form; the crowd adulation disappeared and Crossan, strangely depressed and unhappy, left Manchester City. Alas, there was no quick change of fortunes.

'I was worried sick for the first few months at Maine Road because I was beginning to drift along. I was as disinterested and apathetic as the others,' said Crossan. 'Malcolm Allison came to stop the rot. Otherwise I could have ended on the scrap heap within twelve months. Above all others he gave me faith in myself again.'

Crossan, outwardly the typical Irish extrovert with the ability to crack jokes against himself, next had a spell at Middlesbrough who released him in 1970. Back he went to Belgium — this time to Tongren and, finally, home to Londonderry again.

Crossan, the martyr, has no grudge against life. 'Looking back on it all that ban could have been a blessing in disguise,' he says. 'I developed a maturity, improved my education, made a good living and played football with the stars of Europe. A transfer to an English club from Ireland could so easily have led to oblivion.'

An apt philosophy for a player who succeeded despite all the adversities.

Johnny Crossan grabs the first of his three goals against Albania at Windsor Park in 1965 with Willie Irvine watching from behind. Albania's goalkeeper was Yanku. Northern Ireland won 4-1.

Terry Cochrane, Northern Ireland's first £200,000 plus player when he was transferred from Burnley to Middlesbrough. He was a product of junior football.

Junior, Youth and Schools Football

It is the stars who make the headlines in football — the big names, the big clubs. Yet without the juniors, the game would not have developed as we know it today. Those players and officials are the fabric of Irish football, the basis of the pyramid.

Irish FA junior affairs are, of course, conducted by the Junior Committee who send one delegate to the Council. It is their responsibility to ensure the smooth running of the various competitions — Intermediate, Junior and Youth Cups and, of course, the Junior Internationals.

In the Divisional Associations, in the various leagues around the Province the voluntary time and effort given by officials is quite remarkable. They have a true love of the game, and throughout the years the Irish FA have been fortunate to have in their ranks men who worked tirelessly; indeed it is commonplace to find an official, say, of the Amateur or Churches' Leagues arranging on Friday night for players to report, inflating the ball on a Saturday and even taking the skip home with him to be washed over the weekend!

The Steel Cup, promoted by the County Antrim FA who are also responsible

The Northern Ireland Youth team pictured at Wembley Stadium before their European Youth Cup final against England in 1963. *Back row:* Robin Parke (*Northern Whig*), Claude Wilton (IFA), Dave Clements, Sam Todd, Terry McKeown, Jimmy Nicholl (Capt.), Derek Watson, Wallace Reid, Pat Jennings, Matt McClelland, Vic McKinney, John Napier, Sean Dunlop. *Front row:* Howard McCurley, Jim Stokes, Denis Guy.

for the Senior Shield, remains the prime competition. Each Christmas Day morning thousands attend this traditional fixture. It has become a ritual and for young players a platform for thngs of greater promise.

Proper planning has ensured a progression from schools football to the senior grade. Northern Ireland's Schools' FA, now affiliated to the Irish FA, has competed throughout the years in the Victory Shield internationals, winning in 1979 under manager Ian Russell the European championship promoted to celebrate the 75th anniversary of the English Schools FA. This was the pinnacle of achievement, one of outstanding merit, considering all matches in the previous seasons had to be played away from home because of civil unrest.

Northern Ireland's youth team has proved of invaluable help to senior managers, a nursery for the stars of the future. Here again the handling is professionally organised, at present by Jackie Cummings, with a broad base used for competition at international level.

Northern Ireland have an outstanding record in the European championship. They first entered in 1949, finishing fourth in a series played in Holland. Two years later with France as the venue they were again fourth, and then in 1963, after an absence of some years on economic grounds, they took part in the series staged in England with Bognor Regis as their base.

117

The history-making Dundela team which won the Irish Cup in 1955. *Back row:* Jackie Greenwood, Jimmy McMaster, Jimmy Smyth, Howard Lynch, Dave Gourley, Jimmy Stewart. *Front row:* George Millar, Roy Smyth, Bobby McAuley, Bobby Irvine, Davey Kavanagh, Norman Reid. They defeated Glenavon 2-0.

There were sixteen players in the party — Pat Jennings (Newry Town), Jim Stokes (Post Office SC), Tom Corbett (Ballyclare Comrades), Howard McCurley (Linfield), Jim Nicholl (Coleraine) *Captain*, John Napier (Bolton), Sammy Todd (Burnley), Shaun Dunlop (Coleraine), Eric Ross (Glentoran), Denis Guy (Linfield), Vic McKinney (Glenavon), Derek Watson (Glentoran), Dave Clements (Wolverhampton Wanderers), Matt McClelland (Coleraine), Terry McKeown (Burnley), Wallace Reid (Linfield), with Norman Kernaghan as the manager and Freddie Jardine the trainer.

Northern Ireland defeated Belgium 1-0 at the Oval, Eastbourne, in the first match, due primarily to the tactics adopted by Kernaghan; he decided on a 4-3-3 formation with Dunlop and McKinney playing deep on the wings. And remember, this was three years before Sir Alf Ramsey's similar tactical approach to the 1966 World Cup finals.

Czechoslovakia and Sweden were the other Group D opponents. There was an 1-0 triumph against Czechoslovakia; a 3-3 draw with Sweden after being 3-1 down. Thus Northern Ireland qualified for the semi-finals against Bulgaria at The Dell, Southampton, on Friday, 19 April 1963 — a match in which Nicholl became a central figure as part of the drama of Irish soccer history was unfolded.

The game ended in a 3-3 draw with Northern Ireland's goals coming from McKinney, Guy and Dunlop. It was a dreadful night with Ross losing one of his contact lenses which was later recovered after a search of the pitch by the teams.

118

A moment of triumph — Carrick Rangers with the Irish Cup which they won in 1976, defeating Linfield 2-1. *Back row:* Jimmy Hamilton, Tom Cullen, Albert Macklin, Gary Prenter, Davy McKenzie, Gary Reid, Eddie Connor, Gary Erwin. *Front row:* Ronnie Whiteside, Jeff Cowan, Jimmy Brown, Davy Allen, George Matchett.

Nicholl was called into the referee's room along with his Bulgarian counterpart to toss up for the right to go through into the final against England. The referee did not speak English and could not make his intentions known, but he quietly slipped a piece of paper into each hand. On one was written 'winner', the other remained blank.

A coin was tossed to determine who would draw first. Nicholl, with remarkable calm, considering the emotion of the occasion, called correctly and invited the Bulgarian to select. He called wrongly so Northern Ireland were bound for Wembley where a much more powerful England won 4-0. This was the team that night: Jennings, Corbett, McCurley, Nicholl (*Captain*), Napier, Dunlop, Ross, Guy, Clements, McKinney.

Wilf McGuinness, trainer to the English team, was surprised Northern Ireland had not included a seventeen-year-old from his club — George Best. Brian Dempster, then a secretarial assistant at the Irish FA, informed his Association about this Old Trafford genius who was selected to play against England at Oldham and against Wales in the youth championship at Aberystwyth the next month; Best scored the goal in the 1-1 draw with the Welsh.

The Dell that night will forever live in the memory of those privileged to have been there.

Coaching is, of course, under the control of the Referees and Coaching Committee with courses at primary, secondary and Under Fourteen level. From this is developed the team for international matches, while the Esso Under Seventeen inter-county championship is the ideal build-up for the youth team.

In the early days coaching courses, controlled by Eric Trevorrow and Terry McCavana, were held at Orangefield under the auspices of the IFA and the Education Authority; then in 1959-60 the grade two course had Stranmillis College as the venue with Len Graham in charge. There is now a course to train teachers; a preliminary course, IFA grade One, and FA full badge. In the last-named grade, among the holders in Northern Ireland are Roy Millar, coaching and development officer, Roy Downey, Jackie Gallagher, Jackie Cummings, Gibby MacKenzie, Bob Nesbitt and Arthur Hunter. Northern Ireland's Coaches Association was formed in November 1966 with Ted Smyth as its first chairman, Eric Trevorrow the secretary and Dave Cloughley the treasurer.

Coaching has come a long way since those days when Harry Cavan visited clubs and other organisations with film and a projector. This laid the foundation for what is now an efficient set-up and with the Irish Universities Union who promote the Collingwood Cup which is an all-Ireland competition, there is no area outside Irish FA jurisdiction. Happily, nowadays few youngsters of promise can escape through the net.

The men who ran Irish junior football — the IFA Junior Committee. *Front row:* W.J. Drennan (sec.), George Rankin, William Hamilton, William McElroy, Richard Holmes, Herbert Johnstone, Edward Barry. *Middle row:* Robert Haslett, Derek Solomon, Noel Wright. *Back row:* Edward Pepper, Harold Moore, William Craig, John Tolerton, Gerald Kennedy, Terence Pateman, Joseph Grimes.

Derek Dougan tries to calm a mud-bespattered George Best, ordered off in the game against Scotland at Windsor Park in April 1970. Behind them are team mates Eric McMordie and Jimmy Nicholson.

George Best

Recently after an Irish League match at Ballymena the subject switched to George Best. Was he better than Pelé, Cruyff, Matthews, Finney, Di Stefano and the stars of yesteryear? I put the question to Linfield Manager Roy Coyle. His answer was categorical: 'Best is the most complete footballer I've ever watched — he could do anything — tackle, pass, move into space, score goals, shield the ball. He possessed the lot.'

Best is, like Blanchflower, a native of East Belfast. He is a superstar in the modern idiom: a player symbolic of the age with his life-style, his appearance. Someone who brought ballet to the game. A Nureyev if you like.

George Best, controversial figure of world soccer, rarely visits his native trouble-torn Belfast these days but he never forgets his home town or, more important still his father, his brothers, his sisters. While few people ever get close to George — 'nobody really knows me,' he once said — there is a distinct affinity between all members of the Belfast family of Burren Way on the sprawling Cregagh housing estate.

If you spoke to his late mother, Ann Best, or his father Dick, you realised

there was a close parents-son relationship, a relationship which was not diminished by George's much publicised peregrinations around the world. They always kept in cosntant touch over many problems — those in the crisis-ridden life of George, those in Northern Ireland with its continued civil unrest. Despite the backcloth of the women who pursued him, the love affairs, alcoholism, trendy clothes, night clubs, Best, now married, remains in the eyes of his family, still the easily impressed youngster with the magic in those size seven boots who, in 1962, arrived without fuss at Old Trafford. The *Boys Own* hero who could go on to the pitch, outclass his opponent and score the winning goal as well.

He was born on 22 May 1946, at the Royal Maternity Hospital, Belfast. It was a difficult birth, touch and go whether he would pull through. 'In fact,' said his mother, 'a few years later a man who had been working in the hospital asked me how the boy was keeping. He was amazed he had developed so well.'

George was named after his grandfather, the late George Withers, whom he adored. 'George thought there was nobody like my father,' said Mrs Best. 'He died the day George was doing his 11-plus at Nettlefield School. We decided to keep the news from him until afterwards, but when he went to a local shop for a jotter, the newsagent asked him "When is your grandfather getting buried?" It was the first he knew about it.'

Best's introduction to football was early. . . very early. Photographs show him, aged fourteen months, tackling a ball with skill and balance. 'He was only five when we took him to junior matches at Wilgar Park,' says Dick Best. 'Even then there were signs that an inbred talent existed. He saw nobody when he went there. He followed that ball. . . he lived with the players, even though a mere child. It was quite unbelievable.'

George's boyhood matches were played on a field near Bell's Bridge, Cregagh, a few hundred yards from his home. People often stopped and watched in awe at his artistry and ball control. Quickly he developed into a boy legend with the locals. 'People used to come up and say to me "That wee lad of yours is going to be a footballer",' said Mrs Best. 'I never paid much attention. He was so thin I could never imagine him in the hurly-burly of football, yet he had the heart of a lion.' 'I never could see it either,' recalls his father. 'He was too lightly built, too slim, too small.' Others, however, were impressed: people like Albert Topping, an official of Cregagh Yough Club, who persuaded Dick Best to allow his son to play for the club. That was the first step on the road to soccer fame and fortune; to Old Trafford, into the glamour of global football.

George's development at the youth club was rapid under the guidance of the late Hugh 'Bud' McFarlane. 'He was my boy at the club. If I wanted any messages delivered I just called in George. Off he went, taking a ball with him and dribbling it all the way there and back,' said Bud. George attended Grosvenor High School, but he didn't like it as no football was played there. So he left on transfer to Lisnasharragh Intermediate, Cregagh, where his school work improved and where he became a competent attentive pupil — all because he could take part in soccer matches. Best, a boy star, never got an Ireland schoolboy cap. McFarlane hoped to remedy that. 'I challenged the Ireland schoolboy team with my Under Fifteen XI and we beat them 2-1. The idea was to put George on view and, in my opinion, he was the best forward.'

'Agreed,' says George Smyth, an Ireland schoolboy selector. 'But he was too light. . . too small.' It was the old, old story with the lack of physical attributes likely to hamper his ambition of becoming a footballer.

Scout after scout watched him. All went home without noting his name in their book. . . all except Bob Bishop. Again McFarlane played a key role here. 'Bob asked me about the boy,' said McFarlane. 'As his team, Boyland, played in a different league from us he couldn't get to see Best in action. I arranged a match between our Under Seventeen side and Boyland. George scored two of the goals in a 4-2 win. Bob Bishop realised what gold he had discovered.'

George went back to his Burren Way home. An English club was reported to be interested in him, but he thought it was a leg pull. Off he went, however, to Old Trafford on a two-week trial. He arrived on the Tuesday, caught the home-sickness bug and was back in Belfast by the Thursday. Elation had changed to depression.

'Son, you've done nothing to be ashamed of. . . don't sit brooding there. Get out and play among the boys,' his father told him. So off to Old Trafford he went again with Eric McMordie, his Northern Ireland team-mate and Middlesbrough mid-fielder. The rest of the story is now part of football history.

Best signed amateur forms for United on 16 August 1961: Joe Armstrong, chief scout, took him to the Manchester Canal Co. where he became a part-time clerk. The manager had a quick look at his copperplate handwriting and said, 'He's my boy.'

And he was Sir Matt Busby's boy too. His first match was for the A team against Stockport County in the Lancashire League on 9 September 1961. He made his senior debut on 14 September 1963 against West Bromwich Albion. The boy Best had arrived and United, ever mindful of how youth and boys clubs assisted them, forwarded a cheque for £150 to Cregagh Youth Club in appreciation of the manner in which they had trained young Best in the basics of football.

In *There's Only One United*, the official centenary history of Manchester United, Geoffrey Green writes: 'George Best is a Gemini. He is two people and, like his football, one has never known what the other is about to do at any given moment. He has lived and played with tension and apparently thrived on it. That is the nature of this animal who has always shunned being caged.

'Five years after joining United he was at the height of his powers. The world was at his feet. At that time one only had to thumb through the glossy magazines or the humblest football rag, the odds were he would be staring out of a page, fixing attention with luminous blue eyes, a lush Beatle hairstyle, and a quizzical expression which suggested that, while he alone may know the

A typical action study of George Best, this time in the colours of Manchester United.

hundredth name of Allah, it was all a bit of a joke anyway.'

Words, words, words, analysed, X-rayed and photographed. It has all been said before about this modern phenomenon of the football scene. In six years he became a cult for youth, a rebel, a living James Dean. The cause was clearly defined — the welfare of his club and country, to prove himself the greatest player in all history.

The rebel in him was contrary — the creator of a new image for football, yet one who turned back the clock in a search for individual freedom in an age of conformity and method within the game. He remains a son of instinct rather than logic.

The fact that he was a Pied Piper followed by an ever growing army worried him not a bit. He was touched, mauled, buffeted by the admiring crowd off stage; he faced an equivalent treatment on the field. Yet in neither case did he suffer an inflated ego nor a wounded sense of revenge. Like breathing in and breathing out, it was all merely part of the business of life.

Certainly there were flaws in his complex character. There came the sudden upsurge of angry retaliation to something brutal; sometimes a childish taunting provocation, the figurative thumbing of the nose at some frustrated opponent, a mischievous irreverence, difficulty pinning him down in personal affairs. A Pied Piper in one sense, he was an Elusive Pimpernel in another.

Just where did Best stand in the hierarchy of the game? How did he figure with Stanley Matthews, Tommy Finney? Everything is relative from age to age. 'George was different. All the others were just footballers,' says Malcolm Allison. 'Probably his greatest ability was his courage,' says Stanley Cullis.

Blanchflower, later to be his international manager, rated Best like this: 'Stanley Matthews was a supreme dribbler who would tax even the most ruthless, sophisticated defences of today. But he was primarily a provider. Tommy Finney was, perhaps, a better all-rounder than Matthews.

'He could play anywhere in a forward line and besides that was a free goal-scorer. Best was a master of control and manipulation; he was also a superb combination of creator and finisher; he too could play anywhere along the line.

'But more than the others he seemed to have a wider, more appreciative eye for any situation. Best made a greater appeal to the senses than the other two. His movements were quicker, lighter, more balletic. He offered the greater surprise to the mind and the eye.'

And from Sir Matt came this tribute: 'George Best is, possibly, the greatest player on the ball I've ever seen. You can remember Matthews, Finney, Mannion and all the great players of that era, but I cannot think of one who took the ball so close to an opponent to beat him with it as did Best.'

George was ice-cool. He approached matches with nonchalance, munching a sandwich just twenty minutes before kick off. And he could go out and turn it on immediately. It was in March 1966 at Lisbon's giant Estadio Da Luz where he took Benfica apart in a 5-1 win that *Bola,* Portugal's leading sports paper, proclaimed in screaming black and red headlines, 'A Beatle called Best smashed Benfica'.

In contrast with his European and club exploits, Best's performances for Northern Ireland were a mixture of magnificence and mediocrity. Only once at international level — he was capped thirty-seven times — did he hit the jackpot. That was on Saturday, 21 October 1967, when Northern Ireland defeated Scotland 1-0 at Windsor Park; it was the thirteenth international appearance of the new wonder boy whose rather lengthy pants draping over those thin, spindly legs gave him a slightly old fashioned look. Best gripped the match by the scruff of the neck and made it live in Technicolor.

The Seventies saw the rift with Manchester United, his failure to report for Northern Ireland's match against Scotland at Hampden Park after flying to southern Spain, the spell with Fulham, departure to the United States, controversy with Los Angeles Aztecs and with Fort Lauderdale Strikers, the FIFA ban, and his £2,000 per match contract with Hibernians. Then came his marriage in Las Vegas to model Angela MacDonald James. All these things and more made up the life of a genius who was public property from the moment he woke until he fell asleep again.

Epilogue
The Next Century

It has been a dramatic hundred years: a century of crises, controversy, triumph, tragedy. Yet throughout it all the IFA has succeeded in maintaining its status in British and world football. Its expertise has greatly helped the advancement of the game which was, of course, one of the original objects when the Association was formed in 1880. Football in Ireland has given countless thousands enjoyment either as players or spectators. The Association has more than adequately fulfilled its role.

Now we enter another century. Will it be a period of significant change? Will there be revolutionary ideas or will activities merely plod along in a stereotyped manner? The game has, unquestionably, moved in unison with social changes and the great demand from the public for more leisure time, but it is difficult to envisage any radical alterations at the grass roots level.

The tradition is too firmly grounded for that. Some member clubs will flounder and fade away to be replaced by others. Minor competitions will die and new ventures will take their place. Personalities will make their own contribution on the playing pitches or in the legislative chambers, just as their predecessors did over the last hundred years.

Can Irish football, as some have advocated, become instead of professional and semi-professional a basically amateur game in which everyone is described as 'a player' with expenses allowed similar to the system adopted in some continental countries? Can the burden of inflated transfer fees, spiralling costs and fluctuating attendances be eased — or eliminated altogether?

Sponsorship has played a significant part in the budgetary control of football in the 1970s. Over-dependence on it could be fatal, as IFA president Harry Cavan points out:

'I'm gravely suspicious of the inroads of commercialisation. There should be more of a community involvement and clubs should basically ensure that all costs can be met through gate receipts and other fund raising means. Sponsorship and social clubs, while playing a part, could be a danger. They dominate the situation to such an extent that football itself would be a subsidiary activity.'

Mr. Cavan, one of the game's visionaries, sees another problem arising through the diminished number of young players going to English clubs from school. 'There has to be less reliance on Northern Ireland players in England for they are just not emerging in the same numbers as of recent years. Clearly we have got to allocate money for the development of our local youngsters from an early stage — seven or eight upwards,' says Mr. Cavan.

'My experience in South America proves that this is the only way to ensure proper development. Youngsters can avoid bad habits and learn the basics —

skill, ball control, trapping, heading. That is how players such as Pelé, Madonna, Schiaffino became world figures. They got it right from the start.

'We have got to structure our League competitions so that boys can develop by age groups until they are seventeen or eighteen when they ought to be up to international standard. Naturally there must be a large capital investment from the Association for such a scheme, but it is an essential if Northern Ireland football is to progress.'

What are the prospects of an all-Ireland team? It would seem that this cherished dream of so many will not become a reality in the immediate future at least. 'We have had a series of talks with the Football Association of Ireland in which we both put forward our views on unification of the national side, but there are many snags against this and officials in each Association are fully aware of the circumstances,' says Mr. Cavan.

Statistics

Participants in International Matches

Results of International Matches

Youth Intermediate Junior Cup Results

1: THE IRISH RECORD SINCE 1882

Despite its small size, Northern Ireland has had an amazingly high record of success in full international soccer matches against foreign opposition, but in the Home Championship games this has been more modest.

Northern Ireland have played 330 full soccer internationals since 1882, of which 257 were in the British Home Championship.

We have won 73 games, drawn 61 and lost 196. The goals for are 377 and against 830.

Against the three Home Countries the aggregate results have been —

	P	W	D	L	F	A
England	88	6	13	70	79	311
Wales	86	26	20	40	124	176
Scotland	84	13	12	59	76	249

Two outings against England were in the European Championship which England won 4-0 (Wembley) and 5-1 (Belfast).

Against foreign opposition Northern Ireland has had better results. Since 1921 Northern Ireland has played 71 matches (including 35 World Cup encounters) against 26 nations from outside the United Kingdom.

We have won 28, drawn 16 and lost 27, with 98 goals for and 94 against.

Our full record against foreign nations reads:

	P	W	D	L	F	A
France	5	1	1	3	5	14
Holland	5	1	2	2	4	8
Spain	5	0	2	3	3	11
West Germany	5	0	1	4	6	15
Bulgaria	4	2	1	1	4	3
Cyprus	4	3	0	1	11	1
Italy	4	1	1	2	6	7
Portugal	4	1	3	0	6	3
Russia	4	0	2	2	1	4
Albania	2	1	1	0	5	2
Belgium	2	1	0	1	3	2
Czechoslovakia	2	2	0	0	3	1
Greece	2	1	0	1	3	2
Israel	2	1	1	0	4	3
Iceland	2	1	0	1	2	1
Norway	2	1	0	1	4	2
Poland	2	2	0	0	4	0
Sweden	2	1	0	1	3	2
Switzerland	2	1	0	1	2	2
Turkey	2	2	0	0	7	1
Yugoslavia	2	1	0	1	1	1
Denmark	2	1	0	1	2	5
Argentina	1	0	0	1	1	3
Rep. of Ireland	2	1	1	0	1	0
Mexico	1	1	0	0	4	1
Uruguay	1	1	0	0	3	0

2: INTERNATIONAL GOALSCORERS

12	Joe Bambrick	(Linfield, Chelsea)
12	Billy Gillespie	(Sheffield Utd)
10	Peter McParland	(Dundalk, A. Villa, Wolves, Plymouth)

10	Billy Bingham	(Glentoran, S'land, Luton, Everton)
10	Johnny Crossan	(Derry, Coleraine, Sparta, S. Liège, Man. City, S'land, M'boro)
10	Jimmy McIlroy	(Burnley, Stoke)
9	George Best	(Man. Utd, Fulham)
9	Olphie Stanfield	(Distillery)
8	Billy Irvine	(Burnley, Preston, Brighton)
7	John Peden	(Linfield, Distillery)
7	Billy McAdams	(Dist., Man. City, Bolton, Leeds, Brentford)
7	Derek Dougan	(Dist., P'outh, B'burn, A. Villa, Peterborough, Wolves)
6	Sammy Wilson	(Glenavon, Falkirk, Dundee)
6	Jimmy Nicholson	(Man. Utd)
6	Billy Dalton	(Y.M.C.A.)
5	Alex Stevenson	(Rangers, Everton)
5	Sammy Smyth	(Wolves, Stoke)
5	Davy Walsh	(W.B.A.)
5	Billy Simpson	(Linfield, Rangers, Stirling)
5	Billy Cush	(Glenavon, Leeds)
5	Jimmy McLaughlin	(Derry, Birmingham, Shrewsbury)
5	Gerry Armstrong	(Bangor, Spurs)
3	Peter Doherty	(Blackpool, Man. City, Derby Co., Huddersfield, Doncaster Rovers); he also scored 4 against the Combined Services in 1944.

Note:— These statistics, as of 1 January 1980, apply to the British Championship and all other matches, but not to Victory internationals or those against the Services in war-time.

3: INTERNATIONAL APPEARANCES BY IRISH FOOTBALLERS

This is a list of full international apearances by Irishmen against the Home Countries and foreign nations up to 1 January 1980.

Explanatory code for matches played by Home Countries: A, represents Austria; Alb, Albania; Arg, Argentine; B, Bohemia; Bel, Belgium; Br, Brazil; Bul, Bulgaria; Ch, Chile; Co, Columbia; Cy, Cyprus; Cz, Czechoslovakia; D, Denmark; Ec, Ecuador; Ei, Eire; EG, East Germany; F, France; Fi, Finland; G, Germany (pre-war); Gr, Greece; H, Hungary; Ho, Holland; I, Italy; Ic, Iceland; Ir, Iran, Is, Israel; K, Kuwait; L, Luxembourg; M, Mexico; Ma, Malta; N, Norway; P, Portugal; Par, Paraguay; Pe, Peru; Pol, Poland; R, Rumania, R of E, Rest of Europe; R of W, Rest of World; S, Scotland; Se, Sweden; Sp, Spain; Sw, Switzerland; T, Turkey; U, Uruguay; UK, Rest of United Kingdom; US, United States of America; USSR, Russia; W, Wales; WG, West Germany; Y, Yugoslavia.

Addis, D.J. (Cliftonville), 1922 v N (2) (2)

Aherne, T. (Belfast C.), 1947 v E; 1948 v S; 1949 v W; (with Luton T.), 1950 v W (4)

Alexander, A. (Cliftonville), 1895 v S (1)

Allen, C.A. (Cliftonville), 1936 v E (1)

Allen, J. (Limavady), 1887 v E (1)

Anderson, T. (Manchester U.) 1973 v Cy, E, S, W; 1974 v Bul, P (with Swindon T.), 1975 v S (sub); 1976 v Is; 1977 v Ho, Bel, WG, E, S, Ic; 1978 v Ic, Ho, Bel (with Peterborough U), S, E, W; 1979 v D (21).

Anderson, W. (Linfield), 1898 v W, E, S; 1899 v S(4)

Andrews, W. (Glentoran) 1908 v S; (with Grimsby T.), 1913 v E, S (3)

Armstrong, G. (Tottenham H.), 1977 v WG, E, W (sub), Ic (sub); 1978 v Bel, S, E, W; 1979 v Ei, D, Bul, E, Bul, E, S, W, D, E, Ei (19)

Baird, G. (Distillery), 1896 v S, E, W (3)

Baird, H. (Huddersfield T.), 1939 v E (1)

Balfe, J. (Shelbourne), 1909 v E; 1910 v W (2)

Bambrick, J. (Linfield), 1929 v W, S, E; 1930 v W, S, E; 1932 v W; (with Chelsea), 1935 v W, 1936 v E, S; 1938 v W (11)

Banks, S.J. (Cliftonville), 1937 v W (1)

Barr, H.H. (Linfield), 1962 v E; (with Coventry C.), 1963 v E, Pol (3)

Barron, H. (Cliftonville), 1894 v E, W, S; 1895 v S; 1896 v S; 1897 v E, W (7)

Barry, H. (Bohemians), 1900 v S (1)

Baxter, R.A. (Cliftonville), 1887 v S, W (2)

Bennett, L.V. (Dublin University), 1889 v W (1)

Berry, J. (Cliftonville), 1888 v S, W; 1889 v E (3)

Best, G. (Manchester U.), 1964 v W, U; 1965 v E, Ho (2), S, Sw (2), Alb; 1966 v S, E, Alb; 1967 v E; 1968 v S; 1969 v E, S, W, T; 1970 v S, E, W, USSR; 1971 v Cy (2), Sp, E, S, W; 1972 v USSR, Sp; 1973 v Bul; 1974 v P; (with Fulham), 1977 v Ho, Bel, WG; 1978 v Ic, Ho (37)

Bingham, W.L. (Sunderland), 1951 v F; 1952 v E, S, W; 1953 v E, S, F, W; 1954 v E, S, W; 1955 v E, S, W; 1956 v E, S, W; 1957 v E, S, W, P (2), I; 1958 v S, E, W, I (2), Arg, Cz (2), WG, F; (with Luton T.), 1959 v E, S, W, Sp; 1960 v S, E, W; (with Everton), 1961 v E, S, WG (2), Gr, I; 1962 v E, Gr; 1963 v E, S, Pol (2), Sp; (with Port Vale), 1964 v S, E, Sp (56)

Black, J. (Glentoran), 1901 v E (1)

Blair, H. (Portadown), 1931 v S; 1932 v S; (with Swansea) 1934 v S (3)

Blair, J. (Cliftonville), 1907 v W, E, S; 1908 v E, S (5)

Blair, R.V. (Oldham Ath.), 1975 v Se (sub), S (sub), W; 1976 v Se, Is (5)

Blanchflower, R.D. (Barnsley), 1950 v S, W; 1951 v E, S; (with Aston Villa), F; 1952 v W; 1953 v E, S, W, F; 1954 v E, S, W; (with Tottenham H.), 1955 v E, S, W; 1956 v E, S, W; 1957 v E, S, W, I. P (2); 1958 v E, S, W, I (2), Cz (2), Arg, F, WG; 1959 v E, S, W, Sp; 1960 v E, S, W; 1961 v E, S, W, WG (2); 1962 v E, S, W, Gr, Ho; 1963 v E, S, Pol (2) (56)

Blanchflower, J. (Manchester U.), 1954 v W; 1955 v E, S; 1956 v S, W; 1957 v S, E, P; 1958 v S, E, I (2) (12)

Bookman, L.O. (Bradford C.), 1914 v W; (with Luton T.), 1921 v S, W; 1922 v E (4)

Bothwell, A.W. (Ards), 1926 v S, E, W; 1927 v E, W (5)

Bowler, G.C. (Hull C.), 1950 v E, S, W (3)

Braithwaite, R.S. (Linfield), 1962 v W; 1963 v P, Sp; (with Middlesbrough), 1964 v W, U; 1965 v E, S, Sw (2), Ho (10)

Breen, T. (Belfast C.), 1935 v E, W; 1937 v E, S; (with Manchester U.), 1937 v W; 1938 v E, S; 1939 v W, S (9)

Brennan, B. (Bohemians), 1912 v W (1)

Brennan, R.A. (Luton T.), 1949 v W; (with Birmingham C.), 1950 v E, S, W; (with Fulham), 1951 v E (5)

Briggs, W.R. (Manchester U.), 1962 v W; (with Swansea T.), 1965 v Ho (2)

Brisby, D. (Distillery), 1891 v S (1)

Brolly, T. (Millwall), 1937 v W; 1938 v W; 1939 v E, W (4)

Brookes, E. A. (Shelbourne), 1920 v S (1)

Brown, J. (Glenavon), 1921 v W; (Tranmere R.) 1924 v E, W (3)

Brown, J. (Wolverhampton W.), 1935 v E, W; 1936 v E; (with Coventry C.), 1937 v E. W; 1938 v S, W; (with Birmingham C.), 1939 v E, S, W (10)

Brown, W.G. (Glenavon), 1926 v W (1)

Browne, F. (Cliftonville), 1887 v E, S, W; 1888 v E, S (5)

Browne, R.J. (Leeds U.), 1936 v E, W; 1938 v E, W; 1939 v E, S (6)

Bruce, W. (Glentoran), 1961 v S, 1967 v W (2)

Buckle, H. (Cliftonville), 1882 v E (1)

Buckle, H.R. (Sunderland), 1904 v E; (with Bristol C.), 1908 v W (2)

Burnett, J. (Distillery), 1894 v E, W, S; (with Glentoran), 1895 v E, W (5)

Burnison, J. (Distillery), 1901 v E, W (2)

Burnison, S. (Distillery), 1908 v E; 1910 v E, S; (with Bradford), 1911 v E, S, W; (with Distillery), 1912 v E; 1913 v W (8)

Burns J. (Glenavon), 1923 v E (1)

Butler, M.P. (Blackpool), 1939 v W (1)

Campbell, A.C. (Crusaders), 1963 v W; 1965 v Sw (2)

Campbell, J. (Cliftonville), 1896 v W; 1897 v E, S, W; (with Distillery), 1898 v E, S, W; (with Cliftonville), 1899 v E, 1900 v E; S; 1901 v S, W; 1902 v S; 1903 v E; 1904 v S (15)

Campbell, J.P. (Fulham), 1951 v E, S (2)

Campbell, W.G. (Dundee), 1968 v S, E; 1969 v T; 1970 v S, W, USSR (6)

Carey, J.J. (Manchester U.), 1947 v E, S, W; 1948 v E; 1949 v E, S, W (7)

Carroll, E (Glenavon), 1925 v S (1)

Casey, T. (Newcastle U.), 1955 v W; 1956 v W; 1957 v E, S, W, I, P (2); 1958 v WG, F; 1959 v Sp (sub); (with Portsmouth), 1959 v E (12)

Cashin, M. (Cliftonville), 1898 v S (1)

Caskey, W. (Derby Co.), 1979 v Bul, E, Bul, E, D (sub), E (sub) (6)

Cassidy, T. (Newcastle U.), 1971 v E (sub); 1972 v USSR (sub); 1974 v Bul (sub) S, E, W; 1975 v N; 1976 v S, E, W; 1977 v WG (sub), E, Ei (sub) (13)

Chambers, J. (Distillery), 1921 v W; (with Bury) 1928 v E, S, W; 1929 v E, S, W; 1930 v S, W; (with Nottingham F.), 1932 v E, S, W (12)

Chatton H.A. (Partick T.), 1925 v E, S; 1926 v E (3)

Christian, J. (Linfield), 1889 v S (1)

Clarke, R. (Belfast C.), 1901 v E, S (2)

Clements, D. (Coventry C.), 1965 v W, Ho; 1966 v M; 1967 v S, W; 1968 v S, E; 1969 v T (2), S, W; 1970 v S, E, W, USSR (2); 1971 v Sp, E, S, W, Cz; (with Sheffield W.) 1972 v USSR (2) Sp, E, S, W; 1973 v Bul, Cy (2) P, E, S, W; (with Everton) 1974 v Bul, P, S, E, W; 1975 v N, Y, E, S, W; 1976 v Se, Y (with New York Cosmos), E, W (48)

Clugston, J. (Cliftonville), 1888 v W, 1889 v W, S, E; 1890 v E, S; 1891 v E, W; 1892 v E, S, W; 1893 v E, S, W (14)

Cochrane, D. (Leeds), 1939 v E, W; 1947 v E, S, W; 1949 v E, S, W; 1949 v S, W; 1950 v S, E, (12)

Cochrane, M. (Distillery), 1898 v S, W, E; 1899 v E; 1900 v E, S, W; (with Leicester Fosse), 1901 v S (8)

Cochrane, T. (Coleraine), 1976 v N (with Burnley); 1978 v S (sub), E (sub), W (sub); 1979 v Ei (sub), (Middlesborough), D, Bul, E, Bul, E (10)

Collins, F. (Glasgow C.), 1922 v S(1)

Collins, R. (Cliftonville), 1922 v N (1)

Condy, J. (Distillery), 1882 v W; 1886 v E, S (3)

Connor, J. (Glentoran), 1901 v S, E; (with Belfast C.), 1905 v E, S, W; 1907 v E, S; 1908 v E, S; 1909 v W; 1911 v S, E, W (13)

Connor, M.J. (Brentford), 1903 v S, W; (with Fulham) 1904 v E (3)

Cook, W. (Celtic), 1933 v E, W, S; (with Everton) 1935 v E; 1936 v S, W; 1937 v E, S, W; 1938 v E, S, W; 1939 v E, S, W (15)

Cooke, S. (Belfast YMCA) 1889 v E; (with Cliftonville), 1890 v E, S (3)

Coulter, J. (Belfast C.), 1934 v E, S, W; (with Everton), 1935 v E, S, W; 1937 v S; W; (with Grimsby T.), 1938 v S, W; (with Chelmsford C.), 1939 v S (11)

Cowan, J. (Newcastle U.), 1970 v E (sub) (1)

Cowan, T.S. (Queen's Island), 1925 v W (1)

Coyle, F. (Coleraine), 1956 v E, S; 1957 v P (with Nottingham F.), 1958 v Arg (4)

Coyle, R.I. (Sheffield W.), 1973 v P, Cy (sub), W (sub); 1974 v Bul (sub), P (sub) (5)

Craig, A.B. (Rangers), 1908 v E, S, W; 1909 v S; (with Morton), 1913 v S, W, 1914 v E, S, W (9)

Craig, D.J. (Newcastle U.), 1967 v W; 1968 v W; 1969 v T (2), E, S, W; 1970 v E, S, W, USSR; 1971 v Cy (2), S, S (sub); 1972 v USSR, S (sub); 1973 v Cy (2), E, S, W; 1974 v Bul, P; 1975 v N (25)

Crawford, S. (Distillery), 1889 v E, W; (with Cliftonville), 1891 v E, S, W; 1893 v E, W (7)

Croft, T. (Queen's Island), 1922 v N (2); 1924 v E (3)

Crone, R. (Distillery), 1889 v S; 1890 v E, S, W (4)

Crone, W. (Distillery), 1882 v W; 1884 v E, S, W; 1886 v E, S, W; 1887 v E; 1888 v E, W; 1889 v S; 1890 v W (12)

Crooks, W. (Manchester U.), 1922 v W (1)

Crossan, E. (Blackburn R.), 1950 v S; 1951 v E; 1955 v W (3)

Crossan, J.A. (Sparta-Rotterdam), 1960 v E; (with Sunderland); 1963 v W, P, Sp; 1964 v E, S, W, U, Sp; 1965 v E, S, Sw (2); (with Manchester C.) v W, Ho (2), Alb; 1966 v S, E, Alb, WG; 1967 v E, S; (with Middlesborough), 1968 v S (23)

Crothers, C. (Distillery), 1907 v W (1)

Cumming, L. (Huddersfield T.), 1929 v W, S; (with Oldham Ath.), 1930 v E (3)

Cunningham, R. (Ulster), 1892 v S, E, W; 1893 v E (4)

Cunningham, W.E. (St. Mirren), 1951 v W; 1953 v E; 1954 v S; 1955 v S; (with Leicester C.), 1956 v E, S, W; 1957 v E, S, W, I, P (2); 1958 v S, W, I, Cz (2), Arg, WG, F; 1959 v E, S, W; 1960 v E, S, W; (with Dunfermline Ath.), 1971 v W; 1962 v W, Ho (30)

Curran, S. (Belfast C.), 1926 v S, W; 1928 v S (3)

Curran, J.J. (Glenavon), 1922 v W, N (2); (with Pontypridd), 1923 v E, S; (with Glenavon), 1924 v E (6)

Cush, W.W. (Glenavon), 1951 v E, S; 1954 v S, E; 1957 v W, I, P (2); (with Leeds U.), 1958 v I (2), W, Cz (2), Arg, WG, F; 1959 v E, S, W, Sp; 1960 v E, S, W; (with Portadown), 1961 v WG, Gr; 1962 v Gr (26)

Dalrymple, J.P. (Distillery), 1922 v N (2) (2)

Dalton, W. (YMCA), 1888 v S; (with Linfield), 1890 v S, W; 1891 v S, W; 1892 v E, S, W; 1894 v E, S, W (11)

D'Arcy, S.D. (Chelsea), 1952 v,W; 1953 v E; (with Brentford), 1953 v S, W, F (5)

135

Darling J. (Linfield), 1897 v E, S; 1900 v S; 1902 v E, S, W; 1903 v E, S, W; 1905 v E, S, W; 1906 v E, S, W; 1908 v W; 1909 v E; 1910 v E, S, W; 1912 v S (21)

Davey, H.H. (Reading), 1926 v E; 1927 v E, S; 1928 v E; (with Portsmouth), 1928 v W (5)

Davis, T.L. (Oldham Ath.), 1937 v E (1)

Davison, J.R. (Cliftonville), 1882 v E, W; 1883 v E, W; 1884 v E, W, S; 1885 v E (8)

Devine, W. (Limavady), 1886 v E, S; 1887 v W; 1888 v W (4)

Dickson, D. (Coleraine), 1970 v S (sub), W; 1973 v Cy, P (4)

Dickson, T.A. (Linfield), 1957 v S (1).

Dickson, W. (Chelsea), 1951 v W, F; 1952 v E, S, W; 1953 v E, S, W, F; (with Arsenal); 1954 v E, W; 1955 v E (12)

Diffin, W. (Belfast C.), 1931 v W (1)

Dill, A.H. (Knock and Down Ath.), 1882 v E, W; (with Cliftonville), 1883 v W; 1884 v E, S, W; 1885 v E, S, W (9)

Doherty, I. (Belfast C.), 1901 v E (1)

Doherty, J. (Cliftonville), 1933 v E, W (2)

Doherty, M. (Derry C.), 1938 v S (1)

Doherty, P.D. (Blackpool), 1935 v E, W; 1936 v E, S; (with Manchester C.), 1937 v E, W; 1938 v E, S; 1939 v E, W; (with Derby Co.), 1947 v E; (with Huddersfield T.), 1947 v W; 1948 v E, W; 1949 v S; (with Doncaster R.), 1951 v S (16)

Donnelly, L. (Distillery), 1913 v W (1)

Doran, J.F. (Brighton), 1921 v E; 1922 v E, W (3)

Dougan, A.D. (Portsmouth), 1958 v Cz; (with Blackburn R.), 1960 v S; 1961 v E, W, I, Gr; (with Aston Villa), 1963 v S, P (2); (with Leicester C.), 1966 v S, E, W, M; Alb, WG; 1967 v E, S, (with Wolverhampton W.), 1967 v W; 1968 v S, W, Is, T (2); 1969 v E, S, W; 1970 v S, E, USSR (2); 1971 v Cy (2), Sp, E, S, W; 1972 v USSR (2), E, S, W; 1973 v Bul, Cy (43)

Douglas, J.P., (Belfast C.), 1947 v E (1)

Dowd, H.O. (Glenavon), 1974 v W; 1975 v N (sub), Se (3)

Duggan, H.A. (Leeds U.), 1930 v E; 1931 v E, W; 1933 v E; 1934 v E; 1935 v S, W; 1936 v S (8)

Dunne, J. (Sheffield U.), 1928 v W; 1931 v W, E; 1932 v E, S; 1933 v E, W (7)

Eames, W.L.E. (Dublin U.), 1885 v E, S, W (3)

Eglington, T.J. (Everton), 1947 v S, W; 1948 v E, S, W; 1949 v E (6)

Elder, A.R. (Burnley), 1960 v W; 1961 v S, E, W, WG (2), Gr; 1962 v E, S, Gr; 1963 v E, S, W, P (2), Sp; 1964 v W, U; 1965 v E, S, W, Sw (2), Ho (2), Alb; 1966 v E, S, W, M, Alb; 1967 v E, S, W (with Stoke C.), 1968 v E, W; 1969 v E (sub), S, W; 1970 v USSR (40)

Elleman, A.R. (Cliftonville), 1889 v W; 1890 v E (2)

Elwood, J.H. (Bradford), 1929 v W; 1930 v E (2)

Emerson, W. (Glentoran), 1920 v E, S, W; 1921 v E; 1922 v E, S; (with Burnley), 1922 v W; 1923 v E, S, W; 1924 v E (11)

English, S. (Glasgow R.), 1933 v W, S (2)

Enright, J. (Leeds C.), 1912 v S (1)

Falloon, E. (Aberdeen), 1931 v S; 1933 v S (2)

Farquharson, T.G. (Cardiff C.), 1923 v S, W; 1924 v E, S, W; 1925 v E, S (7)

Farrell, P. (Distillery), 1901 v S, W (2)

Farrell, P. (Hibernian), 1938 v W (1)

Farrell, P.D. (Everton), 1947 v S, W; 1948 v E, S, W; 1949 v E, W (7)

Feeney, J.M. (Linfield), 1947 v S; (with Swansea T.), 1950 v E (2)

Feeney, W. (Glentoran), 1976 v Is (1)

Ferguson, W. (Linfield), 1966 v M; 1967 v E (2)

Ferris, J. (Belfast Celtic), 1920 v E, W; (with Chelsea), 1921 v S, E; (with Belfast C.), 1928 v S (5)

Ferris, R.O. (Birmingham), 1950 v S; 1951 v F; 1952 v S (3)

Finney, T. (Sunderland), 1975 v N; E (sub), S, W; 1976 v N, Y, S, E (8)

Fitzpatrick, J.C. (Bohemians), 1896 v E, S (2)

Flack, H. (Burnley), 1929 v S (1)

Forbes, G. (Limavady), 1888 v W; (with Distillery), 1891 v E, S (3)

Forde, J.T. (Ards), 1959 v Sp; 1961 v E, S, WG (4)

Foreman, T.A. (Cliftonville), 1899 v S (1)

Forsyth, J. (YMCA), 1888 v E, S (2)

Fox, W. (Ulster), 1887 v E, S (2)

Fulton, R.P. (Belfast C.), 1930 v W; 1931 v E, S, W; 1932 v W, E; 1933 v E, S; 1934 v E, W, S; 1935 v E, W, S; 1936 v S, W; 1937 v E, S, W; 1938 v W (20)

Gaffikin, J. (Linfield Ath.), 1890 v S, W; 1891 v S, W; 1892 v E, S, W; 1893 v E, S, W; 1894 v E, S, W; 1895 v E, W (15)

Galbraith, W. (Distillery), 1890 v W (1)

Gallagher, P. (Celtic), 1920 v E, S; 1922 v S; 1923 v S, W; 1924 v S, W; 1925 v S, W, E; (with Falkirk), 1927 v S (11)

Gallogly, C. (Huddersfield T.), 1951 v E, S (2)

Gara, A. (Preston N.E.), 1902 v E, S, W (3)

Gardiner, A. (Cliftonville), 1930 v S, W; 1931 v S; 1932 v E, S (5)

Garrett, J. (Distillery), 1925 v W (1)

Gaston, R. (Oxford U.), 1969 v Is (sub) (1)

Gaukrodger, G. (Linfield), 1895 v W (1)

Gaussen, A, W. (Moyola Park), 1884 v E, S; 1888 v E, W; 1889 v E, W (6)

Geary, J (Glentoran), 1931 v S; 1932 v S (2)

Gibb, J.T. (Wellington Park), 1884 v S, W; 1885 v S, E, W; 1886 v S; 1887 v S, E, W; 1889 v S (10)

Gibb, T.J. (Cliftonville), 1936 v W (1)

Gibson, W.K. (Cliftonville), 1894 v S, W, E; 1895 v S; 1897 v W; 1898 v S, W, E; 1901 v S, W, E; 1902 v S, W (13)

Gillespie, R. (Hertford), 1886 v E, S, W; 1887 v E, S, W (6)

Gillespie, W. (Sheffield U.), 1913 v E, S; 1914 v E, W; 1920 v S, W; 1921 v E; 1922 v E, S, W; 1923 v E, S, W; 1924 v E, S, W; 1925 v E, S; 1926 v S, W; 1927 v E, W; 1928 v E; 1929 v E; 1931 v E (25)

Gillespie, W. (West Down), 1889 v W (1)

Goodall, A.L. (Derby Co.), 1899 v S, W; 1900 v E, W; 1901 v E; 1902 v S; 1903 v E, W; (with Glossop), 1904 v E, W (10)

Goodbody, M.F. (Dublin University), 1889 v E; 1891 v W (2)

Gordon, H. (Linfield), 1891 v S; 1892 v E, S, W; 1893 v E, S, W; 1895 v E, W; 1896 v E, S (11)

Gordon, T. (Linfield), 1894 v W; 1895 v E (2)

Gorman, W.C. (Brentford), 1947 v E, S, W; 1948 v W (4)

Gowdy, J. (Glentoran), 1920 v E; (with Queen's Island), 1924 v W; (with Falkirk), 1926 v E, S; 1927 v E, S (6)

Gowdy, W.A. (Hull C.), 1932 v S; (with Sheffield W.), 1933 v S; (with Linfield), 1935 v E, S, W; (with Hibernian), 1936 v W (6)

Graham, W.G.L. (Doncaster R.), 1951 v W, F; 1952 v E, S, W; 1953 v S, F; 1954 v E, W; 1955 v S, W; 1956 v E, E, S; 1959 v E (14)

Greer, W. (Q.P.R.), 1909 v E, S, W (3)

Gregg, H. (Doncaster R.), 1954 v W; 1957 v E, S, W, I, P (2); 1958 v E, I; (with Manchester U.), 1958 v Cz, Arg, WG, F, W; 1959 v E, W; 1960 v S, E, W; 1961 v E, S; 1962 v S, Gr; 1964 v S, E (25)

Hall, G. (Distillery), 1897 v E (1)

Halligan, W. (Derby Co.), 1911 v W; (with Wolverhampton W.), 1912 v E (2)

Hamill, M. (Manchester U.), 1912 v E; 1914 v E, S; (with Belfast C.), 1920 v E, S, W; (with Manchester C.), 1921 v S (7)

Hamilton, B. (Linfield), 1969 v T; 1971 v Cy (2) E, S, W; (with Ipswich T.), 1972 v USSR (1+1 sub), Sp; 1973 v Bul, Cy (2), P, E, S, W; 1974 v Bul, S, E, W; 1975 v N, Se, Y, E; 1976 v Se, N, Y (with Everton), Is, S, E, W; 1977 v Ho, Bel, WG, E, S, W, Ic (with Millwall); 1978 v S, E, W; 1979 v Ei (sub), (Swindon T.), Bul (2), E, S, W, D (48)

Hamilton, J. (Knock), 1882 v E, W (2)

Hamilton, R. (Distillery), 1908 v W (1)

Hamilton, R. (Glasgow R.), 1928 v S; 1929 v E; 1930 v S, E; 1932 v S (5)

Hamilton, W. (Q.P.R.); 1978 v S (sub) (1)

Hamilton, W.D. (Dublin Association), 1885 v W (1)

Hamilton, W.J. (Dublin Association), 1885 v W (1)

Hampton, H. (Bradford C.), 1911 v E, S, W; 1912 v E, W; 1913 v E, S, W; 1914 v E (9)

Hanna, D.R.A. (Portsmouth), 1899 v W (1)

Hanna, J. (Nottingham), 1912 v S, W (2)

Hannon, D.J. (Bohemian), 1908 v E, S; 1911 v E, S; 1912 v W; 1913 v E (6)

Harkin, J.T. (Southport), 1968 v W; 1969 v T, (with Shrewsbury), W (sub); 1970 v USSR; 1971 v Sp (5)

Harland, A.I. (Linfield), 1922 v N (2), 1923 v E (3)

Harris, J. (Cliftonville), 1921 v W (1)

Harris, V. (Shelbourne), 1906 v E; 1907 v E, W; 1908 v E, W, S; (with Everton); 1909 v E, W, S; 1910 v E, S, W; 1911 v E, S, W; 1912 v E; 1913 v E, S; 1914 v S, W (20)

Harvey, M. (Sunderland), 1961 v I; 1962 v Ho; 1963 v W Sp; 1964 v S, E, W, U, Sp; 1965 v E, S, W, Sw (2), Ho (2), Alb; 1966 v S, E, W, M; Alb, WG; 1967 v E, S; 1968 v E, W; 1969, Is, T (2) v E; 1970 v USSR; 1971 v Cy, W (sub) (33)

Hastings, J. (Knock), 1882 v E, W; (with Ulster), 1883 v W; 1884 v E, S; 1886 v E, S (7)

Hatton, S. (Linfield), 1963 v S, Pol (2)

Hayes, W.E. (Huddersfield T.), 1938 v E, S; 1939 v E, S (4)

Hegan, D. (W.B.A.), 1970 v USSR (with Wolverhampton W.); 1972 v USSR, E, S, W; 1973 v Bul, Cy (7)

Henderson, A.W. (Ulster), 1885 v E, S, W (3)

Hewison, G. (Moyola Park), 1885 v E, S (2)

Hill, M.J. (Norwich C.), 1959 v W; 1960 v W; 1961 v WG; 1962 v S (with Everton), 1964 v S, E, Sp (7)

Hinton, E. (Fulham), 1947 v S, W; 1948 v S, E, W; (Millwall), 1951 v W, F (7)

Hopkins, J. (Brighton), 1926 v E (1)

Houston, J. (Linfield), 1912 v S, W; 1913 v W, (with Everton), 1913 v E, S; 1914 v S (6)
Houston, W. (Linfield), 1933 v W (1)
Houston, W.G. (Moyola Park), 1885 v E, S (2)
Hughes, W, (Bolton W.), 1951 v W (1)
Humphries, W. (Ards), 1962 v W; (with Coventry C.), 1962 v Ho; 1963 v E, S, W, Pol, Sp; 1964 v S, E, Sp; 1965 v S; (with Swansea T.), 1965 v W, Ho, Alb (14)
Hunter, A. (Blackburn R.), 1970 v USSR, 1971 v Cy (2), E, S, W; (with Ipswich T.), 1972 v USSR (2), Sp, E, S, W; 1973 v Bul, Cy (2), P, E, S, W; 1974 v Bul, S, E, W; 1975 v N, Se, Y, E, S, W; 1976 v Se, N, Y, Is, S, E, W; 1977 v Ho, Bel, WG, E, S, W, Ic; 1978 v Ic, Ho, Bel; 1979 v Ei, D, S, W, D, E, Ei (53)
Hunter, A. (Distillery), 1905 v W; 1906 v W, E, S; (with Belfast C.), 1908 v W; 1909 v W, E, S (8)
Hunter, R.J. (Cliftonville), 1884 v E, S, W (3)
Hunter, V. (Coleraine), 1962 v E; 1964 v Sp (2)

Irvine, R.W. (Everton), 1922 v S; 1923 v E, W; 1924 v E, S; 1925 v E; 1926 v E; 1927 v E, W; 1928 v E, S; (with Portsmouth), 1929 v E; 1930 v S; (with Connah's Quay), 1931 v E; (with Derry C.), 1932 v W (15)
Irvine, R.J. (Linfield), 1962 v Ho; 1963 v E, S, W, Pol (2), Sp; (with Stoke C.), 1965 v W (8)
Irvine, W.J. (Burnley), 1963 v W, Sp; 1965 v S, W, Sw, Ho (2), Alb; 1966 v S, E, W, M, Alb; 1967 v E, S; 1968 v E, W; (with Preston N.E.), 1969 v Is, T, E; (with Brighton), 1972 v E, S, W (23)
Irving, S.J. (Dundee), 1923 v S, W; 1924 v S, E, W; 1925 v S, E, W; 1926 v S, W; (with Cardiff C.), 1927 v S, E, W; 1928 v S, E, W; (with Chelsea), 1929 v E; 1931 v W (18)

Jackson, T. (Everton), 1969 v Is, E, S, W; 1970 v USSR (1+1 sub); (with Nottingham F.), 1971 v Sp; 1972 v E, S, W; 1973 v Cy, E, S, W; 1974 v Bul, P, S (sub), E (sub), W (sub); 1975 v N (sub), Se, Y, E, S, W; (with Manchester U.); 1976 v Se, N, Y; 1977 v Ho, Bel, WG, E, S, W, Ic (35)
Jamison, J. (Glentoran), 1976 v N (1)

Jennings, P.A. (Watford), 1964 v W, U; (with Tottenham H.), 1965 v E, S, Sw (2), Ho, Alb; 1966 v S, E, W, Alb, WG; 1967 v E, S; 1968 v S, E, W; 1969 v Is, T (2), E, S, W; 1970 v S, E, USSR (2); 1971 v Cy (2), E, S, W; 1972 v USSR, Sp, S, E, W; 1973 v Bul, Cy, P, E, S, W; 1974 v P, S, E, W; 1975 v N, Se, Y, E, S, W; 1976 v Se, N, Y, Is, S, E, W; 1977 v Ho, Bel, WG, E, S, W, Ic; (with Arsenal), 1978 v Ic, Ho, Bel; 1979 v Ei, D, Bul, E, Bul, E, S, W, D, E, Ei (82)
Johnston, H. (Portadown), 1927 v W (1)
Johnston, R. (Oldpark), 1885 v S, W (2)
Johnston, S. (Distillery), 1882 v W; 1884 v E; 1886 v E, S (4)
Johnston, S. (Linfield), 1890 v W; 1893 v S, W; 1894 v E (4)
Johnston, S. (Distillery), 1905 v W (1)
Johnston, W.C. (Glenavon), 1962 v W; (with Oldham), 1966 v M (sub) (2)
Jones, J. (Linfield), 1930 v S, W; 1931 v S, W, E; 1932 v S, E; 1933 v S, E, W; 1934 v S, E, W; 1935 v S, E, W; 1936 v E, S; (with Hibernian), 1936 v W; 1937 v E, W, S; (with Glenavon), 1938 v E (23)
Jones, J. (Glenavon), 1956 v W; 1957 v E, W (3)
Jones, S. (Distillery), 1934 v E; (with Blackpool), 1934 v W (2)
Jordan, T. (Linfield), 1895 v E, W (2)

Kavanagh, P.J. (Glasgow C.), 1930 v E (1)
Keane, T.R. (Swansea T.), 1949 v S (1)
Kearns, A. (Distillery), 1900 v E, S, W; 1902 v E, S, W (6)
Keith, R.M. (Newcastle U.), 1958 v E, W, Cz (2), Arg, I, WG, F; 1959 v E, S, W, Sp; 1960 v S, E; 1961 v S, E, W, I, WG (2), Gr; 1962 v W, Ho (23)
Kelly, H.R. (Fulham), 1950 v E, W; (with Southampton), 1951 v E, S (4)
Kelly, J. (Glentoran), 1896 v E (1)
Kelly, J. (Derry C.), 1932 v E, W; 1933 v E, W, S; 1934 v W; 1936 v E, S, W; 1937 v S, E (11)
Kelly, P. (Manchester C.), 1921 v E (1)
Kelly, P.M. (Barnsley), 1950 v S (1)
Kennedy, A.L. (Arsenal), 1923 v W; 1925 v E (2)
Kernaghan, N. (Belfast C.), 1936 v W; 1937 v S; 1938 v E (3)
Kirkwood, H. (Cliftonville), 1904 v W (1)
Kirwan, J. (Tottenham H.), 1900 v W; 1902 v E, W; 1903 v E, S, W; 1904 v E, S, W; 1905 v E, S, W; (with Chelsea), 1906 v E, S, W; 1907 v W; (with Clyde), 1909 v S (17)

138

Lacey, W. (Everton), 1909 v E, S, W; 1910 v
    E, S, W; 1911 v E, S, W; 1912 v E; (with
    Liverpool), 1913 v W; 1914 v E, S, W; 1920
    v E, S, W; 1921 v E, S, W; 1922 v E, S;
    (with New Brighton), 1925 v E (23)
Lawther, W.I. (Sunderland), 1960 v W; 1961
    v I; (with Blackburn R.) 1962 v S, Ho (4)
Leatham, J. (Belfast C.), 1939 v W (1)
Ledwidge, J.J. (Shelbourne), 1906 v S, W (2)
Lemon, J. (Glentoran), 1886 v W; 1888 v S;
    (with Belfast YMCA), 1889 v W (3)
Leslie, W. (YMCA), 1887 v E (1)
Lewis, J. (Glentoran), 1889 v S, E, W; (with
    Distillery), 1900 v S (4)
Little, J. (Glentoran), 1898 v W (1)
Lockhart, H. (Rossall School), 1884 v W (1)
Lockhart, N. (Linfield), 1947 v E; (with
    Coventry C.), 1950 v W; 1951 v W; 1952 v
    W; (with Aston Villa), 1954 v S, E; 1955 v
    W; 1956 v W (8)
Lowther, R. (Glentoran), 1888 v E, S (2)
Loyal, J. (Clarence), 1891 v S (1)
Lutton, R.J. (Wolverhampton W.), 1970 v S,
    E; (with West Ham), 1973 v Cy (sub), S
    (sub), W (sub); 1974 v P (6).
Lyner, D. (Glentoran), 1920 v E, W; 1922 v S,
    W; (with Manchester U.); 1923 v E; (with
    Kilmarnock), 1923 v W (6)

McAdams, W.J. (Manchester C.), 1954 v W;
    1955 v S; 1957 v E; 1958 v S, I; (with Bolton
    W.), 1961 v E, S, W, I, WG (2), Gr; 1962 v
    E, Gr, (with Leeds U.), Ho (15)
M'Alery, J.M. (Cliftonville), 1882 v E, W (2)
M'Alinden, J. (Belfast C.), 1938 v S; 1939 v S;
    (with Portsmouth), 1947 v E; (with South-
    end U.), 1949 v E (4)
M'Allen, J. (Linfield), 1898 v E; 1899 v E, S,
    W; 1900 v E, S, W; 1901 v W; 1902 v S (9)
M'Alpine, W.J. (Cliftonville), 1901 v S (1)
M'Arthur, A. (Distillery), 1886 v W (1)
McAuley, P. (Belfast C.), 1900 v S (1)
M'Cabe, J.J. (Leeds U.), 1949 v S, W; 1950 v
    E; 1951 v W; 1953 v W; 1954 v S (6)
M'Cabe, W. (Ulster), 1891 v E (1)
M'Cambridge, J. (Ballymena), 1930 v S, W;
    (with Cardiff C.), 1931 v W; 1932 v E (4)
M'Candless, J. (Bradford), 1912 v W; 1913 v
    W; 1920 v W, S; 1921 v E (5)
McCandless, W. (Linfield), 1920 v E, W;
    1921 v E; (with Rangers), 1921 v W; 1922 v
    S; 1924 v W, S; 1925 v S; 1929 v W (9)
M'Cann, P. (Belfast C.), 1910 v E, S, W; 1911
    v E, (with Glentoran), 1911 v S; 1912 v E;
    1913 v W (7)
M'Cashin, J. (Cliftonville), 1896 v W; 1898 v
    S, W; 1899 v S (4)
M'Cavana, W.T. (Coleraine), 1955 v S; 1956
    v E, S (3)

M'Caw, D. (Distillery), 1882 v E (1)
M'Caw, J.H. (Linfield), 1927 v W; 1930 v S;
    1931 v E, S, W (5)
M'Clatchey, J. (Distillery), 1886 v E, S, W (3)
M'Clatchey, R. (Distillery), 1895 v S (1)
M'Cleary, J.W. (Cliftonville), 1955 v W (1)
M'Cleery, W. (Cliftonville), 1922 v N; 1930 v
    E, W; 1931 v E, S, W; 1932 v S, W; 1938 v
    E, W (10)
McClelland, J. (Arsenal), 1961 v W, I, WG
    (2), Gr; (with Fulham), 1967 v M (6)
M'Cluggage, A. (Cliftonville), 1922 v N (2);
    (with Bradford), 1924 v E; (with Burnley),
    1927 v S, W; 1928 v S, E, W; 1929 v S, E,
    W; 1930 v W; 1931 v E, W (14)
M'Clure, G. (Cliftonville), 1907 v S, W; 1908
    v E; (with Distillery), 1909 v E (4)
M'Connell, E. (Cliftonville), 1904 v S, W;
    (with Glentoran), 1905 v S; (with Sund-
    erland), 1906 v E; 1907 v E; 1908 v S, W;
    (with Sheffield W.), 1909 v S, W; 1910 v S,
    W, E (12)
M'Connell, W.G. (Bohemians), 1912 v W;
    1913 v E, S; 1914 v E, S, W (6)
M'Connell, W.H. (Reading), 1925 v W; 1926
    v E, W; 1927 v E, S, W; 1928 v E, W (8)
M'Court, F.J. (Manchester C.), 1952 v E, W;
    1953 v E, S, W, F (6)

M'Coy, J. (Distillery), 1896 v W (1)
McCracken, R. (Linfield) 1922 v N (2)
M'Cracken, R. (C. Palace), 1921 v E; 1922 v
    E, S, W (4)
M'Cracken, W. (Distillery), 1902 v E, W;
    1903 v E; 1904 v E, S, W; (with Newcastle
    U.), 1905 v E, S, W; 1907 v E; 1920 v E,;
    1922 v E, S, W; (with Hull C.), 1923 v S
    (15)
McCreery, D. (Manchester U.) 1976 v S
    (sub), E, W; 1977 v Ho, Bel, WG, E, S, W,
    Ic; 1978 v Ic, Ho, Bel, S, E, W; 1979 v Ei,
    D, Bul, E, Bul, W, D, E, Ei (25)
McCrory, S. (Southend U.), 1958 v E (1)
McCullough, K. (Belfast C.), 1935 v W; 1936
    v E; (with Manchester C.), 1936 v S; 1937 v
    E, S (5)
McCullough, W.J. (Arsenal), 1961 v I; 1963 v
    Sp; 1964 v S, E, W, U, Sp; 1965 v E, Sw;
    (with Millwall), 1967 v E (10)
M'Donald, R. (Glasgow R.) 1930 v S; 1932 v
    E (2)
M'Donnell, J. (Bohemians), 1911 v E, S; 1912
    v W; 1913 v W (4)
M'Faul, W.S. (Linfield), 1967 v E (sub);
    (with Newcastle U.) 1970 v W; 1971 v Sp;
    1972 v USSR; 1973 v Cy; 1974 v Bul (6)
M'Garry, J.K. (Cliftonville), 1951 v W, F, S
    (3)
M'Gee, G. (Wellington Park), 1885 v E, S, W
    (3)

M'Grath, R.C. (Tottenham H.), 1974 v S, E,
W; 1975 v N; 1976 v Is (sub); (with
Manchester U.), 1977 v Ho, Bel, WG, E,
S, W, Ic; 1978 v Ic, Ho, Bel, S, E, W; 1979
v Bul (sub), E (sub), E (sub) (21)

M'Gregor, S. (Glentoran), 1921 v S (1)

M'Grillen, J. (Clyde), 1924 v S; (with Belfast
C.) 1927 v S (2)

M'Ilroy, H. (Cliftonville), 1906 v E (1)

McIlroy, J. (Burnley), 1952 v E, S, W; 1953 v
E, S, W; 1954 v E, S, W; 1955 v E, S, W;
1956 v E, S, W; 1957 v E, S, W, I, P (2);
1958 v E, S, W, I (2), Cz (2), Arg, WG, F;
1959 v E, S, W, Sp; 1960 v E, S, W; 1961 v
E, W, WG (2) Gr; 1962 v E, S, Gr, Ho;
1963 v E, S, Pol (2); (with Stoke C.), 1963 v
W; 1966 v S, E, Alb (55)

McIlroy, S.B. (Manchester U.), 1972 v Sp, S
(sub); 1974 v S, E, W; 1975 v N, Se, Y, E,
S, W; 1976 v Se, N, Y, S, E, W; 1977 v Ho,
Bel, E, S, W, Ic; 1978 v Ic, Ho, Bel, S, E,
W; 1979 v Ei, D, Bul, E, Bul, E, S, W, D,
E, Ei (40)

M'Ilvenny, J. (Distillery), 1890 v E; 1891 v E
(2)

M'Ilvenny, P. (Distillery), 1924 v W (1)

McKeag, W. (Glentoran), 1968 v S, W (2)

McKee, F.W. (Cliftonville), 1906 v S, W;
(with Belfast C.), 1914 v E, S, W (5)

M'Kelvie, H. (Glentoran), 1901 v W (1)

McKenna, J. (Huddersfield), 1950 v E, S, W;
1951 v E, S, F; 1952 v E (7)

M'Kenzie, H. (Distillery), 1922 v N (2); 1923
v S (3)

McKenzie, R. (Airdrie), 1967 v W (1)

M'Keown, H. (Linfield), 1892 v E, S, W; 1893
v S, W; 1894 v S, W (7)

M'Kie, H. (Cliftonville), 1895 v E, S, W (3)

M'Kinney, D. (Hull C.), 1921 v S; (with
Bradford C.), 1924 v S (2).

McKinney, V.J. (Falkirk), 1966 v WG (1)

M'Knight, J. (Preston N.E.), 1912 v S; (with
Glentoran), 1913 v S (2)

McLaughlin, J.C. (Shrewsbury T.), 1962 v E,
S, W, Gr; 1963 v W; (with Swansea T.),
1964 v W, U; 1965 v E, W, Sw (2); 1966 v W
(12)

M'Lean, T. (Limavady), 1885 v S (1)

M'Mahon, J. (Bohemians), 1934 v S (1)

M'Master, G. (Glentoran), 1897 v E, S, W (3)

McMichael, A. (Newcastle U.), 1950 v E, S;
1951 v E, S, F; 1952 v E, S, W; 1953 v E, S,
W, F; 1954 v E, S, W; 1955 v E, W; 1956 v
W; 1957 v E, S, W, I, P (2); 1958 v E, S, W,
I (2), Cz (2), Arg, WG, F; 1959 v S, W, Sp;
1960 v E, S, W (40)

M'Millan, G (Distillery), 1903 v E; 1905 v W
(2)

McMillan, S. (Manchester U.), 1963 v E, S
(2)

M'Millen, W.S. (Manchester U.), 1934 v E;
1935 v S; 1937 v S; (with Chesterfield),
1938 v S, W; 1939 v E, S (7)

McMordie, A.S. (Middlesbrough), 1969 v Is,
T (2), E, S; 1970 v E, S, W, USSR; 1971
v Cy (2) E, S, W; 1972 v USSR, Sp, E, S,
W; 1973; v Bul (21)

McMorran, E.J. (Belfast C.), 1947 v E; (with
Barnsley), 1951 v E, S, W; 1952 v E, S, W;
1953 v E, S, F; (with Doncaster R.), 1953 v
W; 1954 v E; 1956 v W; 1957 v I, P (15)

M'Mullan, D. (Liverpool), 1926 v E, W; 1927
v S (3)

M'Ninch, J. (Ballymena), 1931 v S; 1932 v S,
W (3)

McParland, P.J. (Aston Villa), 1954 v W;
1955 v E, S; 1956 v E, S; 1957 v E, S, W, P;
1958 v E, S, W, I (2), Cz (2), Arg, WG, F;
1959 v E, S, W, Sp; 1960 v E, S, W; 1961 v
E, S, W, I, WG (2), Gr; (with Wolverhampton W.), 1962 v Ho (34)

M'Shane, J. (Cliftonville), 1899 v S; 1900 v E,
S, W (4)

M'Vickers, J. (Glentoran), 1888 v E; 1889 v S
(2)

M'Wha, W.B.R. (Knock), 1882 v E, W; (with
Cliftonville), 1883 v E, W; 1884 v E; 1885 v
E, W (7)

Macartney, A. (Ulster), 1903 v S, W; (with
Linfield), 1904 v S, W; (with Everton),
1905 v E, S; (with Belfast C.), 1907 v E, S,
W; 1908 v E, S, W; (with Glentoran), 1909
v E, S, W (15)

Macauley, J.L. (Huddersfield T.) 1911 v E,
W; 1912 v E, S; 1913 v E, S (6)

Mackey, J. (Arsenal), 1923 v W; (with
Portsmouth), 1935 v S, W (3)

Madden, O. (Norwich C.) 1938 v E (1)

Magill, E.J. (Arsenal), 1962 v E, S, Gr; 1963 v
E, S, W, Pol (2), Sp; 1964 v E, S, W, U, Sp;
1965 v E, S, Sw (2), Ho, Alb; 1966 v S, Alb;
(with Brighton), 1966 v E, W, WG, M (26)

Maginnis, H. (Linfield), 1900 v E, S, W; 1903
v S, W; 1904 v E, S, W (8)

Maguire, E. (Distillery) 1907 v S (1)

Mahood, J. (Belfast C.), 1926 v S; 1928 v E, S,
W; 1929 v E, S, W; 1930 v W; (with
Ballymena), 1934 v S (9)

Manderson, R. (Glasgow R.), 1920 v W, S;
1925 v S, E; 1926 v S (5)

Mansfield, J. (Dublin Freebooters), 1901 v E
(1)

Martin, C. (Bo'ness), 1925 v S (1)

Martin, C.J. (Glentoran), 1947 v S; (with
Leeds U.), 1948 v E, S, W; (with Aston
Villa), 1949 v E; 1950 v W (6)

Martin, D. (Bo'ness), 1925 v S (1)

Martin, D.C. (Cliftonville), 1882 v E, W; 1883 v E (3)

Martin, D.K (Belfast C.), 1934 v E, S, W; 1935 v S; (with Wolverhampton W.), 1935 v E; 1936 v W; (with Nottingham F.), 1937 v S; 1938 v E, S; 1939 v S (10)

Mathieson, A. (Luton T.), 1921 v W; 1922 v E (2)

Maxwell, J. (Linfield), 1902 v W; 1903 v W, E; (with Glentoran), 1905 v W, S; (with Belfast C.), 1906 v W; 1907 v S (7)

Meek, H.L. (Glentoran), 1922 v N (2); 1925 v W (3)

Mehaffy, J.A.C. (Queen's Island), 1922 v W (1)

Meldon, J. (Dublin Freebooters), 1899 v S, W (2)

Mercer, H.V.A. (Linfield), 1908 v E (1)

Mercer, J.T. (Distillery), 1898 v E, S, W; 1899 v E; (with Linfield), 1902 v E, W; (with Distillery), 1903 v S, W; (with Derby Co.), 1904 v E, W; 1905 v S (11)

Millar, W. (Barrow), 1932 v W; 1933 v S (2)

Miller, J. (Middlesbrough), 1929 v W, S; 1930 v E (3)

Milligan, D. (Chesterfield), 1939 v W (1)

Milne, R.G. (Linfield), 1894 v E, S, W; 1895 v E, W; 1896 v E, S, W; 1897 v E, S; 1898 v E, S, W; 1899 v E, W; 1901 v W; 1902 v E, S, W; 1903 v E, S; 1904 v E, S, W; 1906 v E, S, W (27)

Mitchell, C. (Glentoran), 1934 v W (1)

Mitchell, E.J. (Cliftonville), 1933 v S (1)

Mitchell, W. (Distillery), 1932 v E, W; 1933 v E, W (with Chelsea), 1934 v W. S; 1935 v S, E; 1936 v S, E; 1937 v E, S, W; 1938 v E, S (15)

Molyneux, T.B. (Ligoniel), 1883 v E, W; (with Cliftonville) 1884 v E, W, S; 1885 v E, W; 1886 v E, W, S; 1888 v S (11)

Montgomery, F.J. (Coleraine), 1955 v E (1)

Moore, C. (Glentoran), 1949 v W (1)

Moore, J. (Linfield Ath.), 1891 v E, S, W (3)

Moore, P. (Aberdeen), 1933 v E (1)

Moore, T. (Ulster), 1887 v S, W (2)

Moorehead, F.W. (Dublin University), 1885 v E (1)

Moorhead, G. (Linfield); 1923 v S; 1928 v S; 1929 v S (3)

Moran, J. (Leeds C.), 1912 v S (1)

Moreland, V. (Derby Co.), 1979 v Bul (sub), Bul (sub), E, S, E, Ei (6)

Morgan, F.G. (Linfield), 1922 v N (2); 1923 v E; (with Nottingham F.), 1924 v S; 1927 v E; 1928 v E, S, W; 1929 v E (9)

Morgan, S. (Port Vale), 1972 v Sp; 1973 v Bul (sub), P, Cy, E, S, W; (with Aston Villa), 1974 v Bul, P, S, E; 1975 v Se; 1976 v Se, N, Y; (with Brighton & H.A.), S, W (sub); (Sparta Rotterdam), 1979 v D (18)

Morrison, J. (Linfield Ath.), 1891 v E, W (2)

Morrison, T. (Glentoran), 1895 v E, S, W; (with Burnley); 1899 v W; 1900 v W; 1902 v E, S (7)

Morrogh, E. (Bohemians), 1896 v S (1)

Morrow, W.J. (Moyola Park), 1883 v E, W; 1884 v S (3)

Muir, R. (Oldpark), 1885 v S, W (2)

Mulholland, S. (Celtic), 1906 v S, E (2)

Mulligan, J. (Manchester C.), 1921 v S (1)

Murphy, J. (Bradford C.), 1910 v E, S, W (3)

Murphy, N. (Q.P.R.), 1905 v E, S, W (3)

Murray, J.M. (Motherwell), 1910 v E, S; (with Sheffield W.), 1910 v W (3)

Napier, R.J. (Bolton W.), 1966 v WG (1)

Neill, W.J.T. (Arsenal), 1961 v I, Gr, WG; 1962 v E, S, W, Gr; 1963 v E, W, Pol, Sp; 1964 v S, E, W, U, Sp; 1965 v E, S, W, Sw, Ho (2), Alb; 1966 v S, E, W, Alb, WG, M; 1967 v S, W; 1968 v S, E; 1969 v E, S, W, Is, T (2); 1970 v S, E, W, USSR (2); (with Hull C.), 1971 v Cy, Sp; 1972 v USSR (2), Sp, S, E, W; 1973 v Bul, Cy, (2), P, E, S, W (59)

Nelis, P. (Nottingham F.), 1923 v E (1)

Nelson, S. (Arsenal), 1970 v W, E (sub); 1971 v Cy, Sp, E, S, W; 1972 v USSR (2), Sp, E, S, W; 1973 v Bul, Cy, P; 1974 v S, E; 1975 v Se, Y; 1976 v Se, N, Is, E; 1977 v Bel (sub), WG, W, Ic; 1978 v Ic, Ho, Bel, W (sub); 1979 v Ei, D, Bul, E, Bul, E, S, W, D, E, Ei (43)

Nicholl, C.J. (Aston Villa), 1975 v Se, Y, E, S, W; 1976 v Se, N, Y, S, E, W; 1977 v W; (with Southampton), 1978 v Bel (sub), S, E, W; 1979 v Ei; Bul, E, Bul, E, W, Ei (23)

Nicholl, J.M. (Manchester U.), 1976 v Is, W (sub); 1977 v Ho, Bel, E, S, W, Ic; 1978 v Ic, Ho, Bel, S, E, W; 1979 v Ei, D, Bul, E, Bul, E, S, W, D, E, Ei (25)

Nicholl, H. (Belfast C.), 1902 v E, W; 1905 v E (3)

Nicholson, J.J. (Manchester U.), 1961 v S, W; 1962 v E, W, Gr, Ho; 1963 v E, S, Pol (2); (with Huddersfield T.), 1965 v W, Ho (2); Alb; 1966 v S, E, W, Alb, M; 1967 v S, W; 1968 v S, E, W; 1969 v S, E, W, T (2); 1970 v S, E, W, USSR (2); 1971 v Cy (2), E, S, W; 1972 v USSR (2) (41)

Nixon, R. (Linfield), 1914 v S (1)

Nolan-Whelan, J.V. (Dublin Freebooters), 1901 E, W; 1902 v S, W (4)

O'Brien, M.T. (Q.P.R.), 1921 v S; (with Leicester C.), 1922 v S, W; 1924 v S, W; (with Hull C.), 1925 v S, E, W; 1926 v W; (with Derby Co.), 1927 v W (10)

O'Connell, P. (Sheffield W.), 1912 v E, S; (with Hull C.), 1914 v E, S, W (5)

141

O'Doherty, A. (Coleraine), 1970 v E, W (sub) (2)

O'Driscoll, J.F. (Swansea T.), 1949 v E, S, W (3)

O'Hagan, C. (Tottenham H.), 1905 v S, W; 1906 v S, W, E; (with Aberdeen), 1907 v E, S, W; 1908 v S, W; 1909 v E (11)

O'Hagan, W. (St. Mirren), 1920 v E, W (2)

O'Hehir, J.C. (Bohemians), 1910 v W (1)

O'Kane, W.J. (Nottingham F.), 1970 v E, W, S (sub); 1971 v Sp, E, S, W; 1972 v USSR (2), 1973 v P, Cy; 1974 v Bul, P, S, E, W; 1975 v N; Se, E, S (20)

O'Mahoney, M.T. (Bristol R.), 1939 v S (1)

O'Neill, J. (Sunderland), 1962 v W (1)

O'Neill, M.H. (Distillery), 1972 v USSR (sub); (with Nottingham F.), Sp (sub), W (sub); 1973 v P, Cy, E, S, W; 1974 v Bul, P, E (sub), W; 1975 v Se, Y, E, S; 1976 v Y; 1977 v E (sub), S; 1978 v Ic, Ho, S, E, W; 1979 v Ei, D, Bul, E, Bul, D, Ei (31)

O'Reilly, H. (Dublin Freebooters), 1901 v S, W; 1904 v S (3)

Parke, J. (Linfield), 1964 v S; (with Hibernian), 1964 v E, Sp; (with Sunderland), 1965 v Sw; 1965 v S, W, Ho (2), Alb; 1966 v WG; 1967 v E, S; 1968 v S, E (14)

Peacock, R. (Celtic), 1952 v S; 1953 v F; 1954 v W; 1955 v E, S; 1956 v E, S; 1957 v W, I, P; 1958 v S, E, W, I (2), Arg, Cz (2) WG; 1959 v E, S, W, Sp; 1960 v S, E; 1961 v E, S, I, WG (2), Gr; (with Coleraine), 1962 v S (32)

Peden, J. (Linfield), 1887 v S, W; 1888 v W, E; 1889 v S, E; 1890 v W, S; 1891 v W, E; 1892 v W, E; 1893 v E, S, W; (with Distillery), 1896 v W, E, S; 1897 v W, S; 1898 v W, E, S; (with Linfield), 1899 v W (24)

Percy, J.C. (Belfast YMCA), 1889 v W (1)

Platt, J.A. (Middlesbrough), 1976 v Is (sub); 1978 v S, E, W (4)

Ponsonby, J. (Distillery), 1895 v S; 1896 v E, S, W; 1897 v E, S, W; 1899 v E (8)

Potts, R.M.C. (Cliftonville), 1883 v E, W (2)

Priestley, T.J. (Coleraine), 1933 v S; (with Chelsea), 1934 v E (2)

Pyper, Jas. (Cliftonville), 1897 v S, W; 1898 v S, E, W; 1899 v S; 1900 v E (7)

Pyper, John (Cliftonville), 1897 v E, S, W; 1899 v E, W; 1900 v E, W, S; 1902 v S (9)

Pyper, M. (Linfield), 1931 v W (1)

Rafferty, P. (Linfield), 1979 v E (sub) (1)

Rankine, J. (Alexander), 1883 v E, W (2)

Raper, E.O. (Dublin University), 1886 v W (1)

Rattray, D. (Avoniel), 1882 v E; 1883 v E, W (3)

Rea, B. (Glentoran), 1901 v E (1)

Redmond, J. (Cliftonville), 1884 v W (1)

Reid, G.H. (Cardiff C.), 1923 v S (1)

Reid, J. (Ulster), 1883 v E; 1884 v W; 1887 v S; 1889 v W; 1890 v S, W (6)

Reid, S.E. (Derby Co.), 1934 v E, W; 1936 v E (3)

Reid, W. (Hearts), 1931 v E (1)

Reilly, J. (Portsmouth), 1900 v E; 1902 v E (2)

Renneville, W.T. (Leyton), 1910 v S, E, W; (with Aston Villa), 1911 v W (4)

Reynolds, J. (Distillery), 1890 v E, W; (with Ulster), 1891 v E, S, W (5)

Reynolds, R. (Bohemians), 1905 v W (1)

Rice, P.J. (Arsenal), 1969 v Is; 1970 v USSR; 1971 v E, S, W; 1972 v USSR, Sp, E, S, W; 1973 v Bul, Cy, E, S, W; 1974 v Bul, P, S, E, W; 1975 v N, Y, E, S, W; 1976 v Se, N, Y, Is, S, E, W; 1977 v Ho, Bel, WG, E, S, Ic; 1978 v Ic, Ho, Bel; 1979 v Ei, D, E (2), S, W, D, E (49)

Roberts, F.C. (Glentoran), 1931 v S (1)

Robinson, P. (Distillery), 1920 v S; (with Blackburn R.), 1921 v W (2)

Rollo, D. (Linfield), 1912 v W; 1913 v W; 1914 v W, E; (with Blackburn R.), 1920 v S, W; 1921 v E, S, W; 1922 v E; 1923 v E; 1924 v S, W; 1925 v W; 1926 v E; 1927 v E (16)

Rosbotham, A. (Cliftonville), 1887 v E, S, W; 1888 v E, S, W; 1889 v E (7)

Ross, W.E. (Newcastle U.), 1969 v Is (1)

Rowley, R.W.M. (Southampton), 1929 v S, W; 1930 v W, E; (with Tottenham H.), 1931 v W; 1932 v S (6)

Russell, A. (Linfield), 1947 v E (1)

Russell, S.R. (Bradford C.), 1930 v E, S; (with Derry C.), 1932 v E (3)

Ryan, R.A. (W.B.A.), 1950 v W (1)

Scott, E. (Liverpool), 1920 v S; 1921 v E, S, W; 1922 v E; 1925 v W; 1926 v E, S, W; 1927 v E, S, W; 1928 v E, S, W; 1929 v E, S, W; 1930 v E; 1931 v E; 1932 v S; 1933 v E, S, W; 1934 v E, S, W; (with Belfast Celtic), 1935 v S; 1936 v E, S, W (30)

Scott, J. (Grimsby), 1958 v Cz, F (2)

Scott, J.E. (Cliftonville), 1901 v S (1)

Scott, L.J. (Dublin University), 1895 v S, W (2)

Scott, P.W. (Everton), 1975 v W; 1976 v Y (with York C.), Is, S, E (sub), W; 1978 v S, E, W; (Aldershot), 1979 v S (sub) (10)

Scott, T. (Cliftonville), 1894 v E, S; 1895 v S, W; 1896 v S, E, W; 1897 v E, W; 1898 v E, S, W; 1900 v W (13)

Scott, W. (Linfield), 1903 v E, S, W; 1904 v E, S, W; (with Everton) 1905 v E, S; 1907 v E, S; 1908 v E, S, W; 1909 v E, S, W; 1910 v E, S; 1911 v E, S, W; 1912 v E; (with Leeds City) 1913 v E, S, W (25)

Scraggs, M.J. (Glentoran), 1921 v W; 1922 v E (2)

Seymour, H.C. (Bohemians), 1914 v W (1)

Seymour, J. (Cliftonville), 1907-9 v W (2)

Shanks, T. (Woolwich Arsenal), 1903 v S; 1904 v W; (with Brentford), 1905 v E (3)

Sharkey, P. (Ipswich T.), 1976 v S (1)

Sheehan, Dr. G. (Bohemians), 1899 v S; 1900 v E, W (3)

Sheridan, J. (Everton), 1903 v W, E, S; 1904 v E, S; (with Stoke C.), 1905 v E (6)

Sherrard, J. (Limavady), 1885 v S; 1887 v W; 1888 v W (3)

Sherrard, W. (Cliftonville), 1895 v E, W, S (3)

Sherry, J.J. (Bohemians), 1906 v E; 1907 v W (2)

Shields, J. (Southampton), 1957 v S (1)

Silo, M. (Belfast YMCA), 1888 v E (1)

Simpson, W.J. (Glasgow R.), 1951 v W, F; 1954 v E, S; 1955 v E; 1957 v I, P; 1958 v S, E, W, I; 1959 v S (12)

Sinclair, J. (Knock), 1882 v E, W (2)

Slemin, J.C. (Bohemians), 1909 v W (1)

Sloan, A.S. (London Caledonians), 1925 v W (1)

Sloan, D (Oxford U.), 1969 v Is; 1971 v Sp (2)

Sloan, H.A. de B. (Bohemians), 1903 v E; 1904 v S; 1905 v E; 1906 v W; 1907 v E, W; 1908 v W; 1909 v S (8)

Sloan, J.W. (Arsenal), 1947 v W (1)

Sloan, T. (Cardiff C.), 1926 v S, W, E; 1927 v W, S; 1928 v E, W; 1929 v E; (with Linfield), 1930 v W, S; 1931 v S (11)

Sloan, T. (Manchester U.), 1979 v S, W (sub), D (sub) (3)

Small, J. (Clarence), 1887 v E (1)

Small, J.M. (Cliftonville) 1893 v E, S, W (3)

Smith, E.E. (Cardiff C.), 1921 v S; 1923 v W, E; 1924 v E (4)

Smith, J. (Distillery), 1901 v S, W (2)

Smyth, R.H. (Dublin University), 1886 v W (1)

Smyth, S. (Wolverhampton W.), 1948 v E, S, W; 1949 v S, W; 1950 v E, S, W; (with Stoke C.), 1952 v E (9)

Smyth, W. (Distillery), 1949 v E, S; 1954 v S, E (4)

Snape, A. (Airdrie), 1920 v E (1)

Spence, D.W. (Bury), 1975 v Y, E, S, W; 1976 v Se, Is, E, W, S (sub); (with Blackpool); 1977 v Ho (sub), WG (sub), E (sub), S (sub), W (sub), Ic (sub); 1979 v Ei, D (sub), E (sub), Bul (sub), E (sub), S, W, D, Ei (24)

Spencer, S. (Distillery), 1890 v E, S; 1892 v E, S, W; 1893 v E (6)

Spiller, E.A. (Cliftonville), 1883 v E, W; 1884 v E, W, S (5)

Stanfield, O.M. (Distillery), 1887 v E, S, W; 1888 v E, S, W; 1889 v E, S, W; 1890 v E, S; 1891 v E, S, W, 1892 v E, S, W; 1893 v E, W; 1894 v E, S, W; 1895 v E, S; 1896 v E, S, W; 1897 v E, S, W (30)

Steele, A. (Charlton Ath.), 1926 v W, S; (with Fulham), 1929 v W, S (4)

Stevenson, A.E. (Rangers), 1934 v E, S, W; (with Everton), 1935 v E, S; 1936 v S, W; 1937 v E, W; 1938 v E, W; 1939 v E, S, W; 1947 v S, W; 1948 v S (17)

Stewart, A. (Glentoran), 1967 v W; 1968 v S, E; (with Derby Co.), 1968 v W; 1969 v Is, T (1+1 sub) (7)

Stewart, D.C., (Hull C.), 1978 v Bel (1)

Stewart, R.H. (St. Columb's Court), 1890 v E, S, W; (with Cliftonville), 1892 v E, S, W; 1893 v E, W; 1894 v E, S, W (11)

Stewart, T.C. (Linfield), 1961 v W (1)

Swan, S. (Linfield), 1899 v S (1)

Taggart, J. (Walsall), 1899 v W (1)

Thompson, F.W. (Cliftonville), 1910 v E, S, W; (with Bradford C.), 1911 v E, (with Linfield), v W; 1912 v E, W; 1913 v E, S, W; (with Clyde), 1914 v E, S (12)

Thompson, J. (Distillery), 1897 v S (1)

Thompson, J. (Belfast Ath.), 1889 v S (1)

Thunder, P.J. (Bohemians), 1911 v W (1)

Todd, S.J. (Burnley), 1966 v M (sub); 1967 v E; 1968 v W; 1969 v E, S, W; 1970 v S, USSR (Sheffield W.), 1971 v Cy (2) Sp (sub) (11)

Toner, J. (Arsenal), 1922 v W; 1923 v W; 1924 v W, E; 1925 v E, S; (with St. Johnstone), 1927 v E, S (8)

Torrans, R. (Linfield), 1893 v S (1)

Torrans, S. (Linfield), 1889 v S; 1890 v S, W; 1891 v S, W; 1892 v E, S, W; 1893 v E, S; 1894 v E, S, W; 1895 v E; 1896 v E, S, W; 1897 v E, S, W; 1898 v E, S, W; 1899 v E; 1901 v S, W (26)

Trainor, D. (Crusaders), 1967 v W (1)

Tully, C.P. (Glasgow C.), 1949 v E; 1950 v E; 1952 v S; 1953 v E, S, W, F; 1954 v S; 1956 v E; 1959 v Sp (10)

Turner, E. (Cliftonville), 1896 v E, W (2)

Turner, W. (Cliftonville), 1886 v E; 1887 v S; 1888 v S (3)

Twoomey, J.F. (Leeds U.), 1938 v W; 1939 v E (2)

Uprichard, N. (Distillery, Swindon, Portsmouth), 1951-52, v S, E, W; 1952-53, v E, S, F, W; 1954-55, v E, S, W; 1955-56, v S, E, W; 1957-58, v S, I, Cz; 1958-59, v S, Sp (18)

Vernon, J. (Belfast C.), 1947 v E, S; (with W.B.A.), 1947 v W; 1948 v E, S, W; 1949 v E, S, W; 1950 v E, S; 1951 v E, S, W, F; 1952 v S, E (17)

Waddell, T.M.R. (Cliftonville), 1906 v S (1)
Walker, J. (Doncaster R.), 1955 v W (1)
Walker, T. (Bury), 1911 v S (1)
Walsh, D.J. (W.B.A.), 1947 v S, W; 1948 v E, S, W; 1949 v E, S, W; 1950 v W (9)
Walsh, W. (Manchester C.), 1948 v E, S, W; 1949 v E, S (5)
Waring, R. (Distillery), 1899 v E (1)
Warren, P. (Shelbourne), 1913 v E, S (2)
Watson, J. (Ulster), 1883 v E, W; 1886 v E, S, W; 1887 v S, W; 1889 v E, W (9)
Watson, P. (Distillery), 1971 v Cy (sub), (1)
Watson, T. (Cardiff C.), 1926 v S (1)
Wattie, J. (Distillery), 1899 v E (1)
Webb, C.G. (Brighton), 1909 v S, W; 1911 v S (3)
Weir, E. (Clyde), 1939 v W (1)
Welsh, E. (Carlisle U.), 1966 v W, WG, M; 1967 v W (4)
Whiteside, T. (Distillery), 1891 v E (1)
Whitfield, E.R. (Dublin University), 1886 v W (1)

Williams J.R. (Ulster), 1886 v E, W (2)
Williamson, J. (Cliftonville), 1890 v E; 1892 v S, 1893 v S (3)
Willingham, T. (Burnley), 1933 v W; 1934 v S (2)
Willis, G. (Linfield), 1906 v S, W; 1907 v S; 1912 v S (4)
Wilson, H. (Linfield), 1925 v W (1)
Wilson, M. (Distillery), 1884 v E, S, W (3)
Wilson, R. (Cliftonville), 1888 v S (1)
Wilson, S.J. (Glenavon), 1962 v S; 1964 v S; (with Falkirk), 1964 v E, W, U, Sp; 1965 v E, Sw; (with Dundee), 1966 v W, WG; 1967 v S; 1968 v E (12)
Wilton, J.M. (St. Columb's Court), 1888 v E, W; 1889 v S, E; (with Cliftonville), 1890 v E; (with St. Columb's Court), 1892 v W; 1893 v S (7)
Wright, J. (Cliftonville), 1906 v E, S, W; 1907 v E, S, W (6)

Young, S. (Linfield), 1907 v E, S; 1908 v E, S; (with Airdrie), 1909 v E; 1912 v S; (with Linfield), 1914 v E, S, W (9)

Note:— J. Reynolds also played for England against S, W, I, 1892-1897. His English clubs were W.B.A. and Aston Villa.

4: VICTORY INTERNATIONALS— 1919

Emerson, W. (Glentoran), S (2)
Halligan, W. (Hull City), S (2)
Hamill, M. (Belfast Celtic), S (2)
Kerr, E. (Belfast Celtic), S
Lacey, W. (Linfield and Liverpool), S (2)
Lyner, D. (Glentoran), S
McCandless, W. (Linfield), S
McCracken, W. (Newcastle United), S (2)
McKinney, D. (Belfast Celtic), S (2)
Moore, W. (Glentoran), S
O'Connell, P. (Manchester United), S
Rollo, D. (Linfield), S (2)
Scott, E. (Liverpool), S (2)
Scraggs, J. (Glentoran), S

5: VICTORY INTERNATIONALS— 1946

Aherne, T. (Belfast Celtic), S, W
Bonnar, P. (Belfast Celtic), E, S
Breen, T. (Linfield), E, S, W
Carey, J. (Manchester Utd), S, W
Doherty, P. (Derby Co.), E, W
Feeney, J. (Linfield), E, S
Jones, S. (Blackpool), E
McCarthy, S. (Belfast Celtic), E
McKenna (Linfield), E, W
McMillan, W. (Belfast Celtic), E, S, W
O'Flanagan, Dr. K. (Arsenal), S, W
Sloan, W. (Tranmere Rovers), E, W
Stevenson, A. (Everton), S
Todd, J. (Blackpool), E, S
Vernon, J. (Belfast Celtic), E, S, W
Walsh, D. (Linfield), S, W
Waters, P. (Glentoran), W

Substitutes in brackets

1882 England	1882 Wales	1883 England	1883 Wales	1884 Scotland
1 Hamilton	1 Hamilton	1 Rankine	1 Rankine	1 Hunter
2 McAlevy	2 Crone, W.	2 Watson	2 Watson	2 Wilson
3 Rattray	3 McAlevy	3 Rattray	3 Rattray	3 Crone, W.
4 Martin	4 Martin	4 Molyneux	4 Molyneux	4 Hastings
5 Hastings	5 Hastings	5 Martin	5 Hastings	5 Molyneux
6 Buckle	6 Davison	6 Morrow	6 Morrow	6 Dill
7 McWha	7 McWha	7 Potts	7 Potts	7 Spiller
8 Davison	8 Condy	8 McWha	8 McWha	8 Gibb
9 Sinclair	9 Sinclair	9 Davison	9 Davison	9 Morrow
10 Dill	10 Dill	10 Buckle	10 Spiller	10 Davison
11 McCaw	11 Johnston	11 Dill	11 Dill	11 Gaussen
Belfast **Feb 18: 0-13**	**Wrexham** **Feb 25: 1-7** **Johnston**	**Liverpool** **Feb 24: 0-7**	**Belfast** **Mar 17: 1-1** **Morrow**	**Belfast** **Jan 26: 0-5**

1884 Wales	1884 England	1885 England	1885 Scotland	1885 Wales
1 Hunter	1 Hunter	1 Henderson	1 Henderson	1 Henderson
2 Wilson	2 Wilson	2 Hewison	2 Hewison	2 Johnston
3 Crone, W.	3 Crone, W.	3 Moorehead	3 Johnson	3 Eames
4 Molyneux	4 Hastings	4 Molyneux	4 Muir	4 Molyneux
5 Lockhart	5 Molyneux	5 Houston	5 Houston	5 Muir
6 Redman	6 Dill	6 Eames	6 Eames	6 McWha
7 Davison	7 Spiller	7 McWha	7 McLean	7 Hamilton, W.J.
8 Gibb	8 McWha	8 Davison	8 Sherrard	8 Hamilton, W.D.
9 Reid	9 Johnson	9 Gibb	9 Gibb	9 Gibb
10 Spiller	10 Davison	10 McGee	10 McGee	10 McGee
11 Dill	11 Gaussen	11 Dill	11 Dill	11 Dill
Wrexham **Feb. 9: 0-6**	**Belfast** **Feb. 23: 1-8** **McWha**	**Manchester** **Feb 28: 0-4**	**Glasgow** **Mar 14: 2-8** **Gibb 2**	**Belfast** **April 11: 2-8** **Molyneux, Dill**

1886 Wales	1886 England	1886 Scotland	1887 England	1887 Scotland
1 Gillespie	1 Gillespie	1 Gillespie	1 Gillespie	1 Gillespie
2 Watson	2 Watson	2 Watson	2 Browne	2 Fox
3 Devine	3 Devine	3 Crone, W.	3 Fox	3 Watson
4 Molyneux	4 Molyneux	4 Molyneux	4 Rosbotham	4 Moore
5 Crone, W.	5 Crone, W.	5 Williams	5 Leslie	5 Rosbotham
6 McArthur	6 Hastings	6 Hastings	6 Crone, W.	6 Baxter
7 McClatchey	7 Turner	7 McClatchey	7 Allen	7 Reid
8 Smyth	8 Condy	8 Johnson	8 Gibb	8 Stanfield
9 Whitfield	9 Johnson	9 Gibb	9 Stanfield	9 Browne
10 Lemon	10 McClatchey	10 Condy	10 Small	10 Peden
11 Raper	11 Williams	11 Turner	11 Whitfield	11 Gibb
Wrexham **Feb 27: 0-5**	**Belfast** **Mar 13: 1-6** **Williams**	**Belfast** **Mar 20: 2-7** **Condy, Johnson**	**Sheffield** **Feb 5: 0-7**	**Glasgow** **Feb: 19: 1-4** **Browne**

145

1887 Wales	1888 Wales	1888 Scotland	1888 England	1889 England
1 Gillespie	1 Clugston	1 Lowther	1 Lowther	1 Clugston
2 Browne	2 Forbes	2 Wilson	2 McVickers	2 Goodbody
3 Watson	3 Crone, W.	3 Browne	3 Browne	3 Watson
4 Sherrard	4 Sherrard	4 Forsyth	4 Forsyth	4 Crawford
5 Rosbotham	5 Rosbotham	5 Rosbotham	5 Rosbotham	5 Rosbotham
6 Devine	6 Devine	6 Molyneux	6 Crone, W.	6 Cooke
7 Moore	7 Gaussen	7 Dalton	7 Gaussen	7 Gaussen
8 Baxter	8 Stanfield	8 Stanfield	8 Stanfield	8 Stanfield
9 Gibb	9 Berry	9 Berry	9 Silo	9 Berry
10 Stanfield	10 Wilton	10 Lemon	10 Wilton	10 Wilton
11 Peden	11 Peden	11 Turner	11 Peden	11 Peden
Belfast **Mar 12: 4-1** Stanfield, Browne, Peden, Sherrard	**Wrexham** **Mar 3: 0-11**	**Belfast** **Mar 24: 2-10** Lemon Dalton	**Belfast** **April 7: 1-5** Crone	**Liverpool** **Mar 2: 1-6** Wilton

1889 Scotland	1889 Wales	1890 Wales	1890 England	1890 Scotland
1 Clugston	1 Clugston	1 Galbraith	1 Clugston	1 Clugston
2 McVickers	2 Elleman	2 Crone, R.	2 Stewart	2 Stewart
3 Crone, R.	3 Watson	3 Stewart	3 Crone, R.	3 Crone, R
4 Thomson	4 Crawford	4 Crone, W.	4 Williamson	4 Reid
5 Christian	5 Bennett	5 Reynolds	5 Spencer	5 Spencer
6 Crone, W.	6 Reid	6 Reid	6 Cooke	6 Cooke
7 Torrans, S.	7 Gaussen	7 Dalton	7 Elleman	7 Dalton
8 Stanfield	8 Stanfield	8 Gaffikin	8 Stanfield	8 Gaffikin
9 Gibb	9 Percy	9 Johnston	9 Wilton	9 Stanfield
10 Wilton	10 Lemon	10 Torrans, S.	10 McIlvenny	10 Torrans, S.
11 Peden	11 Gillespie	11 Peden	11 Reynolds	11 Peden
Glasgow **Mar 9: 0-7**	**Belfast** **April 27: 1-3** Lemon	**Shrewsbury** **Feb 8: 2-5** Dalton 2	**Belfast** **Mar 15: 1-9** Reynolds	**Belfast** **Mar 29: 1-4** Peden

1891 Wales	1891 England	1891 Scotland	1892 Wales	1892 England
1 Clugston	1 Clugston	1 Loyal	1 Clugston	1 Clugston
2 Goodbody	2 Forbes	2 Gordon	2 Gordon	2 Gordon
2 Morris	3 Morrison	3 Forbes	3 Stewart	3 Stewart
4 Crawford	4 Crawford	4 Crawford	4 McKeown	4 McKeown
5 Reynolds	5 Reynolds	5 Reynolds	5 Spencer	5 Spencer
6 Moore	6 Moore	6 Moore	6 Cunningham	6 Cunningham
7 Dalton	7 Whitehead	7 Dalton	7 Dalton	7 Dalton
8 Gaffikin	8 Stanfield	8 Gaffikin	8 Gaffikin	8 Gaffikin
9 Stanfield	9 McCabe	9 Stanfield	9 Stanfield	9 Stanfield
10 Torrans, S.	10 McIlvenny	10 Brisby	10 Torrans, S.	10 Torrans, S.
11 Peden	11 Peden	11 Torrans, S.	11 Peden	11 Peden
Belfast **Feb 7: 7-2** Dalton 3 Gaffikin 2 Stanfield 2	**Wolverhampton** **Mar 7: 1-6** Whitehead	**Glasgow** **Mar 28: 2-1** Stanfield	**Bangor** **Feb 27: 1-1** Stanfield	**Belfast** **Mar 5: 0-2**

146

1892 Scotland	1893 England	1893 Scotland	1893 Wales	1894 Wales
1 Clugston	1 Clugston	1 Clugston	1 Clugston	1 Gordon
2 Gordon	2 Gordon	2 Gordon	2 Gordon	2 Stewart
3 Stewart	3 Stewart	3 Torrans, R.	3 Stewart	3 Torrans, S.
4 McKeown	4 Crawford	4 McKeown	4 Crawford	4 McKeown
5 Spencer	5 Spencer	5 Johnston	5 McKeown	5 Burnett
6 Cunningham	6 Cunningham	6 Torrans, S.	6 Johnston	6 Milne
7 Dalton	7 Small	7 Small	7 Small	7 Dalton
8 Gaffikin	8 Gaffikin	8 Gaffikin	8 Gaffikin	8 Gaffikin
9 Williamson	9 Stanfield	9 Williamson	9 Stanfield	9 Stanfield
10 Stanfield	10 Torrans, S.	10 Wilton	10 Wilton	10 Gibson
11 Torrans, S.	11 Peden	11 Peden	11 Peden	11 Baron

Belfast	**Birmingham**	**Glasgow**	**Belfast**	**Swansea**
Mar 19: 2-3	**Feb 25: 1-6**	**Mar 25: 1-6**	**April 5: 4-3**	**Feb 24: 1-4**
Williamson	**Gaffikin**	**Gaffikin**	**Peden 3**	**Stanfield**
Gaffikin			**Wilton**	

1894 England	1894 Scotland	1895 England	1895 Wales	1895 Scotland
1 Scott, T.	1 Scott, T.	1 Gordon, T.	1 Scott, T.	1 Scott, T.
2 Stewart	2 Stewart	2 Gordon, H.	2 Gordon, H.	2 Ponsonby
3 Torrans, S.	3 Torrans, S.	3 Torrans, S.	3 Scott, L.J.	3 Scott, L.J.
4 Johnston	4 McKeown	4 McKie	4 McKie	4 McKie
5 Burnett	5 Burnett	5 Milne	5 Milne	5 Alexander
6 Milne	6 Milne	6 Burnett	6 Burnett	6 McClatchey
7 Dalton	7 Dalton	7 Morrison	7 Morrison	7 Morrison
8 Gaffikin	8 Gaffikin	8 Gaffikin	8 Sherrard	8 Sherrard
9 Stanfield	9 Stanfield	9 Stanfield	9 Jordan	9 Stanfield
10 Gibson	10 Gibson	10 Sherrard	10 Gawkrodger	10 Gibson
11 Barron	11 Barron	11 Jordan	11 Gaffikin	11 Barron

Belfast	**Belfast**	**Derby**	**Belfast**	**Glasgow**
Mar 3: 2-2	**Mar 31: 1-2**	**Mar 9: 0-9**	**Mar 16: 2-2**	**Mar 30: 1-3**
Stanfield	**Stanfield**		**Gawkrodger**	**Sherrard**
Gibson			**Sherrard**	

1896 Wales	1896 England	1896 Scotland	1897 England	1897 Wales
1 Scott, T.	1 Scott, T.	1 Scott, T.	1 Scott, T.	1 Scott, T.
2 Ponsonby	2 Ponsonby	2 Ponsonby	2 Ponsonby	2 Gibson
3 Torrans, S.	3 Torrans, S.	3 Torrans, S.	3 Torrans, S.	3 Torrans, S.
4 McCoy	4 Fitzpatrick	4 Gordon	4 Pyper, John	4 Pyper, John
5 Milne	5 Milne	5 Milne	5 Milne	5 Ponsonby
6 Campbell	6 Gordon, H.	6 Fitzpatrick	6 McMaster	6 McMaster
7 Turner	7 Baird	7 Baird	7 Campbell	7 Campbell
8 Baird	8 Kelly	8 Morrogh	8 Hall	8 Stanfield
9 Stanfield	9 Stanfield	9 Stanfield	9 Stanfield	9 Pyper, James
10 McCashin	10 Turner	10 Barron	10 Darling	10 Peden
11 Peden	11 Peden	11 Peden	11 Barron	11 Barron

Wrexham	**Belfast**	**Belfast**	**Nottingham**	**Belfast**
Feb 29: 1-6	**Mar 7: 0-2**	**Mar 28: 3-3**	**Feb 20: 0-6**	**Mar 6: 4-3**
Turner		**Barron 2**		**Barron, Stanfield,**
		Milne (pen.)		**John Pyper, Peden**

1897 Scotland	1898 Wales	1898 England	1898 Scotland	1899 England
1 Thompson	1 Scott, T.	1 Scott, T.	1 Scott, T.	1 Lewis
2 Ponsonby	2 Gibson	2 Gibson	2 Gibson	2 Pyper, John
3 Torrans, S.	3 Cochrane	3 Torrans, S.	3 Torrans, S.	3 Torrans, S.
4 Pyper, John	4 Anderson	4 Anderson	4 Anderson	4 Ponsonby
5 Milne	5 Milne	5 Milne	5 Milne	5 Milne
6 McMaster	6 Little	6 Cochrane	6 Cochrane	6 Cochrane
7 Campbell	7 Campbell	7 Campbell	7 Campbell	7 Campbell
8 Stanfield	8 Mercer	8 Mercer	8 Mercer	8 Mercer
9 Pyper, James	9 Pyper, James	9 Pyper, James	9 Pyper, James	9 Waring
10 Darling	10 McCartney	10 Peden	10 McCashin	10 McWhattie
11 Peden	11 Peden	11 McAllen	11 Peden	11 McAllen
Glasgow	**Llandudno**	**Belfast**	**Belfast**	**Sunderland**
Mar 27: 1-5	**Feb 19: 1-0**	**Mar 5: 2-3**	**Mar 26: 0-3**	**Feb 18: 2-13**
James Pyper	**Peden**	**Pyper, Mercer**		**McAllen, Campbell**

1899 Wales	1899 Scotland	1900 Wales	1900 Scotland	1900 England
1 Lewis	1 Lewis	1 Scott, T.	1 Lewis	1 Reilly
2 Pyper, John	2 Swan	2 Pyper, John	2 Pyper, John	2 Pyper, John
3 Torrans, S.	3 Forman	3 Cochrane	3 Cochrane	3 Cochrane
4 Goodall	4 Anderson	4 McShane	4 McShane	4 McShane
5 Milne	5 Goodall	5 Goodall	5 Berry	5 Goodall
6 Taggart	6 McShane	6 Maginnis	6 Maginnis	6 Maginnis
7 Morrison	7 Sheehan	7 Sheehan	7 Campbell	7 Sheehan
8 Meldon	8 Meldon	8 Morrison	8 Darling	8 Campbell
9 Hannah	9 Pyper, James	9 Kirwan	9 McAuley	9 Pyper, James
10 McAllen	10 McCashin	10 Kearns	10 McAllen	10 McAllen
11 Peden	11 McAllen	11 McAllen	11 Kearns	11 Kearns
Belfast	**Glasgow**	**Llandudno**	**Belfast**	**Dublin**
Mar 4: 1-0	**Mar 25: 1-9**	**Feb 24: 0-2**	**Mar 3: 0-3**	**Mar 17: 0-2**
Meldon	**Goodall**			

1901 Scotland	1901 England	1901 Wales	1902 Wales	1902 Scotland
1 McAlpine	1 Nolan-Whelan	1 Nolan-Whelan	1 Nolan-Whelan	1 Nolan-Whelan
2 Gibson	2 Gibson	2 Gibson	2 Gibson	2 Gibson
3 Torrans, S.	3 Boyle	3 Torrans, S.	3 McCracken, V.	3 Pyper, John
4 Farrell	4 Connor	4 Farrell	4 Darling	4 Darling
5 Connor	5 Goodall	5 Milne	5 Milne	5 Goodall
6 Cochrane	6 Burnison	6 Burnison	6 Nicholl	6 Milne
7 Scott, J.	7 Black	7 Campbell	7 Mercer	7 Campbell
8 Smith, J.	8 Rea	8 Smith, J.	8 Maxwell	8 Morrison
9 Campbell	9 Mansfield	9 McKelvie	9 Gara	9 Gara
10 O'Reilly	10 Doherty	10 O'Reilly	10 Kearns	10 Kearns
11 Clarke	11 Clarke	11 McAllen	11 Kirwan	11 McAllen
Glasgow	**Southampton**	**Belfast**	**Cardiff**	**Belfast**
Feb 23: 0-11	**Mar 9: 0-3**	**Mar 23: 0-1**	**Feb 22: 3-0**	**Mar 1: 1-3**
			Gara 3	**Milne**

1902 England	1903 England	1903 Scotland	1903 Wales	1904 England
1 Reilly	1 Scott, W.	1 Scott, W.	1 Scott, W.	1 Scott, W.
2 McCracken, W.	2 McCracken	2 McCartney	2 McCartney	2 McCracken
3 Boyle	3 McMillan	3 Boyle	3 Boyle	3 Boyle
4 Darling	4 Darling	4 Darling	4 Darling	4 Milne
5 Milne	5 Milne	5 Milne	5 Goodall	5 Goodall
6 Nicholl	6 Goodall	6 Maginnis	6 Maginnis	6 Maginnis
7 Mercer	7 Campbell	7 Mercer	7 Mercer	7 Mercer
8 Morrison	8 Maxwell	8 Sheridan	8 Maxwell	8 Sheridan
9 Gara	9 Sheridan	9 Connor	9 Connor	9 Connor
10 Kearns	10 Sloan	10 Shanks	10 Sheridan	10 Kirwan
11 Kirwan	11 Kirwan	11 Kirwan	11 Kirwan	11 Buckle
Belfast **Mar 22: 0-1**	**Wolverhampton** **Feb 14: 0-4**	**Glasgow** **Mar 21: 2-0** **Connor** **Kirwan**	**Belfast** **Mar 28: 2-0** **Goodall** **Sheridan**	**Belfast** **Mar 12: 1-3** **Kirwan**

1904 Wales	1904 Scotland	1905 England	1905 Scotland	1905 Wales
1 Scott, W.	1 Scott, W.	1 Scott, W.	1 Scott, W.	1 Reynolds
2 McCracken	2 McCracken	2 McCracken	2 McCartney	2 McCracken
3 McCartney	3 McCartney	3 McCartney	3 McCracken	3 McMillan
4 McConnell	4 McConnell	4 Darling	4 Darling	4 Darling
5 Milne	5 Milne	5 Connor	5 Connor	5 Connor
6 Maginnis	6 Maginnis	6 Nicholl	6 McConnell	6 Johnstone
7 Mercer	7 Campbell	7 Sloan	7 Mercer	7 Hunter
8 Shanks	8 Sheridan	8 Sheridan	8 Maxwell	8 Maxwell
9 Goodall	9 O'Reilly	9 Murphy	9 Murphy	9 Murphy
10 Kirkwood	10 Sloan	10 Shanks	10 O'Hagan	10 O'Hagan
11 Kirwan	11 Kirwan	11 Kirwan	11 Kirwan	11 Kirwan
Bangor **Mar 21: 1-0** **McCracken** **(pen.)**	**Dublin** **Mar 26: 1-1** **Sheridan**	**Middlesbrough** **Feb 25: 1-1** **Williamson o.g.**	**Glasgow** **Mar 18: 0-4**	**Belfast** **April 8: 2-2**

1906 England	1906 Scotland	1906 Wales	1907 England	1907 Wales
1 Sherry	1 McKee	1 McKee	1 Scott, W.	1 Sherry
2 Darling	2 Willis	2 Willis	2 McCracken	2 Seymour
3 McIlroy	3 Darling	3 Darling	3 McCartney	3 McCartney
4 Wright	4 Wright	4 Wright	4 Wright	4 Wright
5 Milne	5 Milne	5 Milne	5 Connor	5 Crothers
6 McDonnell	6 Ledwidge	6 Ledwidge	6 McConnell	6 McClure
7 Hunter	7 Hunter	7 Hunter	7 Blair	7 Blair
8 Mulholland	8 Mulholland	8 Maxwell	8 Harris	8 Harris
9 Harris	9 Waddell	9 O'Hagan	9 Sloan	9 Sloan
10 O'Hagan	10 O'Hagan	10 Sloan	10 O'Hagan	10 O'Hagan
11 Kirwan	11 Kirwan	11 Kirwan	11 Young	11 Kirwan
Belfast **Feb 17: 0-5**	**Dublin** **Mar 17: 0-1**	**Wrexham** **April 2: 4-4** **Maxwell 2** **Sloan 2**	**Liverpool** **Feb 16: 0-1**	**Belfast** **Feb 23: 2-3** **O'Hagan, Sloan**

149

1907 Scotland	1908 England	1908 Scotland	1908 Wales	1909 England
1 Scott, W.	1 Scott, W.	1 Scott, W.	1 Scott, W.	1 Scott, W.
2 Willis	2 Craig	2 Craig	2 Craig	2 Balfe
3 McCartney	3 McCartney	3 McCartney	3 McCartney	3 McCartney
4 Wright	4 Harris	4 Harris	4 Darling	4 Harris
5 Connor	5 Connor	5 Connor	5 McConnell	5 Darling
6 McClure	6 McClure	6 McConnell	6 Harris	6 McClure
7 Blair	7 Blair	7 Blair	7 Hunter	7 Hunter
8 Maxwell	8 Hannon	8 Hannon	8 Hamilton	8 Lacey
9 Maguire	9 Mercer	9 Andrews	9 Sloan	9 Greer
10 O'Hagan	10 Burnison	· 10 O'Hagan	10 O'Hagan	10 O'Hagan
11 Young	11 Young	11 Young	11 Buckle	11 Young
Glasgow	**Belfast**	**Dublin**	**Aberdare**	**Bradford**
Mar 16: 0-3	**Feb 15: 1-3**	**Mar 14: 0-5**	**April 11: 1-0**	**Feb 13: 0-4**
			Sloan	

1909 Scotland	1909 Wales	1910 England	1910 Scotland	1910 Wales
1 Scott, W.	1 Scott, W.	1 Scott, W.	1 Scott, W.	1 O'Hehir
2 Craig	2 Seymour	2 Burnison	2 Burnison	2 Balfe
3 McCartney	3 McCartney	3 McCann	3 McCann	3 McCann
4 Harris	4 Harris	4 Harris	4 Harris	4 Harris
5 McConnell	5 Connor	5 McConnell	5 McConnell	5 McConnell
6 Sloan	6 McConnell	6 Darling	6 Darling	6 Darling
7 Hunter	7 Hunter	7 Renneville	7 Renneville	7 Renneville
8 Lacey	8 Lacey	8 Lacey	8 Lacey	8 Lacey
9 Greer	9 Greer	9 Murray	9 Murray	9 Murray
10 Webb	10 Webb	10 Murphy	10 Murphy	10 Murphy
11 Kirwan	11 Slemin	11 Thompson	11 Thompson	11 Thompson
Glasgow	**Belfast**	**Belfast**	**Belfast**	**Wrexham**
Mar 15: 0-5	**Mar 20: 2-3**	**Feb 12: 1-1**	**Mar 19: 1-0**	**April 11: 1-4**
	Lacey, Hunter	**Thompson**	**Thompson**	**Darling (pen.)**

1911 Wales	1911 England	1911 Scotland	1912 England	1912 Scotland
1 Scott, W.	1 Scott, W.	1 Scott, W.	1 Scott, W.	1 Hanna
2 Burnison	2 Burnison	2 Burnison	2 Burnison	2 Willis
3 Thunder	3 McCann	3 McCann	3 McCann	3 Craig
4 Harris	4 Harris	4 Harris	4 Harris	4 Darling
5 Connor	5 Connor	5 Connor	5 O'Connell	5 O'Connell
6 Hampton	6 Hampton	6 Hampton	6 Hampton	6 Moran
7 Renneville	7 Lacey	7 Lacey	7 Lacey	7 Houston
8 Lacey	8 Hannon	8 Hannon	8 Hamill	8 McKnight
9 Halligan	9 McConnell	9 McConnell	9 Halligan	9 McAuley
10 McAuley	10 McAuley	10 Webb	10 McAuley	10 Enright
11 Thompson	11 Thompson	11 Walker	11 Thompson	11 Young
Belfast	**Derby**	**Glasgow**	**Dublin**	**Belfast**
Jan 28: 1-2	**Feb 11: 1-2**	**Mar 18: 0-2**	**Feb 10: 1-6**	**Mar 16: 1-4**
Halligan	**McAuley**		**Hamill**	**McKnight (pen.)**

1912 Wales	1913 Wales	1913 England	1913 Scotland	1914 Wales
1 Hanna	1 Scott, W.	1 Scott, W.	1 Scott, W.	1 McKee
2 Craig	2 Burnison	2 McConnell	2 McConnell	2 McConnell
3 McConnell	3 McCann	3 Warren	3 Warren	3 Craig
4 Hampton	4 Rollo	4 Hampton	4 Andrews	4 Harris
5 Brennan	5 Donnelly	5 Harris	5 Harris	5 O'Connell
6 Rollo	6 Hampton	6 Andrews	6 Hampton	6 Rollo
7 Houston	7 Houston	7 Houston	7 Houston	7 Seymour
8 Hannon	8 Lacey	8 Hannon	8 McKnight	8 Young
9 McDonnell	9 McDonnell	9 Gillespie	9 Gillespie	9 Gillespie
10 McCandless	10 McCandless	10 McAuley	10 McAuley	10 Lacey
11 Thompson	11 Thompson	11 Thompson	11 Thompson	11 Bookman
Cardiff	**Belfast**	**Belfast**	**Dublin**	**Wrexham**
April 13: 3-2	**Jan 18: 0-1**	**Feb 15: 2-1**	**Mar 15: 1-2**	**Jan 19: 2-1**
McCandless 2		**Gillespie 2**	**McKnight**	**Young**
Brennan				**Gillespie**

1914 England	1914 Scotland	1919 England	1920 Scotland	1920 Wales
1 McKee	1 McKee	1 O'Hagan	1 Scott, E.	1 O'Hagan
2 McConnell	2 McConnell	2 McCandless	2 Manderson	2 Manderson
3 Craig	3 Craig	3 McCracken, W.	3 Rollo	3 Rollo
4 Hampton	4 Harris	4 Emerson	4 Hamill	4 McCandless, W.
5 O'Connell	5 O'Connell	5 Hamill	5 Lacey	5 Hamill
6 Hamill	6 Hamill	6 Lacey	6 Emerson	6 Emerson
7 Rollo	7 Houston	7 Ferris	7 Robinson	7 Lyner
8 Young	8 Nixon	8 Snape	8 Gallagher	8 Lacey
9 Gillespie	9 Young	9 Gowdy	9 Brookes	9 Gillespie
10 Lacey	10 Lacey	10 Gallagher	10 Gillespie	10 Ferris
11 Thompson	11 Thompson	11 Lyner	11 McCandless	11 McCandless, J.
Middlesbrough	**Belfast**	**Belfast**	**Glasgow**	**Belfast**
Feb 14: 3-0	**Mar 14: 1-1**	**Oct 25: 1-1**	**Mar 13: 0-3**	**Feb 14: 2-2**
Lacey 2	**Young**	**Ferris**		**McCandless, J.**
Gillespie				**Emerson**

1920 England	1921 Scotland	1921 Wales	1921 England	1922 Scotland
1 Scott, E.	1 Scott, E.	1 Scott, E.	1 Scott, E.	1 Collins
2 Rollo	2 Mulligan	2 Rollo	2 McCracken, W.	2 McCracken, W.
3 McCandless, W.	3 Rollo	3 McCandless	3 Rollo	3 McCracken, W.
4 McCracken, R.	4 Lacey	4 Lacey	4 McCracken, R.	4 McCracken, R.
5 Lacey	5 Smith, E.E.	5 Scraggs	5 Scraggs	5 O'Brien
6 Emerson	6 O'Brien	6 Harris, J.	6 Emerson	6 Emerson
7 Kelly	7 McGregor	7 Robinson	7 Lacey	7 Lacey
8 Ferris	8 Ferris	8 Brown, J.	8 Gillespie	8 Gallagher
9 Doran	9 McKinney	9 Chambers	9 Doran	9 Irvine
10 Gillespie	10 Hamill	10 Mathieson	10 Mathieson	10 Gillespie
11 McCandless, J.	11 Bookman	11 Bookman	11 Bookman	11 Lyner
Sunderland	**Belfast**	**Swansea**	**Belfast**	**Glasgow**
Oct 23: 0-2	**Feb 26: 0-2**	**April 9: 1-2**	**Oct 22: 1-1**	**Mar 4: 1-2**
		Chambers	**Gillespie**	**Gillespie**

151

1922 Wales	1922 England	1923 Scotland	1923 Wales	1923 England
1 Mehaffy	1 Harland	1 Farquharson	1 Farquharson	1 Farquharson
2 McCracken, W.	2 Rollo	2 McCracken, W.	2 Mackey	2 McCluggage
3 Curran	3 Curran	3 Curran	3 Kennedy	3 Curran
4 McCracken, R.	4 Emerson	4 Irving	4 Irving	4 Irving
5 O'Brien	5 Smith, E.E.	5 Moorhead	5 Smith, E.E.	5 Smith, E.E.
6 Emerson	6 Morgan	6 Emerson	6 Emerson	6 Emerson
7 Lyner	7 Lyner	7 McKenzie	7 Lyner	7 Brown, J.
8 Crooks	8 Irvine	8 Gallagher	8 Gallagher	8 Croft
9 Doran	9 Nelis	9 Reid	9 Irvine	9 Irvine
10 Gillespie	10 Gillespie	10 Gillespie	10 Gillespie	10 Gillespie
11 Toner	11 Burns	11 Moore	11 Toner	11 Toner
Belfast	**West Bromwich**	**Belfast**	**Wrexham**	**Belfast**
April 1: 1-1	**Oct 21: 0-2**	**Mar 3: 0-1**	**April 14: 3-0**	**Oct 20: 2-1**
Gillespie			**Irvine 2**	**Gillespie**
			Gillespie	**Croft**

1924 Scotland	1924 Wales	1924 England	1925 Scotland	1925 Wales
1 Farquharson	1 Farquharson	1 Farquharson	1 Farquharson	1 Scott, E.
2 Rollo	2 Rollo	2 Manderson	2 Manderson	2 Rollo
3 McCandless	3 McCandless	3 Kennedy	3 McCandless	3 McConnell
4 Irving	4 Gowdy	4 Chatton	4 Chatton	4 Garrett
5 O'Brien	5 O'Brien	5 O'Brien	5 O'Brien	5 O'Brien
6 Morgan	6 Irving	6 Irving	6 Irving	6 Irving
7 McKinney	7 Brown, J.	7 Lacey	7 Martin	7 Cowan
8 Gallagher	8 Gallagher	8 Gallagher	8 Gallagher	8 Gallagher
9 Irvine	9 McIlvenny	9 Irvine	9 Carroll	9 Sloan
10 Gillespie	10 Gillespie	10 Gillespie	10 Gillespie	10 Meek
11 McGrillen	11 Toner	11 Toner	11 Toner	11 Wilson
Glasgow	**Belfast**	**Liverpool**	**Belfast**	**Wrexham**
Mar 1: 0-2	**Mar 15: 0-1**	**Oct 22: 1-3**	**Feb 28: 0-3**	**April 18: 0-0**
		Gillespie		

1925 England	1926 Wales	1926 Scotland	1926 England	1927 Scotland
1 Scott, E.	1 Scott, E.	1 Scott, E.	1 Scott, E.	1 Scott, E.
2 Rollo	2 Brown, J.	2 Manderson	2 Rollo	2 McCluggage
3 McConnell	3 McConnell	3 Watson	3 McConnell	3 McConnell
4 Gowdy	4 Irving	4 Irving	4 Gowdy	4 Gowdy
5 Chatton	5 O'Brien	5 Gowdy	5 Morgan	5 Sloan
6 Sloan	6 Sloan	6 Sloan	6 Irving	6 McMullan
7 Bothwell	7 Bothwell	7 Bothwell	7 Bothwell	7 McGrillen
8 Irvine	8 Steele	8 Steele	8 Irvine	8 Gallagher
9 Davey	9 Curran	9 Curran	9 Davey	9 Davey
10 Hopkins	10 Gillespie	10 Gallagher	10 Gillespie	10 Irving
11 McMullan	11 McMullan	11 McLean	11 Toner	11 Toner
Belfast	**Belfast**	**Glasgow**	**Liverpool**	**Belfast**
Oct 24: 0-0	**Feb 13: 3-0**	**Feb 27: 0-4**	**Oct 20: 3-3**	**Feb 26: 0-2**
	Gillespie		**Gillespie**	
	Curran 2		**Irvine**	
			Davey	

1927 Wales	1927 England	1928 Wales	1928 Scotland	1928 England
1 Scott, E.	1 Scott, E.	1 Scott, E.	1 Scott, E.	1 Scott, E.
2 McCluggage	2 McCluggage	2 McCluggage	2 McCluggage	2 McCluggage
3 McConnell	3 McConnell	3 McConnell, W.	3 Hamilton	3 Hamilton
4 Irving	4 Irving	4 Irving	4 Irving	4 Irving
5 Sloan	5 Morgan	5 Morgan	5 Moorehead	5 Sloan
6 O'Brien	6 Sloan	6 Sloan	6 Morgan	6 Morgan
7 Bothwell	7 Chambers	7 Chambers	7 Chambers	7 Chambers
8 Irvine	8 Irvine	8 Dunne	8 Irvine	8 Irvine
9 Johnston	9 Davey	9 Davey	9 Curran	9 Bambrick
10 Gillespie	10 Gillespie	10 McConnell, P.	10 Ferris	10 Gillespie
11 McCaw	11 Mahood	11 Mahood	11 Mahood	11 Mahood
Cardiff	**Belfast**	**Belfast**	**Glasgow**	**Liverpool**
April 9: 2-2	**Oct 22: 2-0**	**Feb 4: 1-2**	**Feb 25: 1-0**	**Oct 22: 1-2**
Johnston 2	**Jones o.g.**	**Chambers**	**Chambers**	**Bambrick**
	Mahood			

1929 Wales	1929 Scotland	1929 England	1930 Wales	1930 Scotland
1 Scott, E.	1 Scott, E.	1 Scott, E,	1 Gardiner	1 Gardiner
2 McCluggage	2 McCluggage	2 Russell	2 McCluggage	2 Russell
3 McCandless	3 Flack	3 Hamilton	3 Fulton	3 Hamilton
4 Miller	4 Miller	4 Miller	4 McCleery	4 McDonald
5 Elwood	5 Moorehead	5 Elwood	5 Cpl. J. Jones	5 Cpl. J. Jones
6 Steele	6 Steele	6 McCleery	6 Sloan	6 Sloan
7 Chambers	7 Chambers	7 Duggan	7 Chambers	7 Chambers
8 Rowley	8 Rowley	8 Rowley	8 Rowley	8 Irvine
9 Bambrick	9 Bambrick	9 Bambrick	9 Bambrick	9 Bambrick
10 Cumming	10 Cumming	10 Cumming	10 McCambridge	10 McCambridge
11 Mahood	11 Mahood	11 Kavanagh	11 Mahood	11 McCaw
Wrexham	**Belfast**	**Belfast**	**Belfast**	**Glasgow**
Feb 2: 2-2	**Feb 23: 3-7**	**Oct 19: 0-3**	**Feb 1: 7-0**	**Feb 22: 1-3**
Mahood	**Bambrick 2**		**Bambrick 6**	**McCaw**
McCluggage	**Rowley**		**McCluggage**	

1930 England	1931 Scotland	1931 Wales	1931 Scotland	1931 England
1 Scott, E.	1 Gardiner	1 Diffin	1 Gardiner	1 Gardiner
2 McCluggage	2 McNinch	2 McCluggage	2 McNinch	2 Russell
3 Fulton	3 Fulton	3 Fulton	3 Hamilton, R.	3 Fulton
4 Jones, J.	4 McCleery	4 Irving	4 McCleery	4 McDonald
5 Reid	5 Jones, J.	5 Jones, J.	5 Jones, J.	5 Jones, J.
6 McCleery	6 Sloan	6 McCleery	6 Gowdy	6 Mitchell
7 Duggan	7 Blair	7 Duggan	7 Blair	7 Chambers
8 Irvine	8 Falloon	8 Rowley	8 Rowley	8 McConnell
9 Dunne	9 Roberts	9 Dunne	9 Dunne	9 Dunne
10 Gillespie	10 Geary	10 McCambridge	10 Geary	10 McCambridge
11 McCaw	11 McCaw	11 McCaw	11 Chambers	11 Kelly
Sheffield	**Belfast**	**Wrexham**	**Glasgow**	**Belfast**
Oct 20: 1-5	**Feb 21: 0-0**	**April 22: 2-3**	**Sept 19: 1-3**	**Oct 17: 2-6**
Dunne		**Dunne, Rowley**	**Dunne**	**Dunne, Kelly**

1931 Wales	1932 Scotland	1932 England	1932 Wales	1933 Scotland
1 Scott, E.	1 Scott, E.	1 Scott, E.	1 Scott, E.	1 Scott; E.
2 McNinch	2 Cook	2 Cook	2 Cook	2 Willingham
3 Fulton	3 Fulton	3 Fulton	3 Willingham	3 Fulton
4 McCleery	4 Falloon	4 Mitchell, W.	4 Mitchell, W.	4 McMahon
5 Pyper	5 Jones, J.	5 Jones, J.	5 Jones, J.	5 Jones, J.
6 Mitchell, W.	6 Gowdy	6 McCleery	6 McCleery	6 Mitchell, W.
7 Chambers	7 Mitchell, E.	7 Duggan	7 Houston	7 Blair
8 Irvine	8 Priestley	8 Moore	8 English	8 Stevenson
9 Bambrick	9 Miller	9 Dunne	9 Dunne	9 Martin
10 Millar	10 English	10 Doherty, J.	10 Doherty, J.	10 Coulter
11 Kelly	11 Kelly	11 Kelly	11 Kelly	11 Mahood

Belfast — Dec 5: 4-0 — Kelly 2, Miller, Bambrick
Belfast — Sept 12: 0-4
Blackpool — Oct 17: 0-1
Wrexham — Dec 7: 1-4 — English
Glasgow — Sept 16: 2-1 — Martin

1933 England	1933 Wales	1934 Scotland	1935 England	1935 Wales
1 Scott, E.	1 Scott, E.	1 Scott, E.	1 Breen	1 Breen
2 Reid	2 Reid	2 Mackey	2 Cook	2 Mackey
3 Fulton	3 Fulton	3 Fulton	3 Fulton	3 Fulton
4 McMillen	4 Mitchell, W.	4 McMillen	4 Gowdy	4 McCullough
5 Jones, J.	5 Jones, J.	5 Jones, J.	5 Jones, J.	5 Jones, J.
6 Jones, S.	6 Jones, S.	6 Mitchell, W.	6 Mitchell, W.	6 Gowdy
7 Duggan	7 Mitchell, C.	7 Duggan	7 Brown, J.	7 Duggan
8 Stevenson	8 Stevenson	8 Gowdy	8 Doherty, P.	8 Brown, J.
9 Martin	9 Martin	9 Martin	9 Martin	9 Bambrick
10 Coulter	10 Coulter	10 Stevenson	10 Stevenson	10 Doherty, P.
11 Priestley	11 Kelly	11 Coulter	11 Coulter	11 Coulter

Belfast — Oct 14: 0-3
Belfast — Nov 4: 1-1 — Jones, S.
Belfast — Oct 20: 2-1 — Martin, Coulter
Liverpool — Feb 6: 1-2 — Stevenson
Wrexham — Mar 27: 1-3 — Bambrick

1935 England	1935 Scotland	1936 Wales	1936 Scotland	1936 England
1 Scott, E.	1 Scott, E.	1 Scott, E.	1 Breen	1 Breen
2 Reid	2 Cook	2 Cook	2 Cook	2 Cook
3 Allen	3 Fulton	3 Fulton	3 Fulton	3 Fulton
4 Mitchell, W.	4 McCullough	4 Gowdy	4 McMillen	4 McCullough
5 Jones, J.	5 Jones, J.	5 Jones, J.	5 Jones, J.	5 Jones, J.
6 Browne, R.	6 Mitchell, W.	6 Browne, R.	6 Mitchell, W.	6 Mitchell, W.
7 Brown, J.	7 Duggan	7 Kernaghan	7 Kernaghan	7 Brown, J.
8 McCullough	8 Stevenson	8 Gibb	8 McCullough	8 Stevenson
9 Bambrick	9 Bambrick	9 Martin	9 Martin	9 Davis
10 Doherty, P.	10 Doherty, P.	10 Stevenson	10 Coulter	10 Doherty, P.
11 Kelly	11 Kelly	11 Kelly	11 Kelly	11 Kelly

Belfast — Oct 19: 1-3 — Brown
Edinburgh — Nov 13: 1-2 — Kelly
Belfast — Mar 11: 3-2 — Gibb, Stevenson Kernaghan
Belfast — Oct 31: 1-3 — Kernaghan
Stoke-on-Trent — Nov 18: 1-3 — Davis

1937 Wales	1937 England	1937 Scotland	1938 Wales	1938 Scotland
1 Breen	1 Breen	1 Breen	1 Twoomey	1 Breen
2 Cook	2 Hayes	2 Hayes	2 Cook	2 Hayes
3 Fulton	3 Cook	3 Cook	3 Fulton	3 Cook
4 Brolly	4 Mitchell, W.	4 Doherty, J.	4 Brolly	4 McMillen
5 Jones, J.	5 Jones, J.	5 McMillen	5 McMillen	5 O'Mahoney
6 Mitchell, W.	6 Browne, R.	6 Mitchell, W.	6 Browne, R.	6 Browne, R.
7 Brown, J.	7 Kernaghan	7 Brown, J.	7 Brown, J.	7 Brown, J.
8 Doherty, P.	8 Stevenson	8 McAlinden	8 Farrell	8 McAlinden
9 Banks	9 Martin	9 Martin	9 Bambrick	9 Martin
10 Stevenson	10 Doherty, P.	10 Doherty, P.	10 Stevenson	10 Stevenson
11 Coulter	11 Madden	11 Coulter	11 Coulter	11 Coulter
Wrexham	**Belfast**	**Aberdeen**	**Belfast**	**Belfast**
Mar 17: 1-4	**Oct 23: 1-5**	**Nov 10: 1-1**	**Mar 16: 1-0**	**Oct 8: 0-2**
Stevenson	**Stevenson**	**Doherty, P.**	**Bambrick**	

1938 England	1939 Wales	1946 England	1946 Scotland	1947 Wales
1 Twoomey	1 Breen	1 Russell	1 Hinton	1 Hinton
2 Hayes	2 Cook	2 Gorman	2 Gorman	2 Gorman
3 Cook	3 Butler	3 Aherne	3 Feeney	3 Carey
4 Brolly	4 Brolly	4 Carey	4 Martin	4 Sloan
5 McMillen	5 Leatham	5 Vernon	5 Vernon	5 Vernon
6 Browne, R.	6 Weir	6 Douglas	6 Farrell	6 Farrell
7 Cochrane	7 Cochrane	7 Cochrane	7 Cochrane	7 Cochrane
8 Stevenson	8 Stevenson	8 McAlinden	8 Carey	8 Stevenson
9 Baird	9 Milligan	9 McMorran	9 Walsh, D.	9 Walsh, D.
10 Doherty, P.	10 Doherty, P.	10 Doherty	10 Stevenson	10 Doherty
11 Brown, J.	11 Brown, J.	11 Lockhart	11 Eglington	11 Eglington
Manchester	**Wrexham**	**Belfast**	**Hampden**	**Belfast**
Nov 16: 0-7	**Mar 15: 1-3**	**Sept 28: 2-7**	**Nov 27: 0-0**	**April 16: 2-1**
	Milligan	**Lockhart 2**		**Stevenson**
				Doherty

1947 Scotland	1947 England	1948 Wales	1948 England	1948 Scotland
1 Hinton	1 Hinton	1 Hinton	1 Smyth	1 Smyth
2 Martin	2 Martin	2 Martin	2 Carey	2 Carey
3 Aherne	3 Carey	3 Gorman	3 Martin	3 Keane
4 Walsh, W.	4 Walsh, W.	4 Walsh, W.	4 Walsh, W.	4 McCabe
5 Vernon	5 Vernon	5 Vernon	5 Vernon	5 Vernon
6 Farrell	6 Farrell	6 Farrell	6 Farrell	6 Walsh, W.
7 Cochrane	7 Cochrane	7 Cochrane	7 O'Driscoll	7 Cochrane
8 Smyth	8 Smyth	8 Smyth	8 McAlinden	8 Smyth
9 Walsh, D.	9 Walsh, D.	9 Walsh, D.	9 Walsh, D.	9 Walsh, D.
10 Stevenson	10 Doherty	10 Doherty	10 Tully	10 Doherty
11 Eglington	11 Eglington	11 Eglington	11 Eglington	11 O'Driscoll
Belfast	**Everton**	**Wrexham**	**Belfast**	**Hampden**
Oct 4: 2-0	**Nov 5: 2-2**	**Mar 10: 0-2**	**Oct 9: 2-6**	**Nov 17: 2-3**
Smyth 2	**Doherty**		**Walsh, D. 2**	**Walsh, D. 2**
	Walsh, D.			

155

1949 Wales	1949 Scotland	1949 England	1950 Wales	1950 England
1 Moore	1 Kelly, P.	1 Kelly	1 Kelly	1 Kelly
2 Carey	2 Bowler	2 Feeney	2 Bowler	2 Gallogly
3 Aherne	3 McMichael	3 McMichael	3 Aherne	3 McMichael
4 McCabe	4 Blanchflower	4 Bowler	4 Blanchflower	4 Blanchflower
5 Vernon	5 Vernon	5 Vernoh	5 Martin	5 Vernon
6 Farrell	6 Ferris	6 McCabe	6 Ryan	6 Cush
7 Cochrane	7 Cochrane	7 Cochrane	7 McKenna	7 Campbell
8 Smyth	8 Smyth	8 Smyth	8 Smyth	8 Crossan
9 Walsh, D.	9 Brennan	9 Brennan	9 Walsh, D.	9 McMorran
10 Brennan	10 Crossan	10 Tully	10 Brennan	10 Brennan
11 O'Driscoll	11 McKenna	11 McKenna	11 Lockhart	11 McKenna
Belfast **Mar 9: 0-2**	**Belfast** **Oct 1: 2-8** **Smyth 2**	**Maine Road** **Manchester** **Nov 6: 2-9** **Smyth, Brennan**	**Wrexham** **Mar 8: 0-0** **Last All-** **Ireland Team**	**Belfast** **Oct 7: 1-4** **McMorran**

1950 Scotland	1951 Wales	1951 France	1951 Scotland	1951 England
1 Kelly	1 Hinton	1 Hinton	1 Uprichard	1 Uprichard
2 Gallogly	2 Graham	2 Graham	2 Graham	2 Graham
3 McMichael	3 Cunningham	3 McMichael	3 McMichael	3 McMichael
4 Blanchflower	4 McCabe	4 Blanchflower	4 Dickson	4 Dickson
5 Vernon	5 Vernon	5 Vernon	5 Vernon	5 Vernon
6 Cush	6 Dickson	6 Ferris	6 Ferris	6 McCourt
7 Campbell	7 Hughes	7 Bingham	7 Bingham	7 Bingham
8 McGarry	8 McMorran	8 McGarry	8 McIlroy	8 Smyth
9 McMorran	9 Simpson	9 Simpson	9 McMorran	9 McMorran
10 Doherty	10 McGarry	10 Dickson	10 Peacock	10 McIlroy
11 McKenna	11 Lockhart	11 McKenna	11 Tully	11 McKenna
Hampden **Nov 1: 1-6** **McGarry**	**Belfast** **Mar 7: 1-2** **Simpson**	**Belfast** **May 12: 2-2** **Ferris, Simpson**	**Belfast** **Oct 6: 0-3**	**Villa Park** **Nov 20: 0-2**

1952 Wales	1952 England	1952 Scotland	1952 France	1953 Wales
1 Uprichard	1 Uprichard	1 Uprichard	1 Uprichard	1 Uprichard
2 Graham	2 Cunningham	2 Graham	2 Graham	2 McCabe
3 McMichael	3 McMichael	3 McMichael	3 McMichael	3 McMichael
4 Blanchflower	4 Blanchflower	4 Blanchflower	4 Blanchflower	4 Blanchflower
5 Dickson	5 Dickson	5 Dickson	5 Dickson	5 Dickson
6 McCourt	6 McCourt	6 McCourt	6 McCourt	6 McCourt
7 Bingham	7 Bingham	7 Bingham	7 Bingham	7 Bingham
8 D'Arcy	8 D'Arcy	8 D'Arcy	8 D'Arcy	8 McIlroy
9 McMorran	9 McMorran	9 McMorran	9 McMorran	9 McMorran
10 McIlroy	10 McIlroy	10 McIlroy	10 Peacock	10 D'Arcy
11 Lockhart	11 Tully	11 Tully	11 Tully	11 Tully
Swansea **Mar 19: 0-3**	**Belfast** **Oct 4: 2-2** **Tully 2**	**Hampden** **Nov 5: 1-1** **D'Arcy**	**Paris** **Nov 11: 1-3** **Tully**	**Belfast** **April 15: 2-3** **McMorran 2**

1953 Scotland	1953 England	1954 England	1954 Wales	1954 Scotland
1 Smyth	1 Smyth	1 Uprichard	1 Gregg	1 Uprichard
2 Cunningham	2 Graham	2 Montgomery	2 Graham	2 Graham
3 McMichael	3 McMichael	3 McMichael	3 McMichael	3 Cunningham
4 Blanchflower	4 Blanchflower	4 Blanchflower	4 Blanchflower	4 Blanchflower
5 McCabe	5 Dickson	5 Dickson	5 Dickson	5 McCavana
6 Cush	6 Cush	6 Peacock	6 Peacock	6 Peacock
7 Bingham	7 Bingham	7 Bingham	7 Bingham	7 Bingham
8 McIlroy	8 McIlroy	8 Blanchflower, J.	8 Blanchflower, J.	8 Blanchflower, J.
9 Simpson	9 Simpson	9 Simpson	9 McAdams	9 McAdams
10 Tully	10 McMorran	10 McIlroy	10 McIlroy	10 McIlroy
11 Lockhart	11 Lockhart	11 McParland	11 McParland	11 McParland

Belfast	**Everton**	**Belfast**	**Wrexham**	**Hampden**
Oct 3: 1-3	Nov 11: 1-3	Oct 2: 0-2	Mar 31: 2-1	Nov 3: 2-2
Lockhart	**McMorran**		**McParland 2**	**Bingham, McAdams**

1955 Wales	1955 Scotland	1955 England	1956 Wales	1956 England
1 Uprichard	1 Uprichard	1 Uprichard	1 Uprichard	1 Gregg
2 Graham	2 Graham	2 Cunningham	2 Cunningham	2 Cunningham
3 McMichael	3 Cunningham	3 Graham	3 McMichael	3 McMichael
4 Blanchflower	4 Blanchflower	4 Blanchflower	4 Blanchflower	4 Blanchflower
5 McCleary	5 McCavana	5 McCavana	5 Blanchflower, J.	5 Blanchflower, J.
6 Casey	6 Peacock	6 Peacock	6 Casey	6 Casey
7 Bingham	7 Bingham	7 Bingham	7 Bingham	7 Bingham
8 Crossan	8 Blanchflower, J.	8 McIlroy	8 McIlroy	8 McIlroy
9 Walker	9 Coyle	9 Coyle	9 Jones, J.	9 Jones, J.
10 McIlroy	10 McIlroy	10 Tully	10 McMorran	10 McAdams
11 Lockhart	11 McParland	11 McParland	11 Lockhart	11 McParland

Belfast	**Belfast**	**Wembley**	**Cardiff**	**Belfast**
April 20: 2-3	Oct 8: 2-1	Nov 2: 0-3	April 11: 1-1	Oct 6: 1-1
Crossan, Walker	**Blanchflower, J.**		**Jones**	**McIlroy**
	Bingham			

1956 Scotland	1957 Portugal	1957 Wales	1957 Italy	1957 Portugal
1 Gregg	1 Gregg	1 Gregg	1 Gregg	1 Gregg
2 Cunningham	2 Cunningham	2 Cunningham	2 Cunningham	2 Cunningham
3 McMichael	3 McMichael	3 McMichael	3 McMichael	3 McMichael
4 Blanchflower	4 Blanchflower	4 Blanchflower	4 Blanchflower	4 Blanchflower
5 Blanchflower, J.	5 Blanchflower, J.	5 Cush	5 Cush	5 Cush
6 Casey	6 Casey	6 Peacock	6 Casey	6 Casey
7 Bingham	7 Bingham	7 Bingham	7 Bingham	7 Bingham
8 McIlroy	8 McIlroy	8 McIlroy	8 Simpson	8 Simpson
9 Shields	9 Coyle	9 Jones	9 McMorran	9 McMorran
10 Dickson	10 Cush	10 Casey	10 McIlroy	10 McIlroy
11 McParland	11 McParland	11 McParland	11 Peacock	11 Peacock

Hampden	**Lisbon**	**Belfast**	**Rome**	**Belfast**
Nov 7: 0-1	Jan 16: 1-1	April 10: 0-0	April 25: 0-1	May 1: 3-0
	Bingham			**Simpson, McIlroy,**
				Casey

1957 Scotland	1957 England	1957 Italy	1958 Italy	1958 Wales
1 Uprichard	1 Gregg	1 Gregg	1 Uprichard	1 Gregg
2 Cunningham	2 Keith	2 Keith	2 Cunningham	2 Cunningham
3 McMichael	3 McMichael	3 McMichael	3 McMichael	3 McMichael
4 Blanchflower	4 Blanchflower	4 Blanchflower	4 Blanchflower	4 Blanchflower
5 Blanchflower, J.	5 Blanchflower, J.	5 Blanchflower, J.	5 Blanchflower, J.	5 Keith
6 Peacock	6 Peacock	6 Peacock	6 Peacock	6 Peacock
7 Bingham	7 Bingham	7 Bingham	7 Bingham	7 Bingham
8 Simpson	8 McCrory	8 McIlroy	8 Cush	8 Cush
9 McAdams	9 Simpson	9 McAdams	9 Simpson	9 Simpson
10 McIlroy	10 McIlroy	10 Cush	10 McIlroy	10 McIlroy
11 McParland	11 McParland	11 McParland	11 McParland	11 McParland
Belfast	**Wembley**	**Belfast**	**Belfast**	**Cardiff**
Oct 5: 1-1	**Nov 6: 3-2**	**Dec 4: 2-2**	**Jan 15: 2-1**	**April 16: 1-1**
Bingham	**McIlroy, McCrory**	**Cush 2**	**McIlroy, Cush**	**Simpson**
Simpson	**Simpson**			

1958 Czechoslovakia	1958 Argentina	1958 W. Germany	1958 Czechoslovakia	1958 France
1 Gregg	1 Gregg	1 Gregg	1 Uprichard	1 Gregg
2 Keith	2 Keith	2 Keith	2 Keith	2 Keith
3 McMichael	3 McMichael	3 McMichael	3 McMichael	3 McMichael
4 Blanchflower	4 Blanchflower	4 Blanchflower	4 Blanchflower	4 Blanchflower
5 Cunningham	5 Cunningham	5 Cunningham	5 Cunningham	5 Cunningham
6 Peacock	6 Peacock	6 Peacock	6 Peacock	6 Cush
7 Bingham	7 Bingham	7 Bingham	7 Bingham	7 Bingham
8 Cush	8 Cush	8 Cush	8 Cush	8 Casey
9 Dougan	9 Coyle	9 Casey	9 Scott	9 Scott
10 McIlroy	10 McIlroy	10 McIlroy	10 McIlroy	10 McIlroy
11 McParland	11 McParland	11 McParland	11 McParland	11 McParland
Halmstad	**Halmstad**	**Malmo**	**Malmo**	**Norrkoping**
June 8: 1-0	**June 11: 1-3**	**June 15: 2-2**	**June 17: 2-1**	**June 19: 0-4**
Cush	**McParland**	**McParland 2**	**McParland 2**	

1958 England	1958 Spain	1958 Scotland	1959 Wales	1959 Scotland
1 Gregg	1 Uprichard	1 Uprichard	1 Gregg	1 Gregg
2 Keith	2 Keith	2 Keith	2 Keith	2 Keith
3 Graham	3 McMichael	3 McMichael	3 McMichael	3 McMichael
4 Blanchflower	4 Blanchflower	4 Blanchflower	4 Blanchflower	4 Blanchflower
5 Cunningham	5 Forde	5 Cunningham	5 Cunningham	5 Cunningham
6 Peacock	6 Casey	6 Peacock	6 Peacock	6 Peacock
7 Bingham	7 Bingham	7 Bingham	7 Bingham	7 Bingham
8 Cush	8 Cush	8 Cush	8 McIlroy	8 Cush
9 Casey	9 McParland	9 Simpson	9 Cush	9 Dougan
10 McIlroy	10 McIlroy	10 McIlroy	10 Hill	10 McIlroy
11 McParland	11 Tully	11 McParland	11 McParland	11 McParland
Belfast	**Madrid**	**Hampden**	**Belfast**	**Belfast**
Oct 4: 3-3	**Oct 15: 2-6**	**Nov 5: 2-2**	**April 22: 4-1**	**Oct 3: 0-4**
Cush, Peacock	**Bingham**	**opponent o.g.**	**McParland 2**	
Casey	**McIlroy**	**McIlroy**	**Peacock**	
			McIlroy	

1959 England	1960 Wales	1960 England	1960 W. Germany
1 Gregg	1 Gregg	1 Gregg	1 McClelland
2 Keith	2 Elder	2 Keith	2 Keith
3 McMichael	3 McMichael	3 Elder	3 Elder
4 Blanchflower	4 Blanchflower	4 Blanchflower	4 Blanchflower
5 Cunningham	5 Cunningham	5 Forde	5 Forde
6 Peacock	6 Cush	6 Peacock	6 Peacock
7 Bingham	7 Bingham	7 Bingham	7 Bingham
8 Crossan	8 McIlroy	8 McIlroy	8 McIlroy
9 Cush	9 Lawther	9 McAdams	9 McAdams
10 McIlroy	10 Hill	10 Dougan	10 Hill
11 McParland	11 McParland	11 McParland	11 McParland
Wembley	**Wrexham**	**Belfast**	**Belfast**
Nov 18: 1-2	**April 6: 2-3**	**Oct 8: 2-5**	**Oct 26: 3-4**
Bingham	**Bingham**	**McAdams 2**	**McAdams 3**
	Blanchflower		

1960 Scotland	1961 Wales	1961 Italy	1961 Greece	1961 W. Germany
1 Gregg	1 McClelland	1 McClelland	1 McClelland	1 McClelland
2 Keith	2 Keith	2 Keith	2 Keith	2 Keith
3 Elder	3 Elder	3 McCullough	3 Elder	3 Elder
4 Blanchflower	4 Blanchflower	4 Harvey	4 Cush	4 Blanchflower
5 Forde	5 Cunningham	5 Neill	5 Neill	5 Neill
6 Peacock	6 Nicholson	6 Peacock	6 Peacock	6 Peacock
7 Bingham	7 Stewart	7 Bingham	7 Bingham	7 Bingham
8 Bruce	8 Dougan	8 Dougan	8 McIlroy	8 Cush
9 McAdams	9 McAdams	9 Lawther	9 McAdams	9 McAdams
10 Nicholson	10 McIlroy	10 McAdams	10 Dougan	10 McIlroy
11 McParland	11 McParland	11 McParland	11 McParland	11 McParland
Hampden	**Belfast**	**Bologna**	**Athens**	**Berlin**
Nov 9: 2-5	**April 12: 1-5**	**April 25: 2-3**	**May 3: 1-2**	**Mar 10: 1-2**
Blanchflower	**Dougan**	**Dougan**	**McIlroy**	**McIlroy**
McParland		**McAdams**		

1961 Scotland	1961 Greece	1961 England	1962 Wales	1962 Netherlands
1 Gregg	1 Gregg	1 Hunter	1 Briggs	1 Irvine, R.
2 Magill	2 Magill	2 Magill	2 Keith	2 Keith
3 Elder	3 Elder	3 Elder	3 Cunningham	3 Cunningham
4 Blanchflower	4 Blanchflower	4 Blanchflower	4 Blanchflower	4 Harvey
5 Neill	5 Neill	5 Neill	5 Neill	5 Blanchflower
6 Peacock	6 Nicholson	6 Nicholson	6 Nicholson	6 Nicholson
7 Wilson	7 Bingham	7 Bingham	7 Humphries	7 Humphries
8 McIlroy	8 McIlroy	8 Barr, H.	8 Johnston, W.	8 Lawther
9 Lawther	9 McAdams	9 McAdams	9 O'Neill	9 McAdams
10 Hill	10 Cush	10 McIlroy	10 McLaughlin	10 McIlroy
11 McLaughlin	11 McLaughlin	11 McLaughlin	11 Braithwaite	11 McParland
Belfast	**Belfast**	**Wembley**	**Cardiff**	**Rotterdam**
Oct 7: 1-6	**Oct 17: 2-0**	**Nov 22: 1-1**	**April 11: 0-4**	**May 9: 0-4**
McLaughlin	**McLaughlin**	**McIlroy**		

| 1962 | 1962 | 1962 | 1962 | 1963 |
Poland	England	Scotland	Poland	Wales
1 Irvine, R.	1 Irvine, R.	1 Irvine, R.	1 Irvine, R.	1 Irvine, R.
2 Magill	2 Magill	2 Magill	2 Magill	2 Magill
3 Elder	3 Elder	3 Elder	3 Elder	3 Elder
4 Blanchflower	4 Blanchflower	4 Blanchflower	4 Blanchflower	4 Harvey
5 Hatton	5 Neill	5 Hatton	5 Neill	5 Campbell
6 Nicholson	6 Nicholson	6 Nicholson	6 Nicholson	6 Neill
7 Humphries	7 Humphries	7 Humphries	7 Bingham	7 Humphries
8 Barr	8 Barr	8 McMillan	8 Crossan	8 Crossan
9 Dougan	9 McMillan	9 Dougan	9 Dougan	9 Irvine, W.
10 McIlroy	10 McIlroy	10 McIlroy	10 McIlroy	10 McIlroy
11 Bingham	11 Bingham	11 Bingham	11 Braithwaite	11 McLaughlin
Katowice	**Belfast**	**Hampden**	**Belfast**	**Belfast**
Oct 10: 2-0	**Oct 20: 1-3**	**Nov 7: 1-5**	**Nov 28: 2-0**	**April 3: 1-4**
Dougan	**Barr**	**Bingham**	**Crossan**	**Harvey**
Humphries			**Bingham**	

| 1963 | 1963 | 1963 | 1963 | 1964 |
Spain	Scotland	Spain	England	Wales
1 Irvine, R.	1 Gregg	1 Hunter	1 Gregg	1 Jennings
2 Magill	2 Magill	2 Magill	2 Magill	2 Magill
3 Elder	3 Parke	3 Parke	3 Parke	3 Elder
4 Harvey	4 Harvey	4 Harvey	4 Harvey	4 Harvey
5 Neill	5 Neill	5 Neill	5 Neill	5 Neill
6 McCullough	6 McCullough	6 McCullough	6 McCullough	6 McCullough
7 Bingham	7 Bingham	7 Bingham	7 Bingham	7 Best
8 Humphries	8 Humphries	8 Humphries	8 Humphries	8 Crossan
9 Irvine, W.	9 Wilson	9 Wilson	9 Wilson	9 Wilson
10 Crossan	10 Crossan	10 Crossan	10 Crossan	10 McLaughlin
11 Braithwaite	11 Hill	11 Hill	11 Hill	11 Braithwaite
Bilbao	**Belfast**	**Belfast**	**Wembley**	**Swansea**
May 30: 1-1	**Oct 12: 2-1**	**Oct 30: 0-1**	**Nov 20: 3-8**	**April 15: 3-2**
Irvine, W.	**Bingham**		**Crossan**	**McLaughlin**
	Wilson		**Wilson 2**	**Wilson, Harvey**

| 1964 | 1964 | 1964 | 1964 | 1964 |
Uruguay	England	Switzerland	Switzerland	Scotland
1 Jennings	1 Jennings	1 Jennings	1 Jennings	1 Jennings
2 Magill	2 Magill	2 Magill	2 Magill	2 Magill
3 Elder	3 Elder	3 Elder	3 Elder	3 Elder
4 Harvey	4 Harvey	4 Harvey	4 Harvey	4 Harvey
5 Neill	5 Neill	5 Neill	5 Campbell	5 Neill
6 McCullough	6 McCullough	6 McCullough	6 Parke	6 Parke
7 Best	7 Best	7 Best	7 Best	7 Best
8 Crossan	8 Crossan	8 Crossan	8 Crossan	8 Humphries
9 Wilson	9 Wilson	9 Wilson	9 Irvine, W.	9 Irvine, W.
10 McLaughlin	10 McLaughlin	10 McLaughlin	10 McLaughlin	10 Crossan
11 Braithwaite	11 Braithwaite	11 Braithwaite	11 Braithwaite	11 Braithwaite
Belfast	**Belfast**	**Belfast**	**Lausanne**	**Hampden**
April 29: 3-0	**Oct 3: 3-4**	**Oct 14: 1-0**	**Nov 14: 1-2**	**Nov 25: 2-3**
Crossan 2	**Wilson**	**Crossan**	**Best**	**Best, Irvine, W.**
Wilson	**McLaughlin 2**			

1965 Netherlands	1965 Wales	1965 Netherlands	1965 Albania	1965 Scotland
1 Briggs	1 Irvine, R.	1 Jennings	1 Jennings	1 Jennings
2 Parke	2 Parke	2 Magill	2 Magill	2 Magill
3 Elder	3 Elder	3 Elder	3 Elder	3 Elder
4 Harvey	4 Harvey	4 Harvey	4 Harvey	4 Harvey
5 Neill	5 Neill	5 Neill	5 Neill	5 Neill
6 Nicholson	6 Nicholson	6 Parke	6 Parke	6 Nicholson
7 Humphries	7 Humphries	7 Best	7 Humphries	7 McIlroy
8 Crossan	8 Crossan	8 Crossan	8 Crossan	8 Crossan
9 Irvine, W.	9 Irvine, W.	9 Irvine, W.	9 Irvine, W.	9 Irvine, W.
10 Clements	10 McLaughlin	10 Nicholson	10 Nicholson	10 Dougan
11 Best	11 Clements	11 Braithwaite	11 Best	11 Best
Belfast	**Belfast**	**Rotterdam**	**Belfast**	**Belfast**
Mar 17: 2-1	**Mar 31: 0-5**	**April 7: 0-0**	**May 7: 4-1**	**Oct 2: 3-2**
Crossan, Neill			**Crossan 3, Best**	**Dougan, Crossan**
				Irvine, W.

1965 England	1965 Albania	1966 Wales	1966 W. Germany	1966 Mexico
1 Jennings	1 Jennings	1 Jennings	1 Jennings	1 McClelland
2 Magill	2 Magill	2 Magill	2 Magill	2 Magill
3 Elder	3 Elder	3 Elder	3 Parke	3 Elder
4 Harvey	4 Harvey	4 Harvey	4 Harvey	4 Harvey
5 Neill	5 Neill	5 Neill	5 Napier	5 Neill
6 Nicholson	6 Nicholson	6 Nicholson	6 Neill	6 Nicholson
7 McIlroy	7 McIlroy	7 Welsh	7 Welsh	7 Welsh
8 Crossan	8 Crossan	8 Wilson	8 Crossan	8 Ferguson
9 Irvine, W.	9 Irvine, W.	9 Irvine, W.	9 Wilson	9 Irvine (Johnston)
10 Dougan	10 Dougan	10 Dougan	10 Dougan	10 Dougan
11 Best	11 Best	11 McLaughlin	11 McKinney	11 Clements
Wembley	**Tirana**	**Cardiff**	**Belfast**	**Belfast**
Nov 10: 1-2	**Nov 24: 1-1**	**Mar 30: 4-1**	**May 7: 0-2**	**June 22: 4-1**
Irvine, W.	**Irvine, W.**	**Irvine, W.**		**Johnston, Elder**
		Welsh, Harvey		**Nicholson, Ferguson**

1966 England	1966 Scotland	1967 Wales	1967 Scotland	1967 England
1 Jennings (McFaul)	1 Jennings	1 McKenzie	1 Jennings	1 Jennings
2 Parke	2 Parke	2 Craig	2 McKeag	2 Parke
3 Elder	3 Elder	3 Elder	3 Parke	3 Elder
4 Todd	4 Harvey	4 Stewart	4 Stewart	4 Stewart
5 Harvey	5 Neill	5 Neill	5 Neill	5 Neill
6 McCullough	6 Nicholson	6 Nicholson	6 Clements	6 Harvey
7 Ferguson	7 Wilson	7 Welsh	7 Campbell	7 Campbell
8 Crossan	8 Crossan	8 Trainor	8 Crossan	8 Irvine
9 Irvine, W.	9 Irvine, W.	9 Dougan	9 Dougan	9 Wilson
10 Dougan	10 Dougan	10 Bruce	10 Nicholson	10 Nicholson
11 Best	11 Clements	11 Clements	11 Best	11 Clements
Belfast	**Hampden**	**Belfast**	**Belfast**	**Wembley**
Oct 22: 0-2	**Nov 16: 1-2**	**April 12: 0-0**	**Oct 21: 1-0**	**Nov 22: 0-2**
	Nicholson		**Clements**	

1968 Wales	1968 Israel	1968 Turkey	1968 Turkey	1969 England
1 Jennings	1 Jennings	1 Jennings	1 Jennings	1 Jennings
2 Craig	2 Rice	2 Craig (Stewart)	2 Craig	2 Craig
3 Elder	3 Jackson	3 Harvey	3 Harvey	3 Harvey (Elder)
4 Harvey	4 Stewart	4 Nicholson	4 Nicholson	4 Todd
5 Todd	5 Neill	5 Neill	5 Neill	5 Neill
6 McKeag	6 Harvey	6 Clements	6 Stewart	6 Nicholson
7 Irvine	7 Sloan	7 Campbell	7 Hamilton	7 McMordie
8 Stewart	8 McMordie	8 McMordie	8 McMordie	8 Jackson
9 Dougan	9 Dougan (Gaston)	9 Dougan	9 Dougan	9 Dougan
10 Nicholson	10 Irvine, W.	10 Irvine, W.	10 Harkin	10 Irvine, W.
11 Harkin	11 Ross	11 Best	11 Clements	11 Best
Wrexham	**Jaffa**	**Belfast**	**Istanbul**	**Belfast**
Feb 28: 0-2	**Sept 10: 3-2**	**Oct 23: 4-1**	**Dec 11: 3-0**	**May 3: 1-3**
	Irvine 2	**Best, McMordie**	**Harkin 2**	**McMordie**
		Dougan, Campbell	**Nicholson**	

1969 Scotland	1969 Wales	1969 USSR	1969 USSR	1970 Scotland
1 Jennings	1 Jennings	1 Jennings	1 Jennings	1 Jennings
2 Craig	2 Craig	2 Rice	2 Craig	2 Craig
3 Elder	3 Elder	3 Elder	3 Harvey	3 Clements
4 Todd	4 Todd	4 Todd	4 Hunter	4 Todd (O'Kane)
5 Neill	5 Neill	5 Neill	5 Neill	5 Neill
6 Nicholson	6 Nicholson	6 Nicholson	6 Nicholson	6 Nicholson
7 Best	7 Best	7 Campbell	7 Hegan	7 Campbell (Dickson)
8 McMordie	8 McMordie	8 McMordie	8 Jackson	8 Lutton
9 Dougan	9 Dougan	9 Dougan	9 Dougan	9 Dougan
10 Jackson	10 Jackson	10 Clements (Jackson)	10 Harkin	10 McMordie
11 Clements	11 Clements (Harkin)	11 Best	11 Clements	11 Best
Hampden	**Belfast**	**Belfast**	**Moscow**	**Belfast**
May 6: 1-1	**May 10: 0-0**	**Sept 10: 0-0**	**Oct 22: 0-2**	**April 18: 0-1**
McMordie				

1970 England	1970 Wales	1970 Spain	1971 Cyprus	1971 Cyprus
1 Jennings	1 McFaul	1 McFaul	1 Jennings	1 Jennings
2 Craig	2 Craig	2 Craig	2 Craig	2 Craig
3 Clements	3 Nelson	3 Nelson	3 Nelson	3 Clements
4 O'Kane	4 O'Kane	4 Jackson	4 Hunter	4 Harvey
5 Neill	5 Neill	5 Neill	5 Neill	5 Hunter
6 Nicholson	6 Nicholson	6 O'Kane	6 Todd	6 Todd (Watson)
7 McMordie	7 Campbell (O'Doherty)	7 Sloan	7 Hamilton	7 Hamilton
8 Best	8 Best	8 Best	8 McMordie	8 McMordie
9 Dougan	9 Dickson	9 Dougan (Todd)	9 Dougan	9 Dougan
10 O'Doherty (Nelson)	10 McMordie	10 Harkin	10 Nicholson	10 Nicholson
11 Lutton (Cowan)	11 Clements	11 Clements	11 Best	11 Best
			Nicosia	**Belfast**
Wembley	**Swansea**	**Seville**	**Feb 3: 3-0**	**April 21: 5-0**
April 21: 1-3	**April 25: 0-1**	**Nov 11: 0-3**	**Nicholson, Dougan**	**Dougan, Best 3**
Best			**Best**	**Nicholson**

162

1971 England	1971 Scotland	1971 Wales	1971 USSR	1971 USSR
1 Jennings	1 Jennings	1 Jennings	1 McFaul	1 Jennings
2 Rice	2 Rice	2 Rice	2 Craig (Hamilton)	2 Rice
3 Nelson	3 Nelson	3 Nelson	3 Neill	3 Nelson
4 O'Kane	4 O'Kane	4 O'Kane	4 Hunter	4 Nicholson
5 Hunter	5 Hunter	5 Hunter	5 Nelson	5 Hunter
6 Nicholson	6 Nicholson	6 Nicholson (Harvey)	6 Hegan	6 O'Kane
7 Hamilton	7 Hamilton	7 Hamilton	7 Clements	7 McMordie
8 McMordie (Cassidy)	8 McMordie (Craig)	8 McMordie	8 Nicholson	8 Hamilton (O'Neill)
9 Dougan	9 Dougan	9 Dougan	9 O'Kane	9 Neill
10 Clements	10 Clements	10 Clements	10 Dougan	10 Dougan (Cassidy)
11 Best	11 Best	11 Best	11 Best	11 Clements
Belfast **May 15: 0-1**	**Hampden** **May 18: 1-0** **Opponent o.g.**	**Belfast** **May 22: 1-0** **Hamilton**	**Moscow** **Sept 22: 0-1**	**Belfast** **Oct 13: 1-1** **Nicholson**

1972 Spain	1972 Scotland	1972 England	1972 Wales	1972 Bulgaria
1 Jennings	1 Jennings	1 Jennings	1 Jennings	1 Jennings
2 Rice	2 Rice	2 Rice	2 Rice	2 Rice
3 Nelson	3 Nelson	3 Nelson	3 Nelson	3 Nelson
4 Neill	4 Neill	4 Neill	4 Neill	4 Hunter
5 Hunter	5 Hunter	5 Hunter	5 Hunter	5 Neill
6 Clements	6 Clements (Craig)	6 Clements	6 Clements	6 Clements
7 Hamilton (O'Neill)	7 Hegan	7 Hegan	7 Hegan	7 Hamilton (Morgan)
8 McMordie	8 McMordie (McIlroy)	8 McMordie	8 McMordie	8 Hegan
9 Morgan	9 Dougan	9 Dougan	9 Dougan (O'Neill)	9 McMordie
10 McIlroy	10 Irvine	10 Irvine	10 Irvine	10 Dougan
11 Best	11 Jackson	11 Jackson	11 Jackson	11 Best
Hull **Feb 16: 1-1** **Morgan**	**Hampden** **May 20: 0-2**	**Wembley** **May 23: 1-0** **Neill**	**Wrexham** **May 27: 0-0**	**Sofia** **Oct 18: 0-3**

1973 Cyprus	1973 Portugal	1973 Cyprus	1973 England	1973 Scotland
1 Jennings	1 Jennings	1 McFaul	1 Jennings	1 Jennings
2 Rice	2 O'Kane	2 O'Kane	2 Rice	2 Rice
3 Neill	3 Nelson	3 Hunter (Coyle)	3 Craig	3 Craig
4 Hunter	4 Neill	4 Neill	4 Neill	4 Neill
5 Craig	5 Hunter	5 Craig	5 Hunter	5 Hunter
6 Hegan	6 Clements	6 Hamilton (Lutton)	6 Clements	6 Clements
7 Clements	7 Hamilton	7 Jackson	7 Hamilton	7 Hamilton
8 Hamilton	8 Coyle	8 Clements	8 Jackson	8 Jackson
9 Dickson	9 Morgan	9 Morgan	9 Morgan	9 Morgan
10 Dougan	10 Dickson	10 O'Neill	10 O'Neill	10 O'Neill
11 Nelson	11 O'Neill	11 Anderson	11 Anderson	11 Anderson (Lutton)
Nicosia **Feb 14: 0-1**	**Coventry** **Mar 28: 1-1** **O'Neill**	**London** **May 8: 3-0** **Morgan** **Anderson 2**	**Liverpool** **May 12: 1-2** **Clements, pen.**	**Glasgow** **May 16: 2-1** **O'Neill, Anderson**

1973 Bulgaria	1973 Portugal	1973 Wales	1974 Scotland	1974 England
1 McFaul	1 Jennings	1 Jennings	1 Jennings	1 Jennings
2 Rice	2 Rice	2 Rice	2 Rice	2 Rice
3 Craig	3 Craig	3 Craig	3 Nelson	3 Nelson
4 O'Kane	4 Jackson	4 Neill	4 O'Kane	(Sub. Jackson)
5 Hunter	(Sub. Coyle)	5 Hunter	5 Hunter	4 O'Kane
6 Clements	5 O'Kane	6 Clements	6 Clements	5 Hunter
7 Hamilton	6 Clements	7 Hamilton	7 Hamilton	6 Clements
8 Jackson	7 Anderson	(Lutton)	(Sub. Jackson)	7 Hamilton
(Sub. Coyle)	8 O'Neill	8 Jackson	8 Cassidy	8 Cassidy
9 Morgan	9 Morgan	9 Morgan	9 Morgan	9 Morgan
10 Anderson	10 Lutton	10 O'Neill	10 McIlroy	10 McIlroy
11 O'Neill	11 Best	11 Anderson	11 McGrath	11 McGrath
(Sub. Cassidy)		(Coyle)		
Hillsborough	**Lisbon**	**Liverpool**	**Hampden**	**Wembley**
Sheffield	**1-0**	**May 19: 1-0**	**May 11: 1-0**	**May 15: 0-1**
Sept 26: 0-0	**O'Kane**	**Hamilton**	**Cassidy**	

1974 Wales	1974 Norway	1974 Sweden	1975 Yugoslavia	1975 England
1 Jennings	1 Jennings	1 Jennings	1 Jennings	1 Jennings
2 Rice	2 Rice	2 O'Kane	2 Rice	2 Rice
3 O'Kane	3 Craig	3 Nelson	3 Nelson	3 O'Kane
4 Hunter	(Dowd)	(Blair)	4 Nicholl	4 Nicholl
5 Dowd	4 O'Kane	4 Nicholl	5 Hunter	5 Hunter
6 Clements	5 Hunter	5 Hunter	6 Clements	6 Clements
7 Hamilton.	6 Clements	6 Dowd	7 Hamilton	7 Hamilton
(Sub: Jackson)	7 Hamilton	7 Hamilton	8 O'Neill	(Finney)
8 Cassidy	8 Cassidy	8 Jackson	9 Spence	8 O'Neill
9 O'Neill	9 McIlroy	9 Morgan	10 McIlroy	9 Spence
10 McIlroy	10 Finney	10 O'Neill	11 Jackson	10 McIlroy
11 McGrath	11 McGrath	11 McIlroy		11 Jackson
	(Jackson)			
Wrexham	**Oslo**	**Stockholm**	**Belfast**	**Belfast**
May 18: 0-1	**Sept 4: 1-2**	**Oct 30: 2-0**	**April 16: 1-0**	**May 17: 0-0**
	Finney	**Nicholl, O'Neill**	**Hamilton**	

1975 Scotland	1975 Wales	1975 Sweden	1975 Norway	1975 Yugoslavia
1 Jennings	1 Jennings	1 Jennings	1 Jennings	1 Jennings
2 Rice	2 Scott	2 Rice	2 Rice	2 Rice
3 O'Kane	3 Rice	3 Nelson	3 Nicholl, C.	3 Scott
4 Nicholl	4 Nicholl	4 Nicholl, C.	4 Nelson	4 Nicholl, C.
5 Hunter	5 Hunter	5 Hunter	5 Hunter	5 Hunter
(Blair)	6 Clements	6 Clements	6 Jackson	6 Clements
6 Clements	7 Blair	7 Blair	7 Hamilton	7 Hamilton
7 Finney	8 Jackson	8 Hamilton	8 McIlroy	8 McIlroy
8 O'Neill	9 Spence	(Morgan)	9 Morgan	9 Morgan
(Anderson)	10 McIlroy	9 Spence	(Cochrane)	10 Jackson
9 Spence	11 Finney	10 McIlroy	10 Jamison	(O'Neill)
10 McIlroy		11 Jackson	11 Finney	11 Finney
11 Jackson				
Hampden	**Belfast**	**Belfast**	**Belfast**	**Belgrade**
May 20: 0-3	**May 23: 1-0**	**Sept 3: 1-2**	**Oct 29: 3-0**	**Nov 19: 0-1**
	Finney	**Hunter**	**Morgan**	
			Hamilton	
			McIlroy	

1976 Israel	1976 Scotland	1976 England	1976 Wales	1976 Holland
1 Jennings	1 Jennings	1 Jennings	1 Jennings	1 Jennings
(Platt)	2 Scott	2 Rice	2 Scott	2 Nicholl, J.
2 Scott	3 Rice	3 Nicholl, C.	3 Rice	3 Rice
3 Nicholl, J.	4 Nicholl, C.	4 Hunter	4 Nicholl, C.	4 Jackson
4 Hunter	5 Hunter	5 Nelson	5 Hunter	5 Hunter (capt.)
5 Rice	6 Sharkey	(Scott)	6 Clements	6 Hamilton
6 Blair	(McCreery)	6 Hamilton	7 Hamilton	7 Best
7 Nelson	7 Hamilton	7 Cassidy	8 McIlroy	8 McIlroy
8 Hamilton	8 McIlroy	8 Clements	9 Spence	9 McGrath
9 Anderson	9 Morgan	9 McCreery	10 Cassidy	(Sub: Spence)
(McGrath)	(Spence)	10 Spence	(J. Nicholl)	10 McCreery
10 Spence	10 Cassidy	11 McIlroy	11 Morgan	11 Anderson
11 Feeney	11 Finney			
Tel Aviv	**Glasgow**	**Wembley**	**Swansea**	**Rotterdam**
Mar 3: 1-1	**May 8: 0-3**	**May 11: 0-4**	**May 14: 0-1**	**Oct 13: 2-2**
Lev (o.g.)				**McGrath**
				Spence

1976 Belgium	1977 W. Germany	1977 England	1977 Scotland	1977 Wales
1 Jennings	1 Jennings	1 Jennings	1 Jennings	1 Jennings
2 Nicholl, J.	2 Rice	2 Nicholl, J.	2 Nicholl, J.	2 Nicholl, J.
3 Hunter (capt.)	3 Hunter (capt.)	3 Hunter (capt.)	3 Hunter (capt.)	3 Hunter (capt.)
4 Jackson	4 Jackson	4 Rice	4 Rice	4 Nicholl, C.
5 Rice	5 Nelson	5 Jackson	5 Jackson	5 Nelson
(Sub: Nelson)	6 Hamilton	6 Hamilton	6 Hamilton	6 Hamilton
6 Hamilton	7 McCreery	7 McCreery	7 O'Neill	7 Jackson
7 McCreery	(Sub: Cassidy)	8 McIlroy	8 McIlroy	8 McIlroy
8 McGrath	8 Best	9 McGrath	9 McGrath	9 McGrath
9 Anderson	9 McGrath	10 Armstrong	10 McCreery	10 Anderson
10 Best	10 Anderson	(Sub: O'Neill)	11 Anderson	(Sub: Spence)
11 McIlroy	11 Armstrong	11 Anderson	(Sub: Spence)	11 McCreery
		(Sub: Spence)		(Sub: Armstrong)
Liège	**Cologne**	**Belfast**	**Glasgow**	**Belfast**
Nov 10: 0-2	**Apr 27: 0-5**	**May 28: 1-2**	**June 1: 0-3**	**June 3:1-1**
		McGrath		**Nelson**

1977 Iceland	1977 Iceland	1977 Holland	1977 Belgium	1978 Scotland
1 Jennings	1 Jennings	1 Jennings	1 Jennings	1 Platt
2 Rice	2 Rice	2 Rice	2 Rice	2 B. Hamilton
3 Hunter (capt.)	3 Nelson	3 Nelson	3 Nelson	(capt.)
4 Nicholl, J.	4 Nicholl, J.	4 Nicholl, J.	4 Nicholl, J.	3 Nicholl, C.
5 Nelson	5 Hunter (capt.)	5 Hunter (capt.)	5 Hunter (capt.)	4 Nicholl, J.
6 Hamilton	6 O'Neill	6 O'Neill	(Sub. C. Nicholl)	5 Scott
7 Jackson	7 McCreery	7 McCreery	6 McIlroy	6 O'Neill
(Sub: Spence)	8 McIlroy	8 McIlroy	7 McGrath	7 McCreery
8 McIlroy	9 McGrath	9 McGrath	8 Stewart	8 McIlroy
9 McGrath	10 Best	10 Best	9 Armstrong	9 Anderson
10 McCreery	11 Anderson	11 Anderson	10 McCreery	Sub: Cochrane)
11 Anderson			11 Anderson	10 Armstrong
(Sub: Armstrong)				11 McGrath
				(Sub: W. Hamilton)
Reykjavik	**Belfast**	**Belfast**	**Belfast**	**Glasgow**
June: 11 0-1	**Sept: 14 2-0**	**Oct: 13 0-1**	**Nov: 16: 3-0**	**May: 13 1-1**
	McGrath		**Armstrong (2)**	**O'Neill**
	McIlroy		**McGrath**	

165

1978 England	1978 Wales	1978 Rep. of Ireland	1978 Denmark	1978 Bulgaria
1 Platt	1 Platt	1 Jennings	1 Jennings	1 Jennings
2 Hamilton (capt.)	2 Hamilton (capt.)	2 Rice	2 Rice	2 Hamilton (capt.)
3 Nicholl, C.	3 Nicholl, C.	3 Hunter (capt.)	3 Nelson	3 Nicholl, J.
4 Nicholl, J.	4 Nicholl, J.	(Sub. Hamilton)	4 Nicholl, J.	4 Nicholl, C.
5 Scott	5 Scott	4 Nicholl, C.	5 Hunter (capt.)	5 Nelson
6 O'Neill	(Sub. Connell)	5 Nelson	6 McCreery	6 O'Neill
7 McCreery	6 O'Neill	6 McIlroy	7 O'Neill	7 McCreery
8 McIlroy	7 McCreery	7 McCreery	8 McIlroy	8 McIlroy
9 Anderson	8 McIlroy	8 O'Neill	9 Armstrong	(Sub. Moreland)
10 Armstrong	9 McGrath	9 Nicholl, J.	10 Morgan	9 Cochrane
11 McGrath	10 Armstrong	10 Armstrong	(Sub. Spence)	(Sub. McGrath)
(Sub. Cochrane)	11 Anderson	11 Spence	(Sub. Anderson)	10 Armstrong
	(Sub. Cochrane)	(Sub. Cochrane)	11 Cochrane	11 Caskey
Wembley	**Wrexham**	**Dublin**	**Belfast**	**Sofia**
May 16: 0-1	**May 19: 0-1**	**Sept 20: 0-0**	**Oct 25: 2-1**	**Nov 29: 2-0**
			Spence, Anderson	**Armstrong, Caskey**

1979 England	1979 Bulgaria	1979 England	1979 Scotland	1979 Wales
1 Jennings (capt.)	1 Jennings	1 Jennings	1 Jennings	1 Jennings
2 Rice	2 Hamilton (capt.)	2 Rice	2 Rice	2 Rice
3 Nelson	3 Nicholl, J.	3 Nicholl, J.	3 Nicholl, J.	3 Nelson
4 Nicholl, J.	(Sub. Moreland)	4 Nicholl, C.	4 Hunter	4 Nicholl, J.
5 Nicholl, C.	4 Nicholl, C.	5 Nelson	5 Nelson	5 Nicholl, C.
6 McCreery	5 Nelson	6 Moreland	6 Sloan	6 Hunter (capt.)
7 O'Neill	6 McCreery	(Sub. McGrath)	7 Hamilton (capt.)	7 Hamilton, B.
8 McIlroy	7 O'Neill	7 Hamilton (capt.)	8 Moreland	8 Armstrong
9 Armstrong	8 McIlroy	8 McIlroy	(Sub. Scott)	9 Spence
10 Caskey	9 Armstrong	9 Armstrong	9 McIlroy	10 McCreery
(Sub. Spence)	10 Caskey	10 Caskey	10 Spence	(Sub. Sloan)
11 Cochrane	(Sub. Spence)	11 Cochrane	(Sub. Caskey)	11 McIlroy
	11 Cochrane	(Sub. Spence)	11 Armstrong	
Wembley	**Belfast**	**Belfast**	**Glasgow**	**Belfast**
Feb 7: 0-4	**May 12: 2-0**	**May 19: 0-2**	**May 22: 0-1**	**May 25: 1-1**
	C. Nicholl,			**Spence**
	Armstrong			

1979 Denmark	1979 England	1979 Rep. of Ireland
1 Jennings	1 Jennings	1 Jennings
2 Rice	2 Rice	2 Nicholl, J.
3 Nelson	3 Nelson	3 Nelson
4 Nicholl, J.	4 Nicholl, J.	4 Nicholl, C.
5 Hunter (capt.)	5 Hunter (capt.)	5 Hunter (capt.)
6 McCreery	(Sub. Rafferty)	6 McCreery
7 O'Neill	6 McCreery	7 O'Neill, M.
(Sub. Sloan)	7 McIlroy	(Sub. Cassidy)
8 McIlroy	8 Cassidy	8 McIlroy
(Sub. Caskey)	9 Armstrong	9 Armstrong
9 Armstrong	10 Finney	10 Spence
10 Spence	(Sub. Caskey)	11 Moreland
11 Hamilton, B.	11 Moreland	
Copenhagen	**Belfast**	**Belfast**
June 6: 0-4	**Oct 17: 1-5**	**Nov 21: 1-0**
	Moreland pen.	**Armstrong**

7: UNDER 23 INTERNATIONALS
(All matches against Wales except where otherwise stated)

Briggs, R. (Manchester Utd.) 1962 (with Swansea T.) 1965.

Burke (Portadown) 1963.

Campbell, W. (Distillery) 1964 (with Sunderland) 1965.

Campbell, W. (Dundee) 1967.

Clarke, F. (Arsenal) 1962-3-4-5.

Clarke, N. (Ballymena) 1962 (with Sunderland) 1963.

Clements, D. (Coventry C.) 1965, 1967-8.

Craig, D. (Newcastle U.) 1965.

Craig, W. (Linfield) 1965, 1967.

Dunlop, S. (Coleraine) 1965, 1968.

Elder, A. (Burnley) 1964.

Elwood, J. (Linfield) 1962.

Gaston, R. (Oxford) 1968-9—IT

Hamilton, T. (Linfield) 1968, 1969—IT.

Harkin, T. (Port Vale) 1963.

Harvey, M. (Sunderland) 1962-3-4.

Hunter, A. (Oldham) 1968-69—IT.

Irvine, R. (Linfield) 1963.

Irvine, W. (Burnley) 1963-4-5.

Jackson, T. (Everton) 1968.

Jennings, P. (Watford) 1964.

Johnston, J. (Blackpool) 1968-9—IT.

Johnston, W. (Glenavon) 1964.

Magill, J. (Arsenal) 1962.

McAvoy, W. (Ards) 1968.

McCaffrey, G. (Leicester C.) 1963.

McKeag, W. (Glentoran) 1967-8.

McKinney, V. (Falkirk) 1967.

McKenzie, R. (Airdrieonians) 1967-8, 1968-9—IT.

McLaughlin, J. (Shrewsbury T.) 1963-4.

McMillan, S. (Wrexham) 1964.

McMordie, E. (Middlesboro) 1967.

McNeill, A. (Middlesboro) 1968.

Morrow, T. (Glentoran) 1968-9—IT.

Mullan, B. (Fulham) 1968-69—IT.

Napier, J. (Bolton W.) 1967 (with Brighton) 1968.

Neill, T. (Arsenal) 1962-3-4-5.

Nelson, S. (Arsenal), 1968-9—IT.

Nicholson, J. (Manchester U.) 1962-3-4-5.

O'Doherty, T. (Coleraine) 1968-9—IT.

O'Neill, J. (Sunderland) 1962.

Rice, P. (Arsenal) 1968-9—IT.

Ross, E. (Glentoran) 1967.

Sloan, D. (Scunthorpe U.) 1964.

Todd, S. (Burnley) 1965-7, 1968-9—IT.

Trainor, D. (Crusaders) 1967.

Welsh, E. (Distillery) 1962.

8: UNDER 21 INTERNATIONAL CAPS

Blackledge, G. (Portadown), 1978, R.I.

Brotherston, N. (Blackburn Rovers), 1978, R.I.

Connell, T. (Coleraine), 1978, R.I.

Donaghy, M. (Larne), 1978, R.I.

Hamilton, W. (Linfield), 1978, R.I.

Harvey, J. (Arsenal), 1978, R.I.

Hayes, T. (Luton Town), 1978, R.I.

Johnston, B. (Cliftonville), 1978, R.I.

McCreery, D. (Man. United), 1978, R.I.

Moreland, V. (Glentoran), 1978, R.I.

Murray, W. (Linfield), 1978, R.I.

Nicholl, J. (Man. United), 1978, R.I.

O'Neill, J. (Leicester City), 1978, R.I.

Sloan, T. (Ballymena United), 1978, R.I.

9: 'B' INTERNATIONAL CAPS

Barr, H. (Ballymena) 1959—F.

Campbell, A. (Crusaders) 1957—Rum:

Chapman, S. (Mansfield Town) 1957—Rum.

Corr, P. (Glenavon) 1957—Rum.

Crossan, J. (Rotterdam Sparta) 1959—F.

Dougan, D. (Portsmouth) 1957—Rum.; 1959—F.

Elder, A. (Burnley) 1959—F.

Elwood, J. (Leyton Orient) 1960—F.

Fraser, J. (Sunderland) 1959—F.

Hamill, T. (Linfield) 1957—F.

Harvey, M. (Sunderland) 1959—F; 1960—F.

Hill, J. (Newcastle Utd.) 1957—Rum; 1960 (Norwich)—F.

Hunter, V. (Coleraine) 1960—F.

Keith, D. (Newcastle Utd.) 1957—Rum.

Lawther, I. (Sunderland) 1959—F; 1960—F.

Lowry, T. (Falkirk) 1960—F.

Marshall, W. (Burnley) 1957—Rum; 1960—F.

Milligan, J. (Cliftonville) 1959—F.

McCullough, W. (Arsenal) 1959—F.

McCrory, S. (Southend Utd.) 1957—Rum.

Nicholson, J. (Manchester Utd.) 1959—F; 1960—F.

Rea, R. (Glenavon) 1957—Rum.

Scott, J. (Grimsby Town) 1957—Rum.

Shiels, D. (Sheffield Utd.) 1960—F.

Shields, J. (Manchester Utd.) 1960—F.

Wilson, S. (Glenavon) 1960—F.

Wilson, W. (Burnley) 1957—Rum.

167

10: NORTHERN IRELAND MANAGERS

Peter Doherty: 1951-62
Bertie Peacock: 1962-67
Billy Bingham: 1967-71
Terry Neill: 1971-75

Dave Clements: 1975-76
Danny Blanchflower: 1976-79
Billy Bingham: 1980

11: BRITISH INTERNATIONAL CHAMPIONSHIPS

11a: IRELAND v ENGLAND

Year	Venue	Ire.	Eng.	Year	Venue	Ire.	Eng.
1882	Belfast	0	13	1930	Sheffield	1	5
1883	Liverpool	0	7	1931	Belfast	2	6
1884	Belfast	1	8	1932	Blackpool	0	1
1885	Manchester	0	4	1933	Belfast	0	3
1886	Belfast	1	6	1934	Everton	1	2
1887	Sheffield	0	7	1935	Belfast	1	3
1888	Belfast	1	5	1936	Stoke	1	3
1889	Everton	1	6	1937	Belfast	1	5
1890	Belfast	1	9	1938	Manchester	0	7
1891	Wolverhampton	1	6	1939-44	Not played		
1892	Belfast	0	2	1945	Belfast	0	1
1893	Birmingham	1	6	1946	Belfast	2	7
1894	Belfast	2	2	1947	Everton	2	2
1895	Derby	0	9	1948	Belfast	2	6
1896	Belfast	0	2	1949	Manchester	2	9
1897	Nottingham	0	6	1950	Belfast	1	4
1898	Belfast	2	3	1951	Aston Villa	0	2
1899	Sunderland	2	13	1952	Belfast	2	2
1900	Dublin	0	2	1953	Liverpool	1	3
1901	Southampton	0	3	1954	Belfast	0	2
1902	Belfast	0	1	1955	Wembley	0	3
1903	Wolverhampton	0	4	1956	Belfast	1	1
1904	Belfast	1	3	1957	Wembley	3	2
1905	Middlesbrough	1	1	1958	Belfast	3	3
1906	Belfast	0	5	1959	Wembley	1	2
1907	Everton	0	1	1960	Belfast	2	5
1908	Belfast	1	3	1961	Wembley	1	1
1909	Bradford	0	4	1962	Belfast	1	3
1910	Belfast	1	1	1963	Wembley	3	8
1911	Derby	1	2	1964	Belfast	3	4
1912	Dublin	1	6	1965	Wembley	1	2
1913	Belfast	2	1	1966	Belfast	0	2
1914	Middlesbrough	3	0	1967	Wembley	0	2
1915-18	Not played			1969	Belfast (May)	1	3
1919	Belfast	1	1	1970	Wembley (April)	1	3
1920	Sunderland	0	2	1971	Belfast (May)	0	1
1921	Belfast	1	1	1972	Wembley	1	0
1922	West Brom	0	2	1973*	Goodison	1	2
1923	Belfast	2	1	1974	Wembley	0	1
1924	Everton	1	3	1975	Belfast	0	0
1925	Belfast	0	0	1976	Wembley	0	4
1926	Liverpool	3	3	1977	Belfast	1	2
1927	Belfast	2	0	1978	Wembley	0	1
1928	Everton	1	2	1979	Belfast	0	2
1929	Belfast	0	3				

*Switched because of civil unrest.

168

11b: IRELAND v. WALES

Year	Venue	Ire.	Wales	Year	Venue	Ire.	Wales
1882	Wrexham	1	7	1931	Belfast	4	0
1883	Belfast	1	1	1931	Wrexham	2	3
1884	Wrexham	0	6	1932	Wrexham	1	4
1885	Belfast	2	8	1933	Belfast	1	1
1886	Wrexham	0	5	1935	Wrexham	1	3
1887	Belfast	4	1	1936	Belfast	3	2
1888	Wrexham	0	11	1937	Wrexham	1	4
1889	Belfast	1	3	1938	Belfast	1	0
1890	Shrewsbury	2	5	1939	Wrexham	1	3
1891	Belfast	7	2	1940-45	Not played		
1892	Bangor	1	1	1947	Belfast	2	1
1893	Belfast	4	3	1948	Wrexham	0	2
1894	Swansea	1	4	1949	Belfast	0	2
1895	Belfast	2	2	1950	Wrexham	0	0
1896	Wrexham	1	6	1951	Belfast	1	2
1897	Belfast	4	3	1952	Swansea	0	3
1898	Llandudno	1	0	1953	Belfast	2	3
1899	Belfast	1	0	1954	Wrexham	2	1
1900	Llandudno	0	2	1955	Belfast	2	3
1901	Belfast	0	1	1956	Cardiff	1	1
1902	Cardiff	3	0	1957	Belfast	0	0
1903	Belfast	2	1	1958	Cardiff	1	1
1904	Bangor	1	0	1959	Belfast	4	1
1905	Belfast	2	2	1960	Wrexham	2	3
1906	Wrexham	4	4	1961	Belfast	1	5
1907	Belfast	2	3	1962	Cardiff	0	4
1908	Aberdare	1	0	1963	Belfast	1	4
1909	Belfast	2	3	1964	Swansea	3	2
1910	Wrexham	1	4	1965	Belfast	0	4
1911	Belfast	1	2	1966	Cardiff	4	1
1912	Cardiff	3	2	1967	Belfast	0	0
1913	Belfast	0	1	1968	Wrexham	0	2
1914	Wrexham	2	1	1969	Belfast (May)	0	0
1915-19	Not played			1970	Swansea (April)	0	1
1920	Belfast	2	2	1971	Belfast (May)	1	0
1921	Swansea	1	2	1972	Wrexham	0	0
1922	Belfast	1	1	1973*	Goodison	1	0
1923	Wrexham	3	0	1974	Wrexham	0	1
1924	Belfast	0	1	1975	Belfast	1	0
1925	Wrexham	0	0	1976	Swansea	0	1
1926	Belfast	3	0	1977	Belfast	1	1
1927	Cardiff	2	2	1978	Wrexham	0	1
1928	Belfast	1	2	1979	Belfast	1	1
1929	Wrexham	2	2				
1930	Belfast	7	0				

*Switched because of civil unrest.

11c: IRELAND v. SCOTLAND

Year	Venue	Ire.	Scot.	Year	Venue	Ire.	Scot.
1884	Belfast	0	5	1890	Belfast	1	4
1885	Glasgow	2	8	1891	Glasgow	1	2
1886	Belfast	2	7	1892	Belfast	2	3
1887	Glasgow	1	4	1893	Glasgow	1	6
1888	Belfast	2	10	1894	Belfast	1	2
1889	Glasgow	0	7	1895	Glasgow	1	3

Year	Venue			Year	Venue		
1896	Belfast	3	3	1939	Belfast	0	2
1897	Glasgow	1	5	1940-45	Not played		
1898	Belfast	0	3	1946	Glasgow	0	0
1899	Glasgow	1	9	1947	Belfast	2	0
1900	Belfast	0	3	1948	Glasgow	2	3
1901	Glasgow	0	11	1949	Belfast	2	8
1902	Belfast	1	5	1950	Glasgow	1	6
1903	Glasgow	2	0	1951	Belfast	0	3
1904	Dublin	1	1	1952	Glasgow	1	1
1905	Glasgow	0	4	1953	Belfast	1	3
1906	Dublin	0	1	1954	Glasgow	2	2
1907	Glasgow	0	3	1955	Belfast	2	1
1908	Dublin	0	5	1956	Glasgow	0	1
1909	Glasgow	0	5	1957	Belfast	1	1
1910	Belfast	1	0	1958	Glasgow	2	2
1911	Glasgow	0	2	1959	Belfast	0	4
1912	Belfast	1	4	1960	Glasgow	2	5
1913	Dublin	1	2	1961	Belfast	1	6
1914	Belfast	1	1	1962	Glasgow	1	5
1915-19	Not played			1963	Belfast	2	1
1920	Glasgow	0	3	1964	Glasgow	2	3
1921	Belfast	0	2	1965	Belfast	3	2
1922	Glasgow	1	2	1966	Glasgow	1	2
1923	Belfast	0	1	1967	Belfast	1	0
1924	Glasgow	0	2	1969	Glasgow (May)	1	1
1925	Belfast	0	3	1970	Belfast (April)	0	1
1926	Glasgow	0	4	1971	Glasgow (May)	1	0
1927	Belfast	0	2	1972*	Glasgow	0	2
1928	Glasgow	1	0	1973	Glasgow	2	1
1929	Belfast	3	7	1974*	Glasgow	1	0
1930	Glasgow	1	3	1975	Glasgow	0	3
1931	Belfast	0	0	1976*	Glasgow	0	3
1932	Glasgow	1	3	1977	Glasgow	0	3
1933	Belfast	0	4	1978*	Glasgow	1	1
1934	Glasgow	2	1	1979	Glasgow	0	1
1935	Belfast	2	1				
1936	Belfast	1	2				
1937	Aberdeen	1	3				
1938	Belfast	1	1				

*Switched because of civil unrest.

12: VICTORY INTERNATIONALS

12a: 1919

At Glasgow—Scotland	2	Ireland	1
At Belfast—Ireland	0	Scotland	0

12b: 1945-46

At Belfast—England	1	Ireland	0
At Belfast—Scotland	3	Ireland	2
At Cardiff—Ireland	1	Wales	0

13: IFA ANNIVERSARY GAME

Held 15 August 1955 at Windsor Park, Belfast

Great Britain	1	Rest of Europe	4

Attendance: 58,000; receipts £13,000

Scorers: Great Britain — Johnstone (Man. City); Rest of Europe — Vukas (Yugoslavia) (3); Vincent (France).

170

v. ALBANIA

Year	Venue	F.	A.
1965*	Belfast	4	1
1965*	Tirana	1	1

v. ARGENTINE

1958*	Halmstad	1	3

v. BELGIUM

1977*	Liège	0	2
1978*	Belfast	3	0

v. BULGARIA

1972*	Sofia	0	3
1973*	Sheffield	0	0
1978	Sofia	2	0
1979	Belfast	2	0

v. CANADA

1891	Belfast	5	2
1973	Belfast	6	4

v. CYPRUS

1971	Nicosia	3	1
1971	Belfast	5	0
1973*	Nicosia	0	1
1973*	Fulham	3	0

v. CZECHOSLOVAKIA

1958*	Halmstad	1	0
1958*	Malmo	2	1

v. DENMARK

1978	Belfast	2	1
1979	Copenhagen	0	4

v. ENGLAND

1979	Wembley	0	4
1979	Belfast	1	5

v. FRANCE

1921	Paris	2	1
1928	Paris	0	4
1951	Belfast	2	2
1952	Paris	1	3
1958*	Norrkoping	0	4

v. GREECE

1961*	Athens	1	2
1961*	Belfast	2	0

v. HOLLAND

1962	Rotterdam	0	4
1965*	Belfast	2	1
1965*	Rotterdam	0	0
1976	Rotterdam	2	2
1978*	Belfast	0	1

v. ICELAND

1977*	Reykjavik	0	1
1977*	Belfast	2	0

v. ISRAEL

1968	Tel Aviv	3	2
1976	Tel Aviv	1	1

v. ITALY

1957*	Rome	0	1
1957	Belfast	2	2
1958*	Belfast	2	1
1961	Bologna	2	3

v. MEXICO

1966	Belfast	4	1

v. NORWAY

1921	Bergen	1	2
1921	Christiansad	2	1
1974	Oslo	1	2
1975	Belfast	3	0

v. PORTUGAL

1957*	Lisbon	1	1
1957*	Belfast	3	0
1973*	Coventry	1	1
1973*	Lisbon	1	1

v. POLAND

1962	Katowice	2	0
1962	Belfast	2	0

v. REP. OF IRELAND

1978	Dublin	0	0
1979	Belfast	1	0

v. SPAIN

1958	Madrid	2	6
1963	Bilbao	0	0
1964	Belfast	0	1
1970	Seville	0	3
1972	Hull	1	1

v. SWEDEN

1974	Stockholm	2	0
1975	Belfast	1	2

v. SWITZERLAND

1964*	Belfast	1	0
1965*	Lausanne	1	2

v. TURKEY

1968*	Belfast	4	1
1968*	Istanbul	3	0

v. URUGUAY

1964	Belfast	3	0

v. U.S.S.R.

1969*	Belfast	0	0
1969*	Moscow	0	2
1971	Moscow	0	1
1971	Belfast	1	1

v. WEST GERMANY

1958*	Malmo	2	2
1960*	Belfast	3	4
1961*	Berlin	1	2
1966	Belfast	0	2
1977	Cologne	0	5

v. YUGOSLAVIA

1975	Belfast	1	0
1975	Belgrade	0	1

*Indicates World Cup Match

14b: 'B'INTERNATIONALS

v. RUMANIA

1957	Belfast	6	0

v. FRANCE

1959	Belfast	1	1
1960	Annecy	0	5

15: 'UNDER 23' AND 'UNDER 21' INTERNATIONALS

15a: 'UNDER 23' INTERNATIONALS

v. WALES

1962	Belfast	0	0
1963	Swansea	1	5
1964	Belfast	3	3
1965	Swansea	2	2
1967	Belfast	2	1
1968	Cardiff	1	0
1969	Belfast — postponed (frost).		
1970	Wrexham — postponed (snow).		

v. ITALY

1969	Brescia	1	2

15b: 'UNDER 21' INTERNATIONALS

v. REP. OF IRELAND

1978	Dublin	1	1

16: REPRESENTATIVE MATCHES

WAR-TIME GAMES

1941 — Ireland 1; Army 4.
1942 — Ireland 3; Army 2.
1943 — Ireland 4; Army 2.
1944 — Prisoners of War Fund. Ireland 6: Combined Services (NI) 1.
1945 — Ireland 4 (Doherty 4); Combined Services 8 (Carter 4, Mullan 2, Mortensen, Lawton). Attendance 49,875. Receipts £4,457.

v. BRITISH ARMY

Year	Date	F.	A.
1950	Sept. 13 Belfast	0	0
1951	Sept. 11 Belfast	2	2
1952	Sept. 10 Belfast	2	3.
1954	May 5 Belfast	1	0
1956	Mar. 21 Preston	3	4
1956	Oct. 24 Belfast	1	2
1957	Nov. 20 Leeds	1	2
1959	Mar. 11 Belfast	2	4
1960	May 4 Belfast	2	0
1961	Mar. 13 Liverpool	0	1

U.S. & CANADIAN TOUR, 1953

May 14	— Liverpool 4, Ireland 0 (New York)
May 18	— Ireland 4, Hamilton & District 1
May 20	— Ireland 2, Ontario 0
May 24	— Ireland 2, Manitoba 0
May 26	— Ireland 10, Saskatchewan 0
May 31	— Ireland 3, Vancouver All Stars 1
June 2	— Ireland 5, Brit. Columbia 1
June 7	— Ireland 2, Brit. Columbia·3
June 8	— Ireland 9; Alberta 1
June 14	— Ireland 1, Liverpool 3 (Toronto)
June 17	— Ireland 1, Berne Young Boys 4

17: AMATEUR INTERNATIONALS

(Abolished 1973 — 74 Season)

17a: IRELAND v. ENGLAND

Year	Venue	Ire.	Eng.	Year	Venue	Ire.	Eng
1906	Dublin	1	2	1947	Southport	1	3
1907	Tottenham	1	6	1948	Belfast	0	5
1908	Dublin	1	5	1949	Norwich	1	0
1909	Leeds	4	4	1950	Belfast	1	3
1910	Belfast	3	2	1951	Coventry	3	6
1911	Huddersfield	0	2	1952	Portadown	1	3
1912	Belfast	3	2	1953	Lincoln	1	4
1913	Belfast	0	2	1953	Coleraine	2	1
1919	Derby	0	5	1954	Selhurst Park	0	5
1920	Belfast	0	4	1955	Belfast	1	4
1921	Leicester	1	4	1956	Bromley	2	5
1922	Preston	0	4	1957	Belfast	0	3
1923	Crystal Palace	0	3	1958	Bournemouth	2	6
1924	Belfast	2	3	1959	Belfast	1	1
1925	Maidstone	4	6	1960	High Wycombe	2	3
1926	Belfast	0	3	1961	Coleraine	0	3
1927	Blackpool	1	1	1962	Dulwich	2	3
1928	Belfast	0	2	1963	Belfast	2	1
1929	Crystal Palace	2	7	1964	Romford	1	2
1930	Belfast	3	1	1965	Ballymena	0	2
1931	York	2	3	1966	Watford	0	2
1933	Belfast	4	3	1967	Ballymena	1	0
1934	Ilford	0	4	1968	Charlton	0	5
1935	Belfast	2	4	1969	Portadown	1	4
1936	Blackpool	0	5	1970	Woking	1	4
1937	Belfast	5	1	1971-72	Hendon	2	1
1938	Leicester	1	1	1972-73*	Norwich	1	2
1939	Belfast	0	1	1973-74	Manchester	0	2

*Switched because of civil unrest

17b: IRELAND v. SCOTLAND

Year	Venue	Ire.	Scot.	Year	Venue	Ire.	Scot
1930	Londonderry	0	3	1956	Kilmarnock	3	1
1931	Aberdeen	0	2	1957	Newtownards	4	1
1932	Belfast	4	0	1958	Airdrie	3	1
1933	Glasgow	1	5	1959	Coleraine	0	0
1934	Belfast	4	1	1960	Glasgow	0	2
1935	Glasgow	3	2	1961	Coleraine	3	3
1936	Belfast	3	5	1962	Falkirk	0	0
1937	Glasgow	0	3	1963	Belfast	5	2
1938	Belfast	2	1	1964	Glasgow	2	2
1939	Glasgow	1	1	1965	Ballymena	1	1
1950	Aberdeen	5	2	1967	Newtownards	1	2
1951	Londonderry	0	1	1968	Greenock	0	2
1952	Glasgow	1	2	1969	Portadown	1	2
1953	Belfast	1	0	1970	Stranraer	1	3
1954	Kilmarnock	0	0	1971	Belfast	1	1
1955	Belfast	2	1	1972	Paisley	1	0
				1973*	Falkirk	0	1
				1974	Not Played		

*Switched because of civil unrest

173

Year	Venue	Ire.	Wales	Year	Venue	Ire.	Wales
1954	Belfast................	3	2	1964	Belfast................	2	2
1955	Llanidloes............	2	1	1965	Newtown	1	1
1956	Belfast................	2	1	1966	Portadown	0	0
1957	Ebbw Vale	1	3	1967	Welshpool	3	3
1958	Coleraine	3	1	1968	Portadown	0	1
1959	Llandudno	4	3	1969	Ton Pentre	0	1
1960	Ballymena	3	2	1970	Ballymena	3	1
1961	Portmadoc	1	4	1971	Llanelli	0	1
1962	Ballymena	3	1	1972	Welshpool	3	0
1963	Wrexham	2	0	1973*	Rhyl	1	2
*Switched because of civil unrest				1974	Denbigh	0	1

17d: IRELAND v. OLYMPIC XI

1948 (Belfast)	Ireland	5	Gold Coast	0
1951	Ireland	5	Gold Coast	2

(Gold Coast XI played in bare feet)

17e: IRELAND v. SOUTH AFRICA

1953 (Belfast)	Ireland	2	South Africa	5
1958 (Belfast)	Ireland	2	South Africa	5

17f: IRELAND v. NEW ZEALAND

1979	Irish FA XI	2	New Zealand	0

18. JUNIOR INTERNATIONALS

18a: IRELAND v. SCOTLAND

1890 — Scotland	11	Ireland	0	1920 — Scotland	3	Ireland	1
1891 — Scotland	1	Ireland	1	1921 — Ireland	1	Scotland	0
1892 — Scotland	6	Ireland	3	1922 — Scotland	0	Ireland	0
1893 — Scotland	4	Ireland	1	1923 — Scotland	4	Ireland	0
1894 — Scotland	6	Ireland	2	1924 — Ireland	2	Scotland	1
1895 — Scotland	4	Ireland	3	1925 — Ireland	2	Scotland	2
1896 — Scotland	2	Ireland	1	1926 — Ireland	5	Scotland	3
1897 — Scotland	3	Ireland	1	1927 — Ireland	3	Scotland	3
1898 — Scotland	3	Ireland	0	1928 — Ireland	2	Scotland	1
1900 — Ireland	1	Scotland	1	1929 — Scotland	3	Ireland	1
1901 — Scotland	3	Ireland	1	1930 — Ireland	2	Scotland	2
1902 — Scotland	5	Ireland	0	1931 — Scotland	4	Ireland	2
1903 — Scotland	4	Ireland	0	1932 — Ireland	2	Scotland	1
1904 — Scotland	4	Ireland	1	1933 — Scotland	5	Ireland	2
1905 — Scotland	3	Ireland	1	1934 — Ireland	2	Scotland	2
1906 — Scotland	2	Ireland	0	1935 — Scotland	1	Ireland	0
1907 — Ireland	4	Scotland	0	1936 — Ireland	4	Scotland	0
1908 — Ireland	3	Scotland	3	1937 — Scotland	3	Ireland	0
1909 — Scotland	3	Ireland	2	1938 — Ireland	3	Scotland	3
1910 — Scotland	2	Ireland	2	1939 — Scotland	3	Ireland	0
1911 — Scotland	1	Ireland	1	1940-45—Not played			
1912 — Scotland	2	Ireland	0	1947 — Scotland	2	Ireland	2
1913 — Ireland	3	Scotland	0	1948 — Ireland	3	Scotland	0
1914 — Scotland	2	Ireland	1	1949 — Scotland	1	Ireland	0
1915 — Ireland	1	Scotland	1	1950 — Ireland	2	Scotland	2
1916 — Scotland	2	Ireland	0	1951 — Scotland	4	Ireland	4
1917 — Ireland	2	Scotland	1	1952 — Ireland	0	Scotland	2
1918 — Scotland	1	Ireland	0	1953 — Scotland	5	Ireland	1
1919 — Scotland	1	Ireland	1	1954 — Ireland	3	Scotland	1

1955 — Scotland	1	Ireland	0
1956 — Ireland	1	Scotland	3
1957 — Scotland	3	Ireland	2
1958 — Ireland	2	Scotland	1
1959 — Scotland	5	Ireland	0
1960 — Ireland	1	Scotland	1
1961 — Scotland	2	Ireland	0
1962 — Ireland	1	Scotland	4
1963 — Scotland	1	Ireland	1
1964 — Ireland	3	Scotland	6
1965 — Scotland	3	Ireland	2
1966 — Ireland	0	Scotland	2

1967 — Scotland	5	Ireland	5
1968 — Ireland	3	Scotland	3
1969 — Scotland	2	Ireland	4
1970 — Not played			
1971 — Scotland	3	Ireland	2
1972 — Not played			
1973 — Not played			
1974 — Not played			
1975 — Not played			
1978 — Ireland	1	Scotland	1

18b: IRELAND v. WALES

1925 — Wales	4	Ireland	1
1926 — Ireland	3	Wales	0
1927 — Ireland	3	Wales	2

1928 — Ireland	2	Wales	0
1929 — Ireland	3	Wales	1
1930 — Wales	2	Ireland	2

19: YOUTH INTERNATIONALS

(Abolished 1973 — 74 season)

19a: IRELAND v. ENGLAND

Year	Venue	Ire.	Eng.	Year	Venue	Ire.	Eng.
1948	Belfast	2	2	1961	Manchester	0	2
1949	Hull	2	4	1962	Londonderry	2	1
1950	Belfast	1	0	1963	Oldham	1	1
1951	Liverpool	2	5	1964	Belfast	1	3
1952	Belfast	2	0	1965	Birkenhead	3	2
1953	Wolverhampton	0	0	1966	Cliftonville	0	4
1954	Newtownards	2	2	1967	Stockport	0	3
1955	Watford	0	3	1968	Belfast	2	0
1956	Belfast	1	0	1969	Birkenhead	2	0
1957	London	2	6	1970	Lurgan	3	1
1958	Bangor	4	2	1971	Blackpool	1	1
1959	Liverpool	0	5	1972	Chester	1	1
1960	Portadown	2	5	1973*	Telford	0	3
				1974	Birkenhead	2	1

*Switched because of civil unrest

19b: IRELAND v. SCOTLAND

Year	Venue	Ire.	Scot.	Year	Venue	Ire.	Scot.
1948	Ayr	2	2	1961	Belfast	1	3
1949	Belfast	1	2	1962	Greenock	1	2
1950	Edinburgh	3	8	1963	Coleraine	1	2
1951	Belfast	1	0	1964	Greenock	0	4
1952	Paisley	2	2	1965	Derry	2	3
1953	Belfast	1	1	1966	Dundee	2	2
1954	Greenock	3	3	1967	Belfast	5	0
1955	Lurgan	4	5	1968	Galashiels	1	5
1956	Greenock	0	2	1969	Belfast	1	1
1957	Portadown	3	0	1970	Clydebank	3	3
1958	Stranraer	2	2	1971	Coleraine	1	5
1959	Belfast	1	4	1972	Not Played		
1960	Perth	1	4	1973	Paisley	0	2
				1974	Stenhousemuir	2	2

175

19c: IRELAND v. WALES

Year	Venue	Ire.	Wales	Year	Venue	Ire.	Wales
1948	Cliftonville	0	4	1961	Wrexham	0	1
1949	Bangor	2	4	1962	Newtownards	3	0
1950	Derry	3	2	1963	Aberystwyth	1	1
1951	Aberystwyth	0	1	1964	Belfast..............	1	3
1952	Belfast..............	1	4	1965	Caernarvon	2	0
1953	Bangor	4	3	1966	Coleraine	2	3
1954	Portadown	2	0	1967	Ton Pentre	2	2
1955	Flint................	3	1	1968	Belfast..............	3	2
1956	Ballymena	4	2	1969	Aberystwyth	2	4
1957	Llandudno	1	3	1970	Coleraine	2	1
1958	Coleraine	2	3	1971	Bangor, N. Wales	2	3
1959	Cardiff	2	3	1972	Wrexham	1	3
1960	Belfast..............	2	1	1973*	Denbigh	1	0
				1974	Rhyl	3	1

*Switched because of civil unrest.

19d: EUROPEAN YOUTH INTERNATIONALS
(NORTHERN IRELAND SCORES FIRST)

v. AUSTRIA

Year	Venue	F.	A.
1964	Holland..............	1	3
1977	Belgium	1	0

v. BELGIUM

1948	Holland..............	1	2
1951	Nice	0	1
1963	Eastbourne..........	1	0
1978	Belgium	1	4
1978	Belgium	1	5
1979	Belgium	0	0
1979	Belfast..............	1	0

v. BULGARIA

1955	Italy................	1	5
1963	Southampton	3	3

(after extra time)

v. CZECHOSLOVAKIA

1963	Woking	1	0

v. DENMARK

1976	Hungary	3	5
1976	Denmark	0	1
1977	Belfast..............	2	0

v. ENGLAND

1948	Holland..............	3	3
1963	Wembley	0	4
1975	Switzerland	3	0

v. HOLLAND

1948	Holland..............	0	2
1951	France	2	0
1976	Hungary	0	3

v. ICELAND

1974	Reykjavik	2	1
1974	Belfast..............	3	1

v. MALTA

1977	Belgium	2	0

v. POLAND

1955	Italy	1	1

v. REPUBLIC OF IRELAND

1963	Dublin..............	1	1
1963	Belfast..............	3	2
1965	Dublin..............	4	2
1967	Belfast..............	3	0
1968	Dublin..............	1	3
1970	Dublin..............	3	2
1975	Switzerland	2	0
1976	Dublin..............	3	1
1976	Portadown	3	1
1979	Dublin..............	3	1
1979	Belfast..............	1	2
1979	Dublin..............	2	4

v. RUMANIA

1964	Holland..............	1	0

v. SPAIN

1955	Italy	0	3

v. SWEDEN

1963	England	3	3

v. SWITZERLAND

1975	Lausanne	1	1

v. USSR

1976	Hungary	0	2
1977	Belgium	0	1

v. YUGOSLAVIA

1951	France	0	1

(after 40mins extra time)

176

(Prior to 1946, the names of the winning team only are available. From 1946 onwards both teams are recorded, together with the goal scorers. From 1971 onwards records of attendances are given.)

1881 Moyola Park, 1; Cliftonville, 0.
Moyola Park—MacKerd; Hewison, Dowd; McLernon, McSwiggin; R. Redmond, McKenna, W. Houston, T. Houston, M. Redmond, Morrow.

1882 Queen's Island, 2; Cliftonville, 1.
Queen's Island—Gilmore; Gouk, Cunningham; Orr, Gilmore, Kerr; Stewart, Munroe, Bell, Drummond, McMillen.

1883 Cliftonville 5; Ulster, 0.
Cliftonville—R.J. Houston; J.M. McAlery, E. Browne; D. Hannay, D.C. Martin, J.R. Davison; W.B.R. McWha, R.M. Potts, J.T. Potts, E.A. Spiller, A.H. Dill.

1884 Distillery, 5; Ulster, 0.
Distillery—Millar; M. Wilson, Cunningham; Baxter, Crone, McClatchey; Hogg, S. Johnston, J. Johnston, Stewart, Beattie.

1885 Distillery, 2; Limavady, 0.
Distillery—Millar; M. Wilson, Cunningham; Baxter, Crone, McClatchey; Hogg, Johnston, Sinclair, Stewart, Beattie.

1886 Distillery, 1; Limavady, 0.
Distillery—Page; M. Wilson, R. Wilson; Baxter, Crone, McClatchey; McArthur, S. Johnston, J. Johnston, Bell, Condy.

1887 Ulster, 3; Cliftonville, 0.
Ulster—Barclay; Fox, Watson; Moore, Hastings, Campbell; Miller, Mears, E. Reid, J. Reid (1), J. Reid (2).

1888 Cliftonville, 2; Distillery, 1.
Cliftonville—Clugston; Wilson, Browne; Williamson, Rosbotham, Molyneaux; Elleman, Macpherson, Barry, Gibb, Turner.

1889 Distillery, 5; Y.M.C.A., 4.
Distillery—Galbraith; R. Crone, Ritchie; Crawford, Spencer, W. Crone; McClatchey, Stanfield, R. Stewart, W. Stewart, McIlvenny.

1890 Gordon Highlanders, 3; Cliftonville, 1.
Gordons—Grant; Buchanan, Thompson; Milne, Johnston, Maguire; Swan, Reid, Hall, McCormick, Beveridge.

1891 Linfield, 4; Ulster, 2.
Linfield—T. Gordon; W. Gordon, Morrison; McKeown, Milne, Moore; Dalton, Gaffiken, Hill, S. Torrans, R. Torrans.

1892 Linfield, 7; The Black Watch, 0.
Linfield—T. Gordon, W. Gordon, Arnott; McKeown, Milne, Johnston; Dalton, Gaffiken, Hill, S. Torrans, R. Torrans.

1893 Linfield, 5; Cliftonville, 1.
Linfield—T. Gordon; W. Gordon, S. Torrans; McKeown, Johnston, R. Torrans; Peden, Gaffiken, Milne, Turley, T. Torrans.

1894 Distillery, 3; Linfield, 2.
Distillery—Thompson; Stilges, McWhinney; Ponsonby, McClatchey, Miles; Thompson, Stanfield, Emerson, Stilges, Burnett.

1895 Linfield, 10; Bohemians, 1.
Linfield—T. Gordon; H. Gordon, S. Torrans; Johnston, Milne, R. Torrans; Williamson, Gaffiken, Gaukrodger, Jordan, McAllen.

1896 Distillery, 3; Glentoran, 1.
Distillery—Thompson; Brown, Ponsonby; McCoy, Farrell, McClatchey; Baird, Rylie, Stanfield, Campbell, Peden.

1897 Cliftonville, 3; Sherwood Foresters, 1.
Cliftonville—Scott; Gibson, Foreman; Jack Pyper, Polland, Campbell; J. Campbell, McCashin, Jim Pyper, Martin, Barron.

1898 Linfield, 2; St. Columb's Hall Celtic, 0.
Linfield—White; Howard, S. Torrans; Anderson, Milne, Magennis; Stevenson, Darling, Jordan, R. Rea, S. Rea.

1899 Linfield, 2; Glentoran, 1.
Linfield—Murray; Swan, Torrans; Magennis, Milne, Wilson; Peden, Darling, Jordan, Doherty, McAllen.

1900 Cliftonville, 2; Bohemians, 1.
Cliftonville—McAlpine; Jack Pyper, Sheppard; Cochrane, McCoull, McShane; Campbell, Wheeler, Jim Pyper, Martin, Thompson.

1901 Cliftonville, 1; Freebooters, 0.
Cliftonville—McAlpine; Gibson, Sheppard; Cochrane, McKee, Anderson; Scott, Wheeler, Jim Pyper, Kirkwood, Campbell.

1902 Linfield, 5; Distillery, 1.
Linfield—Scott; Darling, Torrans; Crothers, Milne, Magennis; Mercer, Maxwell, Carnegie, Peden, McAllen.

1903 Distillery, 3; Bohemians, 1.
Distillery—Andrews; McCracken, McMillan; Hunter, Morton, Burnison; Mercer, Hamilton, Aiken, Kearns, McDougall.

1904 Linfield, 5; Derry Celtic, 1.
Linfield—Scott; McCartney, Sheppard; Anderson, Milne, Magennis; Darling, Hagan, Carnegie, Stewart, Whaits.

1905 Distillery, 3; Shelbourne, 0.
Distillery—Sloan; Watson, McMillan, Grieve, Johnston, Ferguson; Hunter, Andrews, Soye, Murray, Magill.

1906 Shelbourne, 2; Belfast Celtic, 0.
Shelbourne—Rowe; Heslin, Kelly; Abbey, Doherty, Ledridge; John Owens, Byrne, James Owens, Harris, Clery.

1907 Cliftonville, 1; Shelbourne, 0.
Cliftonville—McKee; Seymour, McIlroy; Spence, Martin, McClure; Blair, Robertson, Campbell, Beattie, Shanks.

1908 Bohemians, 3; Shelbourne, 1.
Bohemians—O'Hehir; Balfe, Thunder; Bastow, Healy, McElhinney; W.F. Hooper, Hannon, R.M. Hooper, Sloan, Slemin.

1909 Cliftonville, 2; Bohemians, 1.
Cliftonville—McKee; Neely, Seymour; Martin, Wright, Palmer; McComb, Robertson, Houghton, McAuley, Thompson.

1910 Distillery, 1; Cliftonville, 0.
Distillery—Sloan; Burnison, Creighton; Flannagan, Donnelly, Scott; Wright, Hamilton, Johnston, Uprichard, Heggarty.

1911 Shelbourne, 2; Bohemians, 1.
Shelbourne—Rowe; Dunne, Bennett; Watson, Doherty, Moran; Clarkin, Murphy, Merrigan; Halpin, Devlin.

1912 Final not played. Linfield awarded Cup.

1913 Linfield, 2; Glentoran, 0.
Linfield—Kelly; Darling, Sterling; Rollo, Clifford, Bartlett; Brown, Nixon, Smith, McNeill, McEwan.

1914 Glentoran, 3; Linfield, 1.
Glentoran—Murphy; McCann, Annesley; Ferritt, Scraggs, Emerson; Lyner, J. Lindsay, Napier, Boyd, W. Lindsay.

1915 Linfield, 1; Belfast Celtic, 0.
Linfield—McKee; Rollo, Foye; Wallace, Clifford, Bartlett; Young, Nixon, Hamilton, Bovill, McEwan.

1916 Linfield, 1; Glentoran, 0.
Linfield—McKee; Rollo, Foye; McCandless, Clifford, Bartlett; Houston, Nixon, Bovill, Campbell, McEwan.

1917 Glentoran, 2; Belfast Celtic, 0.
Glentoran—Steele; G. Moore, Grainger; Bennett, Scraggs, Ferritt; Lyner, Seymour, Boyd, Emerson, W. Moore.

1918 Belfast Celtic, 2; Linfield, 0.
Belfast Celtic—Scott; McStay, Barrett; Mulligan, Hamill, Stewart; McKinney, McIlroy, Ferris, Johnston, Frazer.

1919 Linfield, 2; Glentoran, 1.
Linfield—McKee; Rollo, McCandless; Houston, Lacey, Pollins; Campbell, Lindsay, Featherstone, McDonald, McEwan.

1920 Final not played. Cup awarded to Shelbourne.

1921 Glentoran, 2; Glenavon, 0.
Glentoran—McHaffey; McSeveney, Ferguson; Ferritt, Scraggs, Emerson; McGregor, Crooks, Davey, Meek, Snape.

1922 Linfield, 2; Glenavon, 0.
Linfield—Harland; Gaw, Frame; Wallace, Morgan, McIlveen; Cowan, McCracken, Savage, McIlroy, McGrillen.

1923 Linfield, 2; Glentoran, 0.
Linfield—Diffin; Maultsaid, Frame; Wallace, Moorehead, Robinson; Cowan, McCracken, Savage, McIlreavy, McGrillen.

1924 Queen's Island, 1; Willowfield, 0.
Queen's Island—Gough; McKeown, Fergie; Kennedy, Gowdy, Murdough; Cowan, Croft, Burns, McCleery, Morton.

1925 Distillery, 2; Glentoran, 1.
Distillery—Fitzroy; Thompson, Burnison; Garrett, Sloan, Anderson; McKenzie, Dalrymple, Rushe, Blair, McMullan.

1926 Belfast Celtic, 3; Linfield, 2.
Belfast Celtic—Fitzmaurice; Scott, Ferguson; Pollock, Moore, Perry; McGrillen, Ferris, Curran, S. Mahood, J. Mahood.

1927 Ards, 3; Cliftonville, 2.
Ards—McMullan; McKeown, Wilson; Smyth, Risk, Gamble; Bothwell, Patton, McGee, Croft, McIlreavy.

1928 Willowfield, 1; Larne, 0.
Willowfield—McFarlane; Mallon, Vance; Conway, Kirkwood, McClure; Aiken, Young, Hume, Kimlin, Shaw.

1929 Ballymena, 2; Belfast Celtic, 1.
Ballymena—Gough; McNinch, McDiarmid; J. Reid, D. Reid, Howard; Clarke, Mitchell, Shiels, McCambridge, Cassidy.

1930 Linfield, 4; Ballymena, 3.
Linfield—Lawson; Brown, Watson, McCleery, Jones, Sloan; Houston, McCracken, Bambrick, Grice, McCaw.

1931 Linfield, 3; Ballymena, 0.
Linfield—Higgs; Pyper, Curran; McCleery, Jones, Sloan; Houston, McCracken, Hewitt, Grice, McCaw.

1932 Glentoran, 2; Linfield, 1.
Glentoran—Bennett; Allen, Gibson; Turnbull, Mathieson, McClements; Morgan, Geary, Roberts, Borland, Lucas.

1933 Glentoran, 3; Distillery, 1.
Glentoran—Harris; Lyttle, Gibson; Turnbull, Craig, Arrigan; Doherty, Crooks, Roberts, Leathem, Fitzsimmons.

1934 Linfield, 5; Cliftonville, 0.
Linfield—Eckersley; Richmond, Richardson; Edwards, Jones, McCleery; Mackie, McCracken, Bambrick, Donnelly, Caiels.

1935 Glentoran, 1; Larne, 0.
Glentoran—Lewis; Miller, McDiarmid; Arrigan, Beck, Leathem; Goodwin, Aicken, McNeill, Duncan, Smith.

1936 Linfield, 2; Derry City, 1.
Linfield—Frame; Haire, Richardson; Edwards, Bowden, McCleery; Foye, Donnelly, Hume, Baird, McCormick.

1937 Belfast Celtic, 3; Linfield, 0.
Belfast Celtic—K. McAlinden; McMillan, Lavery; H. Walker, Leathem, J. Walker; Kernaghan, McArdle, Turnbull, Bruce, McIlroy.

1938 Belfast Celtic, 2; Bangor, 0.
Belfast Celtic—K. McAlinden; Lavery, R.P. Fulton; H. Walker, Leathem, J. Walker; Kernaghan, J. McAlinden, Kelly, Bruce, McIlroy.

1939 Linfield, 2; Ballymena United, 0.
Linfield—Doak; Thompson, Richardson; Waddell, Perry, Rosbotham; Brownlow, Donnelly, Marshall, Finlay, McCormick.

1940 Ballymena United, 2; Glenavon, 0.
Ballymena Utd.—Redmond; Vincent, Swann; Barr, McCartney, Rosbotham; Grant, Olphert, Sclater, Weir, Moore.

1941 Belfast Celtic, 1; Linfield, 0.
Belfast Celtic—Breen; McMillan, Fulton; Walker, Vernon, Leathem; Kernaghan, Kelly, O'Connor, McAlinden, C. McIlroy.

1942 Linfield, 3; Glentoran, 1.
Linfield—Redmond; Kirkwood, Feeney; McKeown, Mould, Brolly; Thompson, Wright, Peppitt, Ormiston, Baker.

1943 Belfast Celtic, 1; Glentoran, 0.
Belfast Celtic—Kelly; McMillan, Fulton; Walker, Vernon, Douglas; Kernaghan, O'Connor, Byrne, Townsend, Hollinger.

1944 Belfast Celtic, 3; Linfield, 1.
Belfast Celtic—H. Kelly; McMillan, Cullen; Walker, Vernon, O'Connor; Collins, McAlinden, Byrne, A. Kelly, Bonnar.

1945 Linfield, 4; Glentoran, 2.
Linfield—Breen; Henderson, Feeney; H. Walsh, Bryson, McWilliams; Cochrane, McCrory, D. Walsh, Robinson, Lockhart.

1946 Linfield, 3; Distillery, 0.
Linfield—Breen; Henderson, Feeney; Jones, Bryson, McWilliams; McKenna, McCrory, Walsh, Russell, Lockhart.
Distillery—Smythe; Crossley, McAuley; Collins, Bowler, Currie; O'Connor, Kernaghan, Lonsdale, Brennan, Walker.
Scorers—Linfield: Walsh (2), McCrory.

1947 Belfast Celtic, 1; Glentoran, 0.
Celtic—K. McAlinden; McMillan, Aherne; Walker, Currie, R. Lawler Campbell, Tully, McMorran, Denver, Douglas.
Glentoran—McKee; Kane, Neill; Blanchflower, Waters, Hughes; Wright, Kelly, McCormack, J. Lawler, Lavery.
Scorer—Celtic: Tully.

1948 Linfield, 3; Coleraine, 0.
Linfield—A. Russell; McCune, McMichael; Liggett, Bryson, Walsh; Thompson, Bardsley, Simpson, J. Russell, McKenna.
Coleraine—K. McAlinden, O'Connor, Gilmore; Masters, McCavana, Doherty; O'Reilly, Nolan, Clarke, McDowell, Mahood.
Scorers—Linfield: Thompson, O'Connor (o.g.), Simpson.

1949 Derry City, 3; Glentoran, 1.
Derry City—Muir; Cully, Brennan; Doherty, Ferris, McCreary; Hermon, Aitken, Cannon, Colvin, Kelly.
Glentoran—Moore; Neill, McCarthy; Ferran, Hughes, Blanchflower; Nimmick, Peacock, McFarlane, Kerr, Feeney.
Scorers—Derry City: Colvin, Cannon, Herman; Glentoran: Peacock.

1950 Linfield, 2; Distillery, 1.
Linfield—Russell; McCune, Houston; Smyth, Hamill, Walsh; Thompson, Currie, Simpson, McDowell, Dickson.
Distillery—Smyth; Wilson, Mills; Casement, Lonsdale, Gray; Dodds, Mulholland, McClinton, Mycock, Kelly.
Scorers—Linfield: Thompson, McDowell; Distillery: Mycock.

1951 Glentoran, 3; Ballymena United, 1.
Glentoran—Moore; Dunlop, McCarthy; Mulholland, T. Hughes, Ferran; Cunningham, Ewing, S. Hughes, Williamson, Feeney.
Ballymena United—Rodgers; Trevorrow, Barr; Gray, Murphy, Douglas; Morrison, Anderson, Ewart, O'Hara, Currie.
Scorers—Glentoran: S. Hughes (2), Williamson; Ballymena United: Currie.

1952 Ards, 1; Glentoran, 0.
Ards—O'Connell; Moore, Hamill; Tucker, Robinson, Corbett; Lawther, Thompson, Drake, McDowell, Walker.
Glentoran—Clarke; Lucas, King; Neill, T. Hughes, McFarlane; Lowry, Ewing, S. Hughes, Williamson, Feeney.
Scorer—Ards: Thompson.

1953 Linfield, 5; Coleraine, 0.
Linfield—Russell; Keith, Lewis; G. Nixon, Hamill, MacMillen; Thompson, McDowell, Walker, Dickson, Lunn.
Coleraine—Watt; Montgomery, Canning; Brolly, McCavana, McDermott; Cuneen, Colvan, O'Kane, Doherty, McCormick.
Scorers—Linfield: Thompson (2), Walker, McDowell, Dickson.

1954 Derry City, 1; Glentoran, 0. (After two replays)
Derry City—Heffron; Wilson, Houston; Brolly, Curran, Smyth; Brady, Delaney, Forsythe, Toner, O'Neill.
Glentoran—Bond; McCarthy, King; Neill, Murdough, Lewis; Lowry, Scott, Hughes, Cunningham, Feeney.
Scorer—Derry City: O'Neill. After two drawn games — 2-2 and 0-0

1955 Dundela, 3; Glenavon, 0.
Dundela—J. Smyth; R. Smyth, Stewart; McAuley, Lynch, Millar; Greenwood, Reid, Ervine, Kavanagh, Gourley.
Glenavon—Durkan; Greer, Armstrong; Corr, Liggett, Cush; Masters, Denver, Jones, Campbell, McVeigh.
Scorers—Dundela: Ervine (2), Greenwood.

1956 Distillery, 1; Glentoran, 0. (After two replays)
Distillery—Beare; Magee, Brennan; Twinem, Watters, Tait; Curry, Hepburn; Dugan, Dougan, Hamilton.
Glentoran—McMahon; McCarthy, Lucas; Neill, Murdough, Dubois; Lowry, Fogarty, Mulvey, Bruce, Nolan.
Scorer—Distillery: Curry. After two drawn games — 2-2 and 0-0.

1957 Glenavon, 2; Derry City, 0.
Glenavon—Rea; Armstrong, Lyske; Corr, Davis, Cush; Wilson, McVeigh, Jones, Campbell, Elwood.
Derry City—Heffron; Kinnen, Houston; Brolly, Travers, Smyth; Wright, Crossan, Campbell, P. Coyle, Nash.
Scorers—Glenavon: Houston (o.g.), Jones.

1958 Ballymena United—Bond; Trevorrow, Johnston; Brown, Lowry, Cubitt; Egan, Forsyth, McGhee, McCrae, Russell.
Linfield—Russell; Gilliland, Graham; Rodgers, Hamill, Fletcher; Robinson, Parke, Milburn, Dickson, Braithwaite.
Scorers—Ballymena: McGhee, Russell.

1959 Glenavon, 2; Ballymena United, 0. (After one replay)
Glenavon—Rea; Armstrong, Cummings; Masters, Forde, Hughes; Wilson, Magee, Jones, Campbell, McVeigh.
Ballymena United—Bond; Trevorrow, Johnston; Brown, Lowry, Cubitt; Walsh, McCrea, McGhee, Russell, Clarke.
Scorers—Glenavon: Wilson, Magee. After drawn game of 1-1.

1960 Linfield, 5; Ards, 1.
Linfield—Irvine; Gilliland, Graham; Wilson, Hamill, Gough; Stewart, Dickson, Milburn, Ferguson, Braithwaite.
Ards—Moffatt; Patterson, Hunter; McCullough, Reynolds; Hamill; Humphries, Welsh, McCrory, Ewing, Boyd.
Scorers—Linfield: Ferguson (2), Milburn (2), Gough; Ards: Welsh.

1961 Glenavon, 5; Linfield, 1.
Glenavon—Kinkead; Hughes, Armstrong; Dugan, McKinstry, Magee; Wilson, Johnston, Jones, Campbell, Weatherup.
Linfield—Irvine; Gilliland, Graham, Wilson, Parke, Gough, Stewart, Ferguson, Walker, Dickson, Braithwaite.
Scorers—Glenavon; Campbell (3), Jones (2); Linfield: Ferguson.

1962 Linfield, 4; Portadown, 0.
Linfield—Irvine; Gilliland, Graham; Wilson, Hatton, Parke; Stewart, Ferguson, Barr, Dickson, Braithwaite.
Portadown—Kydd; Burke, Loughlin; Cush, Beattie, Campbell; Gillespie, McMillen, Gorman, Wilson, Callan.
Scorers—Linfield: Dickson (2), Barr, Braithwaite.

1963 Linfield, 2; Distillery, 1
Linfield—Irvine; Parke, Graham; Andrews, Hatton, Gough; Stewart, Ferguson, Cairns, Dickson, Braithwaite.
Distillery—Kennedy; D. Meldrum, Ellison; Kennedy, White, Gregg; Welsh, Curley, J. Meldrum, Scott, Hamilton.
Scorers—Linfield: Cairns, Braithwaite; Distillery: Kennedy.

1964 Derry City, 2; Glentoran, 0.
Derry City—Mahon; Campbell, Cathcart; McGeough, Crossan, Wood; McKenzie, Doherty, Coyle, Wilson, Seddon.
Glentoran Finlay; Creighton, Borne, Byrne, McCullough, Bruce, Pavis, Curley, Thompson, Brannigan, Green.
Scorers—Derry City: Wilson, Doherty.

1965 Coleraine, 2; Glenavon, 1.
Coleraine—V. Hunter; McCurdy, Campbell; Murray, A. Hunter, Peacock: Kinsella, Curley, Halliday, Dunlop, Irwin.
Glenavon—McNally; Murphy, E. Johnston; Magee, Lowry, Hughes; Watson, E. Magee, Guy, W. Johnston, Weatherup.
Scorers—Coleraine: Dunlop, Irwin; Glenavon: Johnston.

1966 Glentoran, 2; Linfield, 0.
Glentoran—Finlay; Creighton, Borne, McCullough, Byrne, Bruce, Conroy, Stewart, Thompson, McDonnell, McAlinden.
Linfield—McFaul; Gilliland, White, Gregg, Hatton, Leishman, Ferguson, Thomas, Pavis, Scott, McCambley.
Scorer—Glentoran: Conroy (2)

1967 Crusaders, 3; Glentoran, 1.
Crusaders—Nicholson; Patterson, Lewis; McPolin, Campbell, McCullough (S.); Law, Trainor, Meldrum, McNeill, Wilson.
Glentoran—Finlay; Creighton, McKeag; Jackson, McCullough (W.), Stewart; Morrow, Bruce, Thompson, Ross, Weatherup.
Scorers—Crusaders: Trainor, McNeill, McCullough; Glentoran: Thompson.

1968 Crusaders, 2; Linfield, 0.
Crusaders—Nicholson; Anderson, Cathcart; Campbell, McFarlane, McPolin; Brush, Trainor, Meldrum, Jamison, Wilson.
Linfield—McGonigal; Gilliland, Patterson; Andrews, Hatton, Wood; Ferguson, Hamilton, Pavis, Scott, Cathcart.
Scorer—Crusaders: Meldrum (2)

1969 Ards, 0; Distillery, 0. (Replay: Ards, 4; Distillery, 2).
Ards—Kydd; Johnston, Crothers; Bell, Stewart, Nixon; Shields, McAvoy, Brown, Humphries, Mowat. Sub— Sands.
Distillery—Young; Patterson, Pike; Kennedy, Conlon, McCarroll; Rafferty, McCaffrey, O'Halloran, Brannigan, Lennox.
Scorers—Ards: McAvoy (4); Distillery: McCaffrey, Conlon.
Referee—Malcolm Wright (Portadown).

1970 Ballymena, 1; Linfield, 2.
Linfield—Stewart; Gilliland, Patterson; Andrews, Hatton (capt.), Bowyer; Viollet, Hamilton, Millen, Scott, Pavis, Sub — Lockhart.
Ballymena—Platt; Erwin, Richardson; Torrens, Averell, Russell (capt.); Porter, McGowan, Fleming, Martin, McFall, Sub — Nicholl.
Scorers—Linfield: Scott (2); Ballymena: Fleming.
Referee—M. Fussey (Retford).

1971 Derry City, 0; Distillery, 3.
Derry City—McKibbin; Duffy, McLaughlin; McDowell, White, Wood; Rowland, O'Halloran, Ward, Hale, Smith (Sub— Hill, 49 mins.).
Distillery—McDonald; McCarroll, Meldrum; Brannigan, Rafferty, Donnelly; Law, Watson, Savage, O'Neill, Lennox, Sub — Patterson.
Referee—M. Wright (Portadown).
Scorers—Distillery: O'Neill (2). Savage.
Attendance—6,000.

1972 Coleraine, 2; Portadown, 1.
Coleraine—Crossan; McCurdy, Gordon, Curley, Jackson, Murray, Dunlop, Mullan, Healey, Dickson, Jennings.
Portadown—Carlisle; Strain, McFall, Malcolmson, Lunn, Hutton, R. Morrison, McGowan, Anderson, B. Morrison, Fleming.
Referee—H. Wilson (Belfast).
Scorers—Coleraine: Dickson, Murray; Portadown: Anderson.
Attendance—8,000.

1973 Glentoran, 3; Linfield, 2.
Glentoran—Patterson A., Hill, McKeag, Stewart (Sub — Walker 45 mins.), Murray, McCreary, Weatherup, Anderson, Hall, Jamieson, Feeney.
Linfield—Barclay, Fraser, Patterson J., Sinclair, McAllister, Bowyer, Nixon, Magee, Millen, Malone, Cathcart (Sub — Larmour 45 mins.).
Referee—Malcolm Wright (Portadown).
Scorers—Glentoran: Feeney 2 (one pen.), Jamison; Linfield: P. Malone, Magee.
Footnote—Stewart took over in the Glentoran goal at half-time after Patterson had injured his shoulder in a tackle with Millen.
Attendance—10,000.

1974 Ards, 2; Ballymena United, 1.
At Windsor Park, Belfast
Ards—Matthews, Patton, Patterson, Mowat, McCoy, Nixon, McAteer, McAvoy, Guy, Humphries, Cathcart. (Sub — Graham, 60 mins.).
Ballymena United—McKenzie, Gowdy, McAuley, Stewart, Averell, Brown, Donald, Sloan, Erwin (Sub — Todd, 82 mins.), McFall, Frickleton.
Referee—R. McFadden (Londonderry).
Scorers—Ards: Guy, McAvoy; Ballymena United: Sloan.
Attendance—7,000.

1975 Coleraine, 1; Linfield, 0 (after two replays).
At Ballymena
Coleraine—V. Magee, McCurdy, McNutt, Beckett, Jackson, Murray, Cochrane, Jennings, Smith, Dickson, Gordon, Sub — Guy.
Linfield—Barclay, Fraser, McVeigh, E. Magee, Rafferty, Bowyer, Campbell (Sub — Bell, 70 mins.), Patterson, P. Malone, Graham, Hunter.
Referee—E. Smyton (Dungannon).
Scorer—Coleraine: Smith.
Attendance—5,200.

1976 Carrick Rangers, 2; Linfield, 1.
At the Oval
Carrick Rangers—Cowan, Hamilton, Macklin, Matchett (capt.), Whiteside, Brown, Cullen, Connor, McKenzie, Prenter, Allen (Sub — Erwin).
Linfield—Barclay, Fraser, McVeigh, Coyle, Rafferty, Bowyer, Nixon, Lemon (Sub — McKee, 45 mins.), Bell, Malone, Magee (capt.).
Referee—T. Perry (Newtownabbey).
Scorers—Carrick Rangers: Prenter (2); Linfield: M. Malone.
Attendance—9,500.

1977 Coleraine, 4; Linfield, 1.
At the Oval
Coleraine—V. Magee, Hutton, McNutt, Beckett, Jackson (capt.), Connell, Porter, Jennings, Guy, Dickson, Moffatt, Sub — Mullan.
Linfield—Barclay, Parkes, Garrett, Coyle, Rafferty (capt.), Lemon, Nixon, Dornan, Bell, Martin, E. Magee, Sub — Hamilton.
Referee—M. Moffatt (Gilford).
Scorers—Coleraine: Beckett, Dickson, Moffatt, Guy; Linfield: Lemon.
Attendance—10,000.

1978 Linfield, 3; Ballymena United, 1.
At the Oval
Linfield—Barclay, Fraser, Parks, Coyle, Rafferty (capt.), Dornan, Nixon, Garrett, Martin, Hamilton, Murray, Sub — Hewitt.
Ballymena United—Rafferty, Donald, Spence, McCullough, Jackson, Simpson, Nelson, T. Sloan, Johnston, J. Sloan, McClean. Sub — McAuley.
Referee—M. Wright (Portadown).
Scorers—Linfield: Dornan, Garrett, Rafferty; Ballymena United: Nelson.
Attendance—12,000.

1979 Cliftonville, 3; Portadown, 2.
At Windsor Park
Cliftonville—Johnston; McGuickan, Largey; Flanagan, M. Quinn, McCurry, T. Bell, McCusker, Mills. (Sub — O'Connor 66 mins.), Platt, Adair.
Portadown—McCollum; Smyth, Dougan; Wilson, Kilburn, Cleary; Gordon Magee (Sub — J. Bell 66 mins.), Alexander, Campbell, A. Quinn.
Referee—Malcolm Wright (Portadown).
Scorers—Cliftonville: Platt, Adair, Bell; Portadown: Campbell, Alexander.
Attendance—15,000.

21: IRISH YOUTH CUP

WINNERS

1952-53 — St. John's (Whitehouse)	1960-61 — Linfield Ran.	1969-70 — Coleraine Ran.
1953-54 — Churchill Utd.	1961-62 — Linfield Ran.	1970-71 — Sunnyside C.
1954-55 — Boyland	1962-63 — Ards Boys	1971-72 — Glentoran O.
1955-56 — Ormeau Rec.	1963-64 — Parkgate O.	1972-73 — Coleraine Ran.
1956-57 — Glentoran O.	1964-65 — Parkgate O.	1974-75 — Coleraine Ran.
1957-58 — Linfield Ran.	1965-66 — Ards Boys	1975-76 — Sunnyside C.
1958-59 — Glentoran O.	1966-67 — Linfield Ran.	1976-77 — Linfield Ran.
1959-60 — Linfield Ran.	1967-68 — Coleraine Ran.	1978-79 — Glentoran O.
	1968-69 — Linfield Ran.	

22: IRISH INTERMEDIATE CUP

WINNERS

1893	Distillery Rovers	1920	St. James' Gate	1950-51	Ballyclare C.
1894	Glentoran II	1921	Queen's Island	1952-53	Brantwood
1895	Milltown	1922	Linfield Rangers	1954	Ballyclare C.
1896	Cliftonville O.	1923	Dunmurry	1955	Dundela
1897	Linfield S.	1924	Willowfield	1956-57	Linfield S.
1898	Glentoran II	1925	Linfield Rangers	1958	Newry Town
1899	Linfield S.	1926	Ballyclare C.	1959	Larne
1900	Cliftonville O.	1927	Crusaders	1960-61	Ballyclare C.
1901	Linfield S.	1928	Willowfield	1962	Glentoran II
1902	Cliftonville O.	1929	Linfield S.	1963-64	Ballyclare C.
1903	Distillery II	1930	Dunmurry	1964-65	Coleraine Res.
1904	Y.M.C.A.	1931	Glentoran II	1965-66	Dundela
1905	Woodvale	1932	Broadway Utd.	1966-67	Newry Town
1906-07	Forth River	1933	Dunvilles	1967-68	Chimney C.
1908	Glenavon	1934	Sunnyside	1968-69	Coleraine Res.
1909	Glentoran II	1935-37	Celtic II	1969-70	Larne
1910	St. James' Gate	1938-39	Crusaders	1970-71	Ards II
1911	Glenavon	1940	Celtic II	1971-72	Linfield Swifts
1912	Derry Guilds	1941	Glentoran II	1972-73	Brantwood
1913	Glentoran II	1942	Bangor Res.	1973-74	Limavady Utd.
1914	Celtic II	1943	Larne Olympic	1974-75	Dundela
1915	Uni. Co. Dublin	1944-45	Bangor Res.	1975-76	Carrick Rangers
1916	Glentoran II	1946	Linfield S.	1976-77	Carrick Rangers
1917	Strandville	1947	Dundela	1977-78	Larne Colts
1918	Glentoran II	1948	Distillery II	1978-79	R.U.C.
1919	Cup withheld	1949	Linfield S.		

186